D1565700

Unassailable Ideas

Unassailable Ideas

How Unwritten Rules and Social Media
Shape Discourse in American Higher
Education

ILANA REDSTONE AND JOHN VILLASENOR

OXFORD
UNIVERSITY PRESS

OXFORD
UNIVERSITY PRESS

Oxford University Press is a department of the University of Oxford. It furthers
the University's objective of excellence in research, scholarship, and education
by publishing worldwide. Oxford is a registered trade mark of Oxford University
Press in the UK and certain other countries.

Published in the United States of America by Oxford University Press
198 Madison Avenue, New York, NY 10016, United States of America.

Library of Congress Cataloging-in-Publication Data
Names: Redstone, Ilana, author. | Villasenor, John, author.
Title: Unassailable ideas : how unwritten rules and social media shape
discourse in American higher education / Ilana Redstone and John Villasenor.
Description: New York, NY : Oxford University Press, [2020] |
Includes bibliographical references and index.
Identifiers: LCCN 2020012862 (print) | LCCN 2020012863 (ebook) |
ISBN 9780190078065 (hardback) | ISBN 9780190078089 (epub)
Subjects: LCSH: Academic freedom—United States. |
Social media in education—United States.
Classification: LCC LC72.2 .R44 2020 (print) |
LCC LC72.2 (ebook) | DDC 378.1/21—dc23
LC record available at https://lccn.loc.gov/2020012862
LC ebook record available at https://lccn.loc.gov/2020012863

1 3 5 7 9 8 6 4 2

Printed by Sheridan Books, Inc., United States of America

Contents

Preface

This is not a book about free speech on campus. While there are some chapters where we consider speech, the real focus of the book is much broader: We examine the challenges to free inquiry and discourse that we see in academia and, increasingly, in society more broadly. At many universities today, there is a set of closely held beliefs, enforced through social media, that constrain much of what is taught, studied, and discussed—or not—on campus.

Our goal in this book is to describe the state of affairs in the academy and the ways in which all arms of the academic enterprise are affected. We hope that by exploring the set of beliefs that shape teaching, research, and the campus climate more generally, we can contribute to a broader discussion on free inquiry, knowledge creation, knowledge dissemination, and the role of higher education.

For readers who share our general concerns about the current academic climate, our hope is that this book can provide new and useful information and perspectives on some of the specific factors that are shaping that climate. For readers who are inclined to disagree with us—those, for example, who think that free inquiry and discourse on American college campuses is not too narrowly constrained—we hope that this book will be viewed as a respectful counterpoint to an on-campus narrative that we believe would benefit from a broader range of views.

America's higher education system is in many ways extraordinary, and we share with everyone with a stake in that system the goal of making it even better. Writing this book has been a learning process for us, and we are quite sure that we still have more to learn. We look forward to continuing that process as we engage in the discussions that we hope this book will help spur.

Before We Begin

In this book, we cite numerous research articles, books, and popular press articles, some of them relatively recent and some from decades ago. When we refer to the authors and their affiliations, we do so using the names and affiliations that were listed at the time of the publication we are citing.

We refer to institutions of higher education as both "colleges" and "universities," and generally use these terms interchangeably despite some difference in scope in their formal definitions. We have adopted this approach because it leaves more flexibility to use the term that best comports with common usage. For example, it is more common to write of "university research" than of "college research," and of "college campuses" than of "university campuses."

When describing on-campus events and controversies, we have endeavored to ensure that our descriptions are accurate as of the time of writing, while also recognizing that in some cases there will be further developments not reflected in the narrative we present.

A note about Covid-19: While this book was produced in 2020, we completed the manuscript in 2019, well before the Covid-19 pandemic shuttered American college campuses in March 2020. To put it mildly, the dynamics of campus discourse are very different when dorms have been largely emptied and instruction has been moved to Zoom. Of course, at present we do not know when students will be able to return to campus in significant numbers. That said, we are confident that our call for a culture of more open discourse in higher education will remain relevant both during the pandemic and after it has passed.

Acknowledgments

We are grateful to the many people with whom we have had conversations as we considered the issues described in this book. We provide the list below with two important caveats. First, the opinions we express here are our own, and are not intended to represent the views of anyone listed below. Second, while we have endeavored to make the list below as complete as possible, we may have inadvertently omitted some names that should have been included. Our heartfelt thanks go to Ahmad Atif Ahmad, Randall Akee, Richard Arum, Bradley Campbell, Michelle Deutchmann, Tara Helfman, James Kierstead, Lisa Littman, Joseph Lowndes, Eileen McDonagh, Pat McDonagh, Manu Meel, Andrew (Yair) Michaels, Joshua Redstone, Paul Redstone, Lawrence Ian Reed, Richard Shweder, Geoffrey Stone, Dovid Tiechtel, Mark Urista, James Matthew Wilson, and to anyone not listed here who has been kind enough to engage in discussions with us on the topics we address. Special thanks also go to James Cook, our editor at Oxford University Press, for his consistent support and enthusiasm.

1

Introduction

A few years ago, the University of California system published a document on "microaggressions." In a section titled "myth of meritocracy," one of the supposedly offensive remarks listed was "I believe the most qualified person should get the job." That statement, according to the primer on microaggressions that was also provided in the document, is a "snub" or an "insult."

It's tempting to write this off as just one more of many examples of the wacky assertions that get made by people on the academic fringe. But this isn't the academic fringe. This was a publication promulgated by one of the country's largest and most well-respected public university systems and containing an explicit denunciation of praise for meritocratic hiring.

In the up-is-down and down-is-up campus environment that produced such a claim, logic itself sometimes takes a backseat to a set of beliefs that act as a filter shaping what can be taught, the research that can be performed and published, and the opinions that can be expressed. Of course, complaints about campus "political correctness" go back decades. But the growth of social media has made academia today fundamentally different and less welcoming to open inquiry and to a diversity of perspectives than in the past.

Ironically, examples of universities *claiming* to support diverse perspectives abound. Consider the University of Illinois' campus "commitment statement" of "I will encourage the expression of different voices, perspectives, and ideas" (1). While this sounds expansive, in reality it is constrained by a list of unwritten prohibitions that are well known to most people in academia. How welcome is that "different" voice if it is articulating, for example, a position against the constitutionality of using race in college admissions in order to further affirmative action goals?[1] In fact, the University of Illinois' exhortation to "encourage the expression of different voices, perspectives, and ideas" has an asterisk attached to it. To receive encouragement, those

---

[1] While the Supreme Court addressed important aspects of this question in *Fisher v. University of Texas at Austin* in 2016, it remains an area of ongoing litigation in lower courts.

Unassailable Ideas. Ilana Redstone and John Villasenor, Oxford University Press (2020). © Oxford University Press.
DOI: 10.1093/oso/9780190078065.001.0001.

voices can only be "different" within a highly prescribed set of boundaries that reflect the worldview that is dominant on campus, but that not everyone shares.

Campuses have long had unwritten rules about what can and can't be said. But in recent years, social media have changed how we communicate and have emerged as a powerful tool both for direct censorship and for strengthening the incentives for self-censorship, some of which is encouraged and supported by people within academia itself.

Both on campus and off, this is most visible through social media–driven public shaming campaigns launched in response to perceived transgressions. In addition, and arguably more importantly in the long run, there is an indirect effect that operates through the fear of potentially being targeted by social media "call-out culture." That fear leads people to preemptively modify their behavior in order to avoid becoming a focus of attack. This means that the pressure to conform goes up, tolerance for dissenting views goes down, and the range of permissible opinions is narrowed.

In the campus context, this applies to research, teaching, and academic discourse more generally. In the pre–social media age, publication of a controversial research result would generally lead, some number of months later, to the publication of articles presenting rebuttals, to a period of debate among experts in the field, and more often than not to an eventual resolution. This is how knowledge advances.

Today, publication of controversial research can lead to a social media backlash that builds within weeks or even days. Faced with the pressure of a social media mob, academic journals will backtrack, questioning the very work that they had already subjected to peer review and deemed worthy of publication. University administrators will rapidly distance themselves from faculty members who publish research results that the Twittersphere has declared off-limits, even before any academic process has been completed to evaluate whether the attacks on the research have merit. In this climate, the pressure to self-censor is enormous.

Moreover, social media play an indirect role through the creation and sustenance of an "outrage culture" that produces incentives not to risk taking any position or making any statement that runs counter to the dominant beliefs. No faculty members want to be attacked on social media and left spinning in the wind by their university administrations. It's far easier, and far better for one's future career prospects, to adopt a new rule: Don't perform or publish research that could lead to results that people on social media might not like. In other words, in determining what research gets performed, the Twittersphere now has a seat at the table.

Similar dynamics act to constrain teaching, where saying anything in the classroom that is deemed hostile to the dominant campus orthodoxy can lead to formal complaints, calls for punishment, social media shaming, and demands for apologies. In short, the loudest and most indignant voices on social media are shaping the college classroom environment, just as they are so often shaping contemporary discourse beyond the campus.

The censorious nature of academia is a consequence of a social media–reinforced campus culture in which there is enormous social and professional pressure to adhere to a particular worldview. That pressure arises in significant part because the costs of publicly questioning that worldview can be high. And, this culture tends to get further strengthened through a positive feedback cycle that makes the campus a more welcoming place for people who see the world similarly, and a far less welcoming place for those who don't.

1.1 Our Thesis

Our thesis is that much of the contemporary academic environment is shaped by three foundational beliefs, all of which are grounded in good intentions and reflect understandable responses to historical and continuing societal wrongs.[2] However, when enforced in absolutist and uncompromising terms, the beliefs negatively impact campus climate. One consequence is that discourse becomes unreasonably constrained on issues that in fact merit more nuanced analysis.

As we describe in more detail in the next chapter, the first belief is that any action that aims to undermine traditional frameworks or power structures is automatically deemed to be good. We hasten to add that in articulating this belief we are *not* in any way promoting nostalgia for past eras in which discrimination based on race, gender, sexual orientation, etc., was far more pervasive than it is today. And we are not defending the exclusionary power structures associated with historical or continuing discrimination. Rather, we are pointing out that not all proposed solutions to pressing, longstanding

---

[2] In a 2018 commentary in the *Chronicle of Higher Education*, we briefly described some aspects of the issues we discuss at length in this book (2).

problems are good solutions. Framing a proposed initiative as an antidote to problematic traditional frameworks should not be a basis to automatically deem it worthy of adoption. Or, to use a medical analogy: Not all proposed cures to a disease are effective; in fact, some may end up doing more harm than good.

The second belief is that discrimination is behind all unequal group outcomes. Of course, both historically and today, discrimination has been and continues to be a major cause of differences in group-level outcomes. However, the second belief goes further than this and asserts that discrimination is the cause of *all* such unequal group outcomes, without leaving room to consider the influence of factors such as culture or preferences that are not clearly ascribable to discrimination.[3]

The third belief is in the primacy of identity along the lines of race, gender, gender identity, etc. Under this belief, there is strong cultural pressure to insist on seeing *everything* through the lens of identity, including when there are also reasonable, non–identity-centered ways of examining an issue. We are not arguing that identity isn't important, or that it should never play a central role. Clearly, identity is a vitally important lens through which to analyze a wide range of complex issues. However, support for the value of identity-centered perspectives should not require viewing all non–identity-centered perspectives as presumptively less worthy of consideration.

On university campuses, these beliefs, which are bolstered and enforced in significant part through social media, have such a strong moral valence that the mere act of questioning them can have significant negative professional consequences. The result is a powerful set of incentives shaping what university instructors, researchers, and students say and write.

The effects of this climate have impacts far beyond the campus. Why? Because the academic enterprise in the United States is both enormous and enormously influential. If the free inquiry that has played such a central role in creating America's culture of innovation, openness, and opportunity is lost at universities, the sheer size of the academic enterprise ensures that it will be lost outside of universities as well.

---

[3] As we note when we discuss the second belief in more detail in the next chapter, we are not suggesting or supporting—in fact, we strongly reject—any assertion of racial differences in intelligence. But there are some group-level differences—such as the vastly higher rate at which men (relative to women) commit violent crime—in regard to which reasonable debates can and should occur regarding the underlying causes.

To give an idea of the numbers involved, consider that, according to the National Center for Education Statistics, in 2017 there were approximately 1,500 two-year and 2,800 four-year colleges and universities in the United States (3). Among four-year institutions, just over half are private nonprofit, about one-fourth are public, and about 17 percent are private for-profit. The total number of enrolled students (including undergraduate and graduate students) in 2017 was just under 20 million (3). This means that millions of people are leaving universities each year to enter the workforce, and bringing with them the worldviews that were shaped while they were students.

The number of faculty members (who not only teach but who in many cases also are responsible for advancing knowledge through their research) is also very large. In the 2017–2018 academic year, the American Association for University Professors (AAUP) put the number of full-time U.S. faculty members at just under 380,000 (4, p. 4). According to the National Science Foundation's National Center for Science and Engineering Statistics, "in FY 2017, federal agencies obligated $32.4 billion to institutions of higher education in support of science and engineering (S&E)" (5, p. 1).

As these numbers show, higher education is a multi-billion-dollar-a-year endeavor that we entrust for both education and knowledge generation, and that is moving millions of people into the workforce each year. As a natural consequence of this continued infusion, the climate at universities foreshadows the climate in society more broadly. What happens in universities should matter to us all.

In the chapters that follow, we'll explain that the challenges we identify can be traced to a particular way of seeing the world that has become *de rigueur* throughout the American higher education system. We'll describe the contours of the underlying beliefs, what their components are, and how the incentives they have created directly and indirectly shape the academic endeavor. We'll explore how these assumptions have made academic freedom no longer particularly free.

We'll examine the censorship and the self-censorship that shape who gets hired into tenure-track positions at universities, and who earns the right to keep working through the award of tenure. We'll see how tenure isn't what it used to be—why a framework that was specifically designed to protect academic freedom now comes with an increasing number of caveats. We'll see why these same pressures for self-censorship shape what research does and doesn't get done and the material that is taught—and avoided—in the classroom. And we'll look at how this climate impacts the adjunct instructors who are playing an increasingly important role in undergraduate teaching, and whose lack of long-term job security gives them a particularly strong incentive to avoid bringing any perspectives into their classroom that might put their future employment opportunities at risk.

1.2 What Is Different About This Book?

There is a whole genre of publications that have addressed various challenges relating to the social and political climate at universities. Previous books include Greg Lukianoff and Jonathan Haidt's *The Coddling of the American Mind*, Frank Furedi's *What's Happened to the University?*, Sigal Ben-Porath's *Free Speech on Campus*, Keith Wittington's *Speak Freely: Why Universities Must Defend Free Speech*, Bradley Campbell and Jason Manning's *The Rise of Victimhood Culture*, Jonathan Zimmerman's *Campus Politics: What Everyone Needs to Know*, Allan Bloom's *The Closing of the American Mind*, Heather Mac Donald's *The Diversity Delusion*, and Roger Kimball's *Tenured Radicals: How Politics Has Corrupted Our Higher Education* (6–14).

This book is complementary to those other works in several ways. First, a number of the events we describe have occurred recently, after the publication of some (but not all) of the books mentioned in the previous paragraph. Second, we focus less on students, and more on faculty, administrators, and the ecosystem more broadly, with particular attention to the impacts on academic research, hiring, and tenure. In taking this approach, we are not suggesting that students are unimportant; in fact, they are clearly the most important constituency in any university. But faculty and administrators play a central role in deciding what research does and doesn't get done and which courses do or don't get taught. Thus, we believe that a broad view of the higher education community warrants the attention we provide here.

Third, the role of social media in shaping the climate at universities is relatively recent and still evolving. We believe that role merits attention and have attempted to illustrate it through analysis and examples. Fourth, we have aimed to provide a holistic view that looks at how the trends we have described are impacting not only academia but society more broadly.

1.3 Why Us?

One might reasonably ask why we are the right people to write this book. As a team, we bring over 40 years of combined experience teaching at large, public research institutions in different parts of the country. One of us has worked for many years at a large university in the Midwest; the other of us has had an academic career in California. We also bring a wide range of perspectives from disciplinary experience in sociology, demography, law, public policy, and engineering. As individuals, Ilana Redstone has long been concerned about the preponderance of overly simplistic and one-dimensional explanations that are advanced for social problems in sociology and related disciplines. John Villasenor has a longstanding focus in the broader societal impacts of technology, and has been particularly interested in the interplay between technology, law, and the digital ecosystem.

1.4 Solutions

We offer a comprehensive set of recommendations that we believe could substantially improve campus climate. While we discuss these recommendations in detail at the end of the book, we summarize them here.

1. We believe that for courses on topics in which the content is related to and potentially shaped by sociopolitical considerations, faculty should be explicitly encouraged to keep in mind the value of providing their students the opportunity to engage with a wider range of political views than typically occurs today.
2. We urge all people with positions of authority in universities—a group that includes faculty, department chairs, deans, and university executives—to give greater thought to how their own public and private communications might inadvertently narrow the range of dialog deemed permissible. A dean who, in an official communication to faculty, expresses support for one particular side of a contentious current social or political issue that admits multiple reasonable perspectives in effect creates a social penalty for those who might want to voice support for a different view. At the very least, such expressions should be accompanied by a statement recognizing that others might reasonably hold a different view.

3. We explicitly oppose *mandating* any form of viewpoint diversity. We support an approach that encourages, but does not require, members of a campus community to engage with a broader set of views.

4. We encourage fostering an increased recognition of intellectual humility as integral to the promotion of viewpoint diversity, and more generally, to productive dialog. Without humility, the incentive to value other viewpoints vanishes.

5. We believe that university administrators and others in positions of power on campus should not let their decisions be driven by fear of social media mobs.

6. Students, faculty, and administrators alike should make it regular practice to personalize connections with people with whom they disagree.

7. We believe that members of campus communities should be encouraged to be more willing to accept a greater degree of discomfort in dialog than is currently the norm, opening the door to conversations that may at times be difficult, but that would in the long run enhance mutual understanding.

8. We recommend that universities revise their formal definitions of "diversity" to include viewpoint diversity—a step that would complement as opposed to compete with efforts to increase other types of diversity.

1.5 The Role of the University

In order to address the challenges to the academic enterprise, it is helpful to provide some context regarding what its mission is. The question of the role of higher education for *students* leads to a range of answers, although most thoughtful responses include a combination of knowledge acquisition, career preparation, the expansion of critical thinking skills, personal development, and the facilitation of economic mobility. There is also the related but separate question of the role of the university in *society*, over and above the benefits provided to students. Answers to that question generally cite knowledge creation and dissemination as well as contribution to overall intellectual discourse.

All of these goals will be better achieved in an environment that features free inquiry, open discourse, and tolerance of a diverse set of perspectives. At the level of individuals in campus communities, this neither favors nor disfavors engagement with contemporary political and social issues. In other words, there should be room in a university for people who choose to do their work in a manner largely disconnected from the political and social issues of the moment. And there should also be ample room for people who view their engagement in research or teaching as inseparable from these issues. What is problematic, in our view, is when the work of members of a university community becomes explicitly or implicitly circumscribed by a dominant narrative that impedes the academic freedom that should be a core value at every university.

2

The Three Beliefs

A core argument of this book is that three beliefs shape much of what occurs on campuses. Taken together, these three beliefs make up a worldview that readily compromises certain values (like respect for open discourse and viewpoint diversity) when they are viewed as conflicting with the goals of protecting against claims of harm.[1]

Anything short of an enthusiastic endorsement of assertions arising from the beliefs can lead to charges of bias, often amplified through social media. The result is an academic environment with substantial restrictions on free inquiry, negatively impacting teaching, research, and discourse more broadly.

2.1 The First Belief: Anything That Aims to Undermine Traditional Frameworks Is Automatically Deemed Good

The first belief is that any action to undermine or replace traditional frameworks or power structures is by definition a good thing. This belief is grounded in the view—that we share—that many of society's problems and inequalities can be attributed to historical power structures that have favored members of the white, cisgender, heteronormative patriarchy. But that does not mean that all proposals to address historical inequities constitute good solutions.

We emphasize that our goal is not to defend traditional power structures. To state the obvious, there is nothing redeeming about historical (or present-day) discrimination, including sexism, racism, intolerance toward members of the LGBTQ community, and so on. One can rightly condemn those ills

---

[1] Apart from the issue of what these beliefs are and how they impact campus discourse, there is a separate and interesting question of *why* these three beliefs have gained such a strong foothold. That is a worthy area of inquiry that could no doubt fill an entire separate book.

Unassailable Ideas. Ilana Redstone and John Villasenor, Oxford University Press (2020). © Oxford University Press.
DOI: 10.1093/oso/9780190078065.001.0001.

while at the same time recognizing that not all initiatives undertaken with the goals of combating them will be effective. Some will be, and some won't be.

The fact that an initiative aims to counteract historical wrongs doesn't mean that, on that basis alone, it should be exempt from an objective evaluation of its merits and drawbacks. A similar observation was articulated by Conor Friedersdorf, who wrote in the *Atlantic* that "[t]o object to a means of achieving x is not to be anti-x" (15). In other words, as Friedersdorf suggests, there is a distinction to be made between criticizing a proposed means to achieve an end and criticizing the goal of achieving that end.

The campus culture of providing unquestioning endorsement of anything presented as a mechanism to undermine, remake, or remove society's real or perceived hierarchies (including the corporate and/or governmental entities and structures that are viewed as enablers of those hierarchies) has broad reach, creating considerable collateral damage. For instance, because this belief is applied to *any* societal feature perceived (whether correctly or not) as having its provenance in historically dominant cultural frameworks, it can lead to absurd consequences, such as assertions that math and logic are inherently racist.

One of many ways this belief has manifested is through the on-campus debate on undergraduate curricula, in which it can be socially unacceptable to assert that classic Western works of literature, philosophy, political theory, and so on have any value at all. The choice that is presented is binary: Members of the campus community are called on to either offer a wholesale rejection and condemnation of Western literary, philosophical, or political thought, or to decline to do so and then be branded as racist, sexist, etc. What is lost is nuance—in this case, the ability to assert without social penalty that, yes, while there is enormous value in globally oriented, holistic curricula that include a substantial focus on non-Western works, that does not have to be at the expense of also reading classic Western works, which, as many others have observed, have something to teach us *despite* their flaws, not because of them.

2.2 The Second Belief: Discrimination Is the Cause of All Unequal Group Outcomes

The second belief is that, absent the hand of discriminatory actors, all group-level outcomes would be equal. However, this belief precludes *this feels ~racist~*

fully considering the role of potential differences in preferences, priorities, and culture that might also contribute to unequal outcomes. It also doesn't fully recognize the complex ways in which different factors (including but not limited to discrimination) might interact in shaping group outcomes, and the challenges of distinguishing correlation from causation.

To take one example, consider a culture in which music plays a particularly large and central role. Such a culture might be expected to produce a disproportionately large number of people who become accomplished musicians. Now, it might also be true that the members of this culture experience discrimination. One can then ask whether they have notably high levels of musical achievement *as a consequence* (among others) of discrimination. Or is this outcome *independent of* discrimination? Or, perhaps the role of music in this culture can be tied in part to cultural factors independent of discrimination and in part to discrimination. Under the second belief, the unequal group outcome—in this case, a higher level of musical achievement among members of this culture—*must* be due to discrimination. But as the foregoing example illustrates, this assumption forecloses a more expansive inquiry that is more open to recognizing culturally driven differences without necessarily tying them to narratives of oppression.

Another factor sometimes raised in relation to group differences is biology. This is a particularly fraught topic, and understandably so given the frequency with which spurious biological explanations for group differences have been used for nefarious purposes in the past. And to be clear, we are *not* suggesting that there is any validity to flawed assertions regarding, for example, purported racial or gender differences in intelligence.

But the fact that claims regarding purported group differences have often been driven by some combination of racism, sexism, and bad science doesn't mean that *all* attempts to explore group differences are attributable to such bias. It seems reasonable to posit, for example, that the dramatic statistical overrepresentation of men among violent criminals has at least some basis in biology. A similar assertion regarding an underlying biological role could also be made regarding the fact—reflected in car insurance rates— that young male drivers tend to get in more accidents than do young female drivers. Yet under the second belief, these suggestions are deemed improper. Instead, it is only permissible to seek explanations based on socialization and gender norms.

or it's cultural.

2.3 The Third Belief: The Primacy of Identity

The third belief is in the primacy of identity, which is commonly invoked through race, ethnicity, gender, religion, sexual orientation, or gender identity. In articulating this belief we are in no way suggesting that identity isn't important. Rather, we are asserting that although it is completely reasonable—and in some cases absolutely necessary—to see things through the lens of identity, that does not mean that an identity-centered view is the *only* legitimate way of examining all issues. While adherence to the third belief has the very positive consequence of ensuring that identity-centered perspectives have a seat at the table, it is often invoked in a way that excludes non–identity-centered perspectives from discourse—despite the value that those perspectives can often add.

Today's identity politics are an understandable reaction to historical (and continuing) patterns of discrimination through which oppressed groups have often been marginalized in the past precisely because those in power placed primacy on these axes of identity and used it in despicable ways (e.g., slavery). Part of the movement to reclaim historically marginalized identities includes elevating them. Yet, as a result of this belief, it has become increasingly unacceptable to make statements suggesting that identity should not *always* have primacy. This shift has been relatively recent, and it is not limited to the campus. At the 2004 Democratic National Convention, then-Senator Barack Obama said, "There's not a black America and white America and Latino America and Asian America; there's the United States of America" (16). It's hard to imagine a major political figure making a statement like that today, as it would immediately be attacked as a devaluation of group-specific experiences. It is even harder to imagine a university dean or president today making such a statement.

Francis Fukuyama, who has written extensively on identity, has argued that its pull stems from a deeper, unfulfilled need for dignity:

> Most economists assume that human beings are motivated by the desire for material resources or goods. This conception of human behavior has deep roots in Western political thought and forms the basis of most contemporary social science. But it leaves out a factor that classical philosophers realized was crucially important: the craving for dignity. Socrates believed that such a need formed an integral "third part" of the human soul, one that coexisted with a "desiring part" and a "calculating part." In Plato's *Republic*,

craving for dignity

he termed this the *thymos*, which English translations render poorly as "spirit." (17, p. 93)

Fukuyama has also noted the tendency to "focus on ever-smaller groups that found themselves marginalized in specific and unique ways." The result, he notes, is that "the principle of universal and equal recognition mutated into calls for special recognition" (17, p. 96).

In an academic culture in which identity is given primacy, it stands to reason that efforts to advance a particular group's interests should take priority, with less attention given to ways in which those efforts may themselves be exclusionary. And, this comes at the price of deemphasizing the opportunities for engagement among members of different identity groups, which in theory is one of most important benefits of a university education. Another consequence of the on-campus focus on identity is that racism, sexism, and other forms of discrimination are often the only causal mechanisms advanced for a complex set of problems, not all of which are ascribable solely to discrimination.

2.4 Are They Beliefs or Unquestionable Truths?

Of course, it could be argued that what we have characterized as beliefs that can reasonably be questioned are instead truths that reflect the "right" way, in an objective sense, to view the world. If that is the case, then any attempt to label them as beliefs and open them to questioning is by definition flawed and misguided. If, on the other hand, they are beliefs rather than nondebatable truths, it becomes possible to ask how widely they are held and to argue for greater recognition that they reflect a particular perspective that not everyone shares.

The "beliefs or unquestionable truths" issue relates to the much broader question of how we develop our opinions on all manner of subjects. In his 1987 book *A Conflict of Visions*, Thomas Sowell of the Hoover Institution argued that the divergence in perspectives among different people runs deep (18). Part of Sowell's inspiration for the book was the observation that people generally coalesce in groups on a multitude of issues. This leads to the interesting observation that by knowing people's position on, for instance, gun control, you can deduce their positions with reasonable confidence on issues such as abortion, charter schools, and affirmative action. As Sowell noted, "it happens too often to be a coincidence and it is too uncontrolled to be a plot" (18, p. 3).

Sowell described a spectrum of views on human nature, ranging from constrained on one side to unconstrained on the other. He wrote, "When Rousseau said that man 'is born free' but 'is everywhere in chains,' he expressed the essence of the unconstrained version, in which the fundamental problem is not nature or man but institutions" (18, p. 30).

"By contrast," Sowell argued, "the constrained vision sees the evils of the world as deriving from the limited and unhappy choices available, given the inherent moral and intellectual limitations of human beings" (18, p. 33). Sowell described the resulting correlation with differences in policy prescriptions:

> Running through the tradition of the unconstrained vision is the conviction that foolish or immoral choices explain the evils of the world—and that wiser or more moral and humane social policies are the solution. (18, p. 32)

He also wrote that:

> In the constrained vision, social processes are described not in terms of intentions or ultimate goals, but in terms of the systematic characteristics deemed necessary to contribute to those goals— "property rights," "free enterprise," or "strict construction" of the Constitution, for example . . . The unconstrained vision speaks directly in terms of desired results, the constrained vision in terms of process characteristics considered conducive to desired results, but not directly or without many unhappy side effects, which are accepted as part of a trade-off. (18, pp. 31–32)

foundations of views

More broadly, Sowell's analysis illustrates that the foundations for the different worldviews are often both unacknowledged and implicit. It can be difficult to recognize the assumptions underlying one's own strongly held views, making it that much harder to understand those who are looking at the same issues from a completely different vantage point.

In a *Washington Post* commentary Megan McArdle made a related point in relation to an invitation offered to Steve Bannon to speak at the 2018 *New Yorker* Festival (19). Although Bannon's history and views were well known to festival organizers when his invitation was extended, in the face of the subsequent social media backlash, *New Yorker* editor David Remnick rescinded it, writing in an e-mail to *New Yorker* staff that "I've changed my mind" and "I don't want well-meaning readers and staff members to think that I've ignored their concerns" (20).

In a *Washington Post* commentary on this set of events, McArdle highlighted the complete separation between the two sides of the political spectrum:

> [B]y leaving less and less room for dissenters, the hegemons created a counter-tribe of outsiders who reject their authority as vehemently as they exert it. And thus, for the same reasons that the beliefs of *New Yorker* readers are in no danger from Steve Bannon, the views of Trump fans are entirely safe from David Remnick.
>
> What's left is a kind of ceremonial cleansing of the sacred city, a mighty labor to make sure that the two circles on the Venn diagram never, ever come into contact. There's something admirable about uncompromising ethical purity, but also something rather dangerous. For it means that outside your circle, there's an entirely different normal. (19)

McArdle's commentary was about the *New Yorker*'s leadership, staff, and readers. But the observation that "outside your circle, there's an entirely different normal" applies in other contexts as well, including on campus. Academic communities can exist in their own circles outside of which there is a different normal. And, like many other communities, they can be places where unacknowledged assumptions can impede dialog, and in some cases can entirely prevent it from occurring.

3

Campus Culture and the Three Beliefs

Each of the three beliefs can be viewed as a reaction to important problems. The first belief, which asserts that any action taken to undermine traditional frameworks and power structures is automatically deemed good, is an understandable reaction to the biases that have historically influenced much of American academia (and society), under which white, male, Western cultures, perspectives, and value systems were explicitly or implicitly assumed to be inherently superior to all others.

The second belief, which asserts that absent the hand of discriminatory actors, all outcomes across groups would be equal, is a reasonable reaction to the many historical and present-day examples in which discrimination has in fact been the direct cause of differences in group outcomes. The third belief—the insistence in the primacy of identity—can be understood as a reaction to the multiple centuries during which American culture devalued (and to a significant extent still does devalue) people based on identity.

The problem is not the fact of recognizing these historical failings and attempting to remedy them in the academy and beyond. Of course, both recognition and remedy are necessary. But in the eagerness to avoid falling into the trap of our predecessors who blithely excused or were incapable of recognizing their own moral failings, there is a reluctance to acknowledge some of the contradictions and detrimental aspects of the current campus climate.

3.1 Claims of Harm

The three beliefs are tied to well-intentioned concerns over the well-being of populations considered vulnerable. How we think about harm in that context shapes the way we evaluate claims of wrongdoing. This in turn has important implications for how we communicate. Part of shielding people from harm means attempting to keep them safe—which is why the word "safe" is frequently invoked in the conversations around campus climate. But, "harm" has taken on a definition so expansive and its prevention a prioritization so

Unassailable Ideas. Ilana Redstone and John Villasenor, Oxford University Press (2020). © Oxford University Press.
DOI: 10.1093/oso/9780190078065.001.0001.

lofty that the question of whom to protect from what has become both critical and polemical.

Concerns about harm to vulnerable groups can be a powerful psychological motivator. Not surprisingly, how we think about harm plays a critical role in impacting our understanding regarding social issues and in determining which problems gain attention and traction. One consequence of the harm-centered narrative in the current campus environment is the erasure of the distinction between subjective and objective claims. This is the premise beneath the now-removed language from the University of Michigan's Bias Response Team website that stated "the most important indication of bias is your own feelings" (21). In citing this, we are not suggesting that feelings generally, or subjective claims of harm, aren't important. Clearly, they are. And, it is easy to imagine any number of scenarios where both a subjective and an objective evaluation will conclude that harm has been caused. Rather, the point is that when academic culture makes no attempt to contextualize and evaluate claims of harm in objective terms, it opens the door to expansive and inconsistent standards of what it means.

inconsistency

The goal of addressing harm can be impeded in multiple ways. On the one hand, when harm is denied or downplayed, it becomes harder to recognize the existence and magnitude of the problem and therefore more difficult to identify appropriate mitigation strategies. On the other hand, overstating harms also has negative consequences. As University of Chicago human and community development professor Richard Shweder said in a 1993 "Aims of Education" address (an annual event at the university's Orientation Week for incoming students on "the aims of a liberal education" (22)):

> If you exaggerate too much the idea that you should be protected from harm, you have a recipe for creating a society of thin-skinned complainers. For every parody, lampoon, or personal slight (you "snake," you "pig," you "animal"), there would be an accusation of "harassment" or "abuse." For every act of criticism, someone would rise up to claim they were being "victimized." Hate groups and anti-defamation leagues would quickly organize and keep each other in business. Eventually, the members of such a society would learn to keep their mouths closed, their ears covered, and their doors shut for fear of the consequences. (23, p. 19)

When claims of harm are placed at the center of a discussion, dialog can be impeded. Consider a classroom debate regarding whether a college should institute a new diversity requirement under which, in order to graduate, all undergraduates would be required to take at least one course addressing diversity. Proponents of the proposal might make reasonable arguments citing the potential value of such courses in broadening student perspectives and understanding regarding complex social issues. Opponents of the proposal might argue that such courses should be available as options, but that they should not be mandatory.

However, some proponents might then respond by asserting that the very fact of expressing opposition to a mandatory diversity requirement is damaging, as it perpetuates some of the very same harms that motivated what they see as a need for a new diversity course requirement. And once opponents of the proposal have been told they are contributing to harm in expressing their opinion, they will understandably be more reticent to engage fully in the debate. As this example illustrates, harm on campus can be conceptualized purely on the basis of what is deemed offensive, regardless of how easily offended the person making the accusation might be.

Assertions that dialog is damaged by excessive invocations of harm are sometimes met with rebuttals arguing that a ground rule of on-campus dialog is that it should be conducted in a manner that avoids devaluing any of the participants—and anything subjectively deemed harmful can of course be cited as a source of devaluation. But this simply restates the issue rather than addressing or explaining it, because the authority to decide what constitutes "devaluing" is implicitly held by the same people who might have an overly broad view of harm. The result is that entire reasonable lines of argument get excluded from discourse.

Assertions of harm often go hand in hand with accusations of bias, which are one of the most potent and commonly deployed weapons used to attack anyone viewed as asserting opinions that run afoul of any of the three beliefs. Thus, a person who questions the effectiveness of a particular affirmative action program might be branded by its defenders as "racist." A person who suggests that, all else being equal, increasing age tends to lead to decreased stamina to work 80-hour weeks is called "ageist." And so on. The social and professional scarring that result from being labeled as biased can persist long after the discussion that led to the labeling. This serves as a powerful deterrent for the people who are unwilling to take on that risk.

It is difficult to engage in debate with people who are both 1) quick to publicly denounce anyone who disagrees with them as biased, and 2) 100 percent certain they are right. In a climate in which claims of harm are often placed at the center of discourse, there can be complex rules over who gets to invoke those claims. Using the earlier example of the classroom debate on the merits of instituting a requirement that all undergraduates take at least one diversity course, the tendency is to focus on the claims of harm voiced by people who feel that opposition to the diversity proposal is offensive. Little or no concern would likely be given to claims of harm by the people who, having been accused of offering harmful opinions, are now excluded from the dialog.

The culture on many campuses centers around listening to, and often meeting, student demands with the priority placed on those demands that are consistent with the three beliefs. An academic culture focused on competing claims of harm has also reshaped the dynamics of student activism. A comparison between the present and the 1960s can shed some light on this. In the 1960s, student protests regarding free speech were aimed at *expanding* that right. At UC Berkeley, students responded to regulations that prohibited organizations from soliciting funds or membership on campus (24). Students wanted to be able to organize tables and raise support for the civil rights movement. This led to demands to relax the restrictions to allow greater freedom for political fundraising on campus. At Berkeley, students wanted the administration to allow them *more* freedom on campus, and wanted *less* control and intervention by the university administration.

This stands in stark contrast with much of today's on-campus activism, which often includes demands that freedoms be *removed* or constrained in exchange for an increase in protections and an increase in what might fifty years ago have been described as paternalism. This is partly because conceptions of identity are often closely intertwined with subjectivism and the veneration of lived experiences. In practice this means that attempts to build understanding and engagement with members of groups other than one's own are often impeded because of assumptions that experiences can't be understood by someone outside the group. As Alex Dean writes on lived experience:

> [The idea] is aimed at ensuring that those affected by problems have a voice in discussions about fixing them, and giving women, ethnic minorities and gay people control of their own narratives. In some ways, this is a great thing: those who have suffered oppression must be able to talk about it if they wish, particularly if throughout history their stories have been twisted by parties with their own agendas. An attempt to break from this, whatever its drawbacks, deserves some praise.

But that's where the emphasis on "lived experience" stops being sensible. It's clearly not the case that we *only* learn from direct experience. To suggest that we do is to stray into a belief that abstract thinking, working a problem out through reflection and reading, is insufficient. It is the idea that feeling, not thinking, is the most important thing when solving a problem. (25, emphasis in original)

The view that feelings are the most important way to understand a problem is tied to the broader idea that only fellow group members can effectively comment on, teach, write, or speak about the experience of members in that group. This has real consequences for the dynamics of how universities are run. For instance, in the current academic climate, a faculty member who does not have Asian heritage might, on that basis, be viewed as automatically less qualified to teach a class on Asian literature or history.

3.2 Microaggressions and Trigger Warnings

People in academia understandably want to avoid getting caught up in university disciplinary proceedings. As a consequence of the dominance of the three beliefs in defining on-campus culture, they learn to safeguard themselves, often through filtering their speech to avoid saying or presenting anything that might be viewed as upsetting. This requires steering clear of language that might be interpreted as a microaggression, as well as being attentive to expectations about the perceived necessity to provide trigger warnings.

Merriam-Webster (online) defines a microaggression as "a comment or action that subtly and often unconsciously or unintentionally expresses a prejudiced attitude toward a member of a marginalized group (such as a racial minority)" (26) and a trigger warning as "a statement cautioning that content (as in a text, video, or class) may be disturbing or upsetting" (27).

Of course, attention to microaggressions and trigger warning has reasonable justifications. For instance, discussions about microaggressions can lead to greater awareness regarding statements that might be unintentionally hurtful, and in doing so can promote greater civility in dialog. As Jesse Singal wrote for *New York* magazine in 2016:

Students, particularly those for whom the diversity of their college campus is novel, really do say dumb things to one another. So if the concept of microaggression merely pointed to these sorts of ignorant remarks, it probably wouldn't have kicked up so much controversy. (28)

There are certainly some phrases that have been characterized as microaggressions that most people would recognize as highly offensive. Raising awareness among the subset of people who might not have otherwise realized that such speech can be insulting is a positive thing. Thus, the problem is not with identifying and calling attention to unintentionally offensive speech, but rather with expanding the definition of microaggressions to encompass even clearly innocuous statements such as "I believe the most qualified person should get the job."

Trigger warnings emerged from a growing understanding of the effects of posttraumatic stress disorder and a desire to avoid the "triggers" that could cause a trauma survivor to "re-experience an incident, go into avoidance mode, or 'numb out'" (29). In a 2014 article in the *Guardian*, Jill Filipovic wrote, "It's perfectly reasonable for a survivor of violence to ask a professor for a heads up if the reading list includes a piece with graphic descriptions of rape or violence, for example" (30).

Yet both trigger warnings and accusations of microaggressions can be overapplied. The word "microaggressions" primes people to view interactions through a lens in which one person is the victim and the other is the perpetrator. This creates a climate that tends to be overly inclusive when assessing whether or not a statement is a microaggression. As Singal wrote, "microaggressions are being defined so broadly and so subjectively that students who are exposed to them are likely to come away very, very confused about what constitutes acceptable speech on campus" (28). Filipovic observed that "generalized trigger warnings" are "a low-stakes way to use the right language to identify yourself as conscious of social justice issues." She also wrote that:

> Trigger warnings, and their cousin the "content note," are now included for a whole slew of potentially offensive or upsetting content, including but not limited to: misogyny, the death penalty, calories in a food item, terrorism, drunk driving, how much a person weighs, racism, gun violence, Stand Your Ground laws, drones, homophobia, PTSD, slavery, victim-blaming, abuse, swearing, child abuse, self-injury, suicide, talk of drug use, descriptions

of medical procedures, corpses, skulls, skeletons, needles, discussion of "isms," neuroatypical shaming, slurs (including "stupid" or "dumb"), kidnapping, dental trauma, discussions of sex (even consensual), death or dying, spiders, insects, snakes, vomit, pregnancy, childbirth . . . (30)

overly broad

The overly broad labeling of microaggressions and trigger warnings is a tangible manifestation of the three beliefs. For example, in accordance with the second belief, in discussions about group outcomes, care must be taken not to make any assertion—however innocuous—that suggests that a particular difference is not purely ascribable to discrimination. Failure to adhere to that rule risks having the offender accused of committing a microaggression. Accusations of microaggressions that implicate identity are related to the third belief, which places primacy on identity and, relatedly, on identity-based claims of harm. To be sure, claims of and concerns over harm on campus have the laudable goal of protecting students from psychological pain. But the label of "harm" is expansive, and when its definition becomes too broad and too subjective, invocations of harm risk becoming a tool for silencing opinions deemed uncomfortable.

Because the speaker's intention is assumed, even in the case where perceived microaggressions stem from a simple misunderstanding or from a reasonable difference in perspectives, they are characterized as harmful attacks. Consider the statement "America is the land of opportunity," which is included in the University of California document discussed earlier as an example of a microaggression (31). While people might reasonably differ in their level of agreement or disagreement with that assertion, the act of voicing it shouldn't be off limits. People who agree with the assertion should be able to freely state it without social penalty, and cite as evidence, for example, America's longstanding status as a destination of choice for immigrants seeking to better their lives and those of their children. People who disagree with it should also be able to do so freely and without social penalty, citing, for example, the innumerable historical and contemporary examples of opportunity in America denied on the basis of attributes such as race, gender, sexual orientation, religion, or gender identity.

Further complicating things, sometimes microaggressions are associated with inconsistencies that make their labeling and interpretation even more confusing. Take, for instance, a compliment regarding the English skills of a non-native English speaker who is a student at a U.S. university. Many people in academia would consider the act of making such a compliment, however well intentioned, to be a microaggression—one that could be interpreted as an identity-based insult intended to "otherize." As a result, such compliments have become rare in on-campus conversations. It is safer to say nothing at all.

Yet this *de facto* on-campus prohibition of the "microaggression" of complimenting someone's mastery of English as a second language illustrates one of the multiple inconsistencies that define current campus culture: There is no outcry regarding the nearly universal requirement for non–U.S.-based, non-native-English-speaker applicants to U.S. degree programs to submit Test of English as a Foreign Language (TOEFL) scores. The fact that it is considered perfectly acceptable to compel (non-native-speaker) applicants to sit through a test designed specifically to score them on their English skills is an acknowledgment that English proficiency matters. When the score is too low, a college can and often does deny admission on that basis. As a matter of logic, it follows that it shouldn't be off limits to compliment someone who has clearly and successfully invested enormous effort in mastering English as a foreign language.

3.3 The Dynamics of Diversity Proposals

Suggesting that any of the mushrooming number of campus programs and initiatives with "diversity" in their title may be anything but perfect is to invite a range of hostile responses. With that in mind, let us first clarify that both of the authors of this book are strong believers in the benefits of diversity in the campus context and beyond. For example, we believe that students, universities, and society as a whole benefit when members of the university community are diverse racially, ethnically, religiously, in relation to gender identity and sexual orientation, and with respect to their viewpoints and socioeconomic backgrounds. But one should be able to hold that view without being required to automatically give enthusiastic endorsement to *every* proposal that is floated or every policy that is adopted with the stated aim of improving diversity.

Proposals for new on-campus initiatives to improve diversity are like those to advance any other cause: Some are well thought out and deserve to be adopted and implemented, some are good but redundant with initiatives that are already in place, some are mediocre, and some are downright bad. With campus diversity proposals, however, purely objective evaluation is elusive, with the result that the barriers to adoption are lower and the incentives for proliferation are higher than with proposals in other areas. To question such proposals runs counter to both the first belief (that anything that aims to undermine traditional frameworks or power structures is automatically deemed to be good) and the third belief (the primacy of identity). As a result, well-intentioned criticism of any proposal involving diversity is perilous. *optics*

One challenge is ~~optics~~. To oppose any such proposal is to risk being branded a bigot by its proponents, even if the opposition is not to the goal of the proposal itself but rather to the specific framework it articulates for achieving that goal. Few faculty members are willing to expend their political capital opposing a substandard diversity proposal that they know is going to get adopted regardless of any opposition they might raise. When faced with such a proposal, the choice, in simple terms, is often between 1) opposing it, being unfairly branded as a bigot, and having it get approved anyway, and 2) staying silent and watching as it gets approved.

In either case, the proposal gets approved, but in the first case the faculty member emerges with a record of being unfriendly to diversity initiatives—something that might well be detrimental to his or her reputation and future career growth. Faced with this choice, it's understandable that would-be faculty opponents of an ill-thought-out proposal for a new diversity initiative might choose to stay silent rather than voice an objection that will have no impact on the approval decision. As an inevitable consequence, this increases the odds that substandard proposals will be approved.

Second, members of the university community, including university presidents, deans, department chairs, faculty members, and students, have powerful incentives to grow diversity programs. When administrators and faculty members seek promotions within the university or posts at other universities, and when students apply to graduate school or for employment, one of the most risk-free ways to curry favor with an evaluating committee is to tally the diversity initiatives they helped create or grow. Moreover, credit is given for the creation of a program, quite apart from any results it might generate downstream. These incentives add to the pressure to create an ever-growing number of diversity programs.

A third factor is that a diversity program, once created, is almost impossible to phase out even if it is not successful. The same factors that lead to a lowering of the barriers to adoption also increase the barriers to cancellation. Even if a program is clearly and demonstrably not successful, the social pressures to continue supporting it are enormous. No one wants to be the person who denies the application for renewal funding for an existing diversity program.

3.4 Campus Similarities with Authoritarian Countries

In some respects, being a member of a campus community—whether as a student, instructor, researcher, or staff member—is like living in an authoritarian country. Residents of authoritarian countries are well schooled in the list of taboo topics and opinions. Those who keep their head down and avoid publicly voicing any opinions that could draw negative attention from authorities are well positioned to thrive. Millions of people lead highly satisfying professional and personal lives in authoritarian countries, in significant part because they are careful to avoid saying or doing anything that touches any of the third rails that all residents of an authoritarian country know exist.

By analogy, the same is true on campuses. There are thousands of people on U.S. college campuses who are thriving. They do good work, get recognized for doing so, and are rewarded with continued professional advancement and opportunities. If they opine at all regarding the beliefs we identify here, it is to endorse them, either because doing so is genuinely consistent with their own beliefs or because they have correctly calculated that doing so will be beneficial to their career and on-campus reputation.

In authoritarian countries there are also dissidents. These are people who, to varying degrees, have chosen to voice taboo opinions. Dissent in authoritarian countries spans a spectrum. On the one end, there are the accidental or mild dissenters. These are people who, perhaps unwittingly, have strayed across the line and voiced a taboo opinion on one or a very few occasions. For them, there is at least the possibility of forgiveness and repentance. Their transgression will be pointed out, and they will be given the opportunity to voice contrition and to pledge to avoid a repeat occurrence. If they stick to that pledge, their professional opportunities might suffer little to no long-term damage. On the other end of the dissent spectrum are those residents of authoritarian countries who choose to confront the government head on. They know that in doing so, they will pay a price that includes being characterized as an outcast and having their professional opportunities wither.

By analogy, campuses also have their dissidents, and as in authoritarian countries, there is a spectrum. There are the accidental or mild dissenters— a professor, for example, who on one occasion voices an opinion to a small group of colleagues that runs counter to one of the three core beliefs discussed above. If the transgression is mild enough, it may lead to few or no negative consequences. At the other end of the spectrum are those who repeatedly and publicly make statements that collide with one or more of the three beliefs.

Faculty members who are repeated and vocal dissidents risk grave damage to their professional opportunities. If they have tenure, they will generally (but not always, as we discuss later) be able to continue in their jobs. But they will likely be ostracized by their colleagues as well as their students, and they will be unlikely to ever be appointed to a higher administrative position, such as department chair or dean. In addition, if they are ever interested in making a lateral move to a tenured position at another university, they will have an extraordinarily difficult time. This is because faculty appointments generally require a vote from faculty in the department that an applicant aspires to join—a hurdle that a "dissident" would almost never be able to clear.

If a faculty dissident who has loudly questioned any of the three beliefs does not have tenure, his or her odds of getting it become dramatically lower. This is likely one of the reasons why almost no untenured, tenure-track faculty do so. Like denizens of an authoritarian country, they know where the boundaries lie, and they are careful to stay on the correct side of them.

For adjunct instructors, the dynamics operate even more quickly. While a tenure-track assistant professor who voices opinions that challenge the beliefs might be denied tenure years later, an adjunct who behaves similarly will likely find that he or she is not rehired for the next academic term, which in general is no more than a few months in the future. The adjunct teaching market is such that the supply of potential instructors vastly exceeds demand. The people making adjunct hiring decisions will naturally gravitate away from hiring an adjunct who has in the past questioned any of the three beliefs.

Students who express positions that run afoul of one or more of the beliefs face both the short-term risk of being ostracized by their peers and potential longer-term reputational costs. Students understand that, along with their education, one of the most valuable things they will acquire at college is a network of peers—a network that will be substantially less valuable if they are viewed as not holding sufficiently conformist views. For those contemplating expressing opinions not aligned with the dominant on-campus narrative, this creates strong social pressure to stay quiet.

4

Social Media

In recent years, social media have become a powerful force in shaping discourse. The impact is particularly strong on campus given the high rates of social media usage among college students. With social media, anyone can be a publisher with the potential to instantly reach a worldwide audience. This enables extraordinarily fast dissemination of information. In some circumstances this is an enormous advantage—for example, when providing information that can help people stay safe before, during, and in the wake of a natural disaster. But while social media bring benefits, spurring real-time, thoughtful, in-person discussions is generally not one of them. In addition, the speed of social media can be problematic when it is used to disseminate false information or information that, while true, is stripped of the context necessary to fully interpret it.

More fundamentally, social media have transformed the way we think and interact with others. Many people—and particularly young people, who tend to spend a lot of time on their smartphones—have come to rely on the validation that comes from positive online feedback such as "likes" and retweets. Social media make it far easier than in the past to construct entire digital universes populated largely by people who are aligned regarding a particular issue. And, social media make it easier to express anger, providing sustenance and support for those who wish to be cheered on as they lob online potshots at people viewed as "others."

An enormous amount of interaction occurs via digital communications tools such as social media postings and text messages. While text messages aren't a form of social media, they share some key attributes with many forms of social media, including the reliance on written expression and the fact that they are often used in ways that replace interactions that might otherwise have occurred via a phone conversation or an in-person discussion.

Some statistics can help convey how much communication is occurring in online contexts. According to a 2013 survey, smartphone owners in the 18-to-24-year age range were sending and receiving a combined total of nearly 130 text messages per day. For those in the 25-to-34, 35-to-44, and

Unassailable Ideas. Ilana Redstone and John Villasenor, Oxford University Press (2020). © Oxford University Press.
DOI: 10.1093/oso/9780190078065.001.0001.

45-to-54 age groups, the corresponding numbers were about 75, 52, and 33 text messages per day respectively (32). These numbers are almost certainly higher today, as the total number of monthly text messages sent in the United States reportedly grew by over 50% in the four years from June 2013 to June 2017 (33). While this overall growth number doesn't include a per-age-group breakdown, given how large it is, it seems likely that texting activity in all of these age groups experienced growth from 2013 to 2017.

For the fourth quarter of 2018, Twitter reported having 66 million monthly active users (34; see page 11, stating that "Average US MAU were 66 million for Q4") in the United States, a number that is impressive even if not all "users" are individuals (some accounts belong to companies and other organizations; some are bots, etc.). Snap, Inc., the company that offers Snapchat, reported 80 million daily active users in North America in the first quarter of 2019 (35). According to Hootsuite, as of January 2019, Instagram had a reach of 120 million people in the United States (36, p. 111). More broadly, again according to Hootsuite, in January 2019 there were 230 million active social media users in the United States, corresponding to a penetration of 70% (37, p. 15). Hootsuite pegged the "average amount of time per day spent using social media" at over two hours (37, p. 32). With these numbers as context, in the remainder of this chapter we discuss how social media have changed the dynamics of communication in society at large as well as in academia.

4.1 Online Communication

While applications such as FaceTime and Skype enable real-time video interactions, most online communications involve writing and occur in non-real time (i.e., asynchronously). As a result, they are often (though not always; e.g., when emojis are used, or when a social media user posts a selfie to be seen by his or her followers) devoid of the facial expressions, body language, and tone of voice that are all features of in-person interactions that convey meaning beyond the words that are verbalized.

The contribution of nonverbal factors to communication is significant, though difficult to quantify. In the 1971 book *Silent Messages*, UCLA psychology professor Albert Mehrabian described a pair of studies that explored relationships—including potential contradictions—between single words and the tone of voice and/or facial expressions employed when voicing those words. In that highly constrained context, he concluded that tone of voice *importance of nonverbal communication*

and body language accounted for considerably more of what was communicated than the words themselves (38–40).

Mehrabian's work has often been misrepresented in both the popular press and in the later academic literature, leading, for example, to blanket (and misleading) assertions that only 7% of the information in communications is verbal. Such extrapolations are problematic because Mehrabian's work was based on the study of single words in isolation. For example, one of his academic papers explained that "3 degrees of attitude (i.e., positive, neutral, and negative) in facial expression were each combined with 3 degrees of attitude communicated vocally. The vocal communications of attitude were superimposed on a neutral word" (39, p. 248).

Mehrabian recognized the problem with extrapolating his work more broadly. In a 2007 article, Augsburg College professor David Lapakko cited a private communication from Mehrabian in 1995 in which Mehrabian explained that "My findings are often misquoted . . . Clearly, it is absurd to imply or suggest that the verbal portion of all communication constitutes only 7% of the message" (41). Despite the limitations of Mehrabian's work and the high frequency with which it is misrepresented, when properly contextualized it remains an interesting—though very narrowly constrained—examination of how people can interpret mismatches between a spoken word and the tone of voice and/or facial expression used when speaking it.

Other studies have also highlighted the importance of nonverbal communication. In a 1980 study of interviews (42) for an engineering apprenticeship, the authors found that "direct eye contact occurs more often in the accept interviews, avoidance gaze occurs more often in the reject interviews, and eye wandering occurs less in accept interviews than in the other two groups of interviews" (42, p. 69) (where "accept interview" refers to an interview in which an offer is later made, and "reject interview" refers to the opposite).

A 2009 study of nonverbal communication in a university classroom found that it can be "an important source of motivation and concentration for students' learning as well as a tool for taking and maintaining attention" (43, see abstract). In sum, it's clear that in face-to-face conversation, nonverbal information such as tone of voice and facial expression matters. Conversely, when we engage in online written communication, nonverbal information that would otherwise help shape our interpretation is lost. In the absence of this information, we fill in the blanks inefficiently—and sometimes incorrectly.

In the best-case scenario, online written expression complements in-person communication, helping us to remain in touch with friends and family when time and distance prevent face-to-face interactions and providing a wealth of options for efficient, cost-effective business communications. However, as MIT professor Sherry Turkle described in her 2015 book *Reclaiming Conversation* (44, p. 137), online communication often functions as a *replacement* for in-person communication. Turkle related the story of Trevor, who recalled that when he was a college senior in 2009—when smartphones were far less advanced and pervasive than they are today—the norm was "Don't talk it. Post it. Share it." Trevor described his experience at a graduation farewell party in the following manner:

ok boomer.

> People barely spoke. They ordered drinks and food. Sat with their dates. Looked at their phones. They didn't even try. Everyone knew that when they got home they would see pictures of the party. They could save the comments until then. We weren't really saying good-bye. It was just good-bye until we got to our rooms and logged onto Facebook. (44, p. 138)

As this anecdote illustrates, the online world provides an alternative venue for engagement and affirmation. The appeal of this venue and its constant siren call of availability and affirmation decrease the incentives to engage more fully in the offline world. When a greater fraction of our communication is happening online, something broader shifts in our relationships with other people.

This change has unfolded in the context of an increase in broader concerns over incivility. Clark University political science professor Robert Boatwright, one of the editors of the 2019 anthology *A Crisis of Civility?*, wrote that "in December 2016 . . . 75% of Americans agreed that there is a 'crisis' of civility'" (45, p. 2). One of the book's contributors, Southwestern University political science professor Emily Snydor, made the following observation:

> Many empirical tests of the effects of incivility focus on incivility as the style or tone of political discourse, rather than its content or substance. From this perspective, civility describes the manner in which political discussions are conducted, emphasizing adherence to cultural norms for polite, face-to-face conversation. (45, p. 62)

As such, the movement toward online communication amplifies, feeds into, and responds to the existing trend toward incivility, and thus polarization, more generally—a change with far-reaching implications.

4.1.1 Changes to How We Think and Communicate

Efforts to add nuance to online written interactions have come not only through predigital keyboard options such as capitalization and punctuation, but also through newer mechanisms such as emojis. Yet even a written communication constructed with skillful use of all these tools falls far short of what in-person interaction can allow. In *Reclaiming Conversation*, Turkle wrote of the learning curve she experienced when communicating with her daughter through text messages:

online etiquette

> If you don't know the rules and you make the wrong assumptions, meaningful conversations can stop. When it comes to texting, a lack of fluency with the rules can divide generations and families . . . Why does my daughter think I am angry with her when I text? She explains: "Mom, your texts are always, like, 'Great.' And I know it's not great. What's happening? What are you really thinking?" There is no convincing her. When I texted her "Great," it was because that really was what I meant. If she were here with me in person, that is what I would have said. But "Great" as a text message is cold. At the very least it needs a lot of exclamation points.
>
> My first—and it turns out, clumsy—move was to include terms of endearment in my texting. To little avail. She said that a text from me ("May I speak with you tonight, sweetheart?") came off "like a death in the family." I learn from my research that "Call??? When good for you????" would have been better. (44, p. 132)

Nicholas Carr has argued in his 2011 book *The Shallows* that the internet hasn't just changed the way we communicate, but it has also fundamentally altered the way we think. Carr observed that in his own experience, it has diminished the ability to focus:

> I'm not thinking the way I used to think. I feel it most strongly when I am reading. I used to find it easy to immerse myself in a book or a lengthy article. My mind would get caught up in the twists of the narrative or the

less concentration

turns of the argument, and I'd spend hours strolling through long stretches of prose. That's rarely the case anymore. Now my concentration starts to drift after a page or two. I get fidgety, lose the thread, begin looking for something else to do . . . I think I know what's going on. For well over a decade now, I've been spending a lot of time online, searching and surfing and sometimes adding to the great databases of the Internet. (46, p. 5–6)

Spending significant amounts of time online of necessity means dividing our attention differently than in the predigital age. Writing about the experiments of University of Southern California neuroscience professor Antonio Damasio, Carr considered the impact of a greater number of distractions on our capacity for empathy. Damasio and colleagues "had subjects listening to stories describing people experiencing physical or psychological pain." As described by Carr, "the experiment, say the scholars, indicates that the more distracted we become, the less able we are to experience the subtlest, most distinctively human forms of empathy, compassion, and other emotions" (46, p. 221). Weakening our ability to feel empathy makes it easier to view whomever we're interacting with as less human, and easier to insult and demean them. *online objectification*

Turkle came to a related conclusion in arguing that online interactions make it easier to view people as objects. She wrote that "we are tempted, summoned by robots and bots, objects that address us as if they were people. And just as we imagine things as people, we invent ways of being with people that turn them into something close to things" (47, p. 224). To illustrate this, she described Chatroulette, a website that was launched in 2009 and randomly pairs users around the world who are simultaneously logged in to the site. They can see, talk, and write to each other in real time, with the interaction lasting until one user clicks "next" to move on to the next partner. Turkle observed that "Chatroulette takes things to an extreme: faces and bodies become objects" (47, p. 225).

4.1.2 The Need for Validation

Our susceptibility to the feedback from apps and the online world is further apparent in the story Turkle recounted of Cara, a college student who was using Happiness Tracker, an app that asks the user to input her level of happiness, what she's doing, where she is, and whom she's with (44, p. 95).

Over a period of a few weeks, Cara's Happiness Tracker reported a decline in her happiness with no clear indication of why. Seeing the app's report made Cara think about her relationship to her boyfriend, despite the fact that he hadn't been mentioned specifically by the app. She found herself feeling less happy with him and wondered if he was the cause of her loss in contentment. Ultimately, Cara decided to end the relationship. Turkle wrote that "[Cara] saw the number she got from the program as a 'failing grade' and it sparked a desire to get a better one" (44, p. 95–96).

Turkle's observations are consistent with what we know about the underlying biology and the relationship between dopamine and social rewards (48). Social media services are designed so that social media companies can get more traffic, users, and data, and, as a result, higher revenue and market value. As designers of social media services have long known, products that exploit (and contribute to) our distractibility by capitalizing on the human tendency to seek affirmation can be highly successful in the marketplace. For users, the currency of the realm in social media is likes, shares, comments, and retweets, which in combination satisfy a need for validation and attention.   *self-esteem*

In a study published in 2016, Anthony Burrow and Nicolette Rainone of the Department of Human Development at Cornell University found that the "number of likes individuals received on their Facebook profile pictures was positively associated with self-esteem" (49, p. 1). The connection between self-esteem and online feedback raises the natural question of which types of posts receive the most attention online. This was explored in a limited context in a paper published in 2013 by Sounman Hong, a professor in the College of Social Sciences at Yonsei University in Korea. Hong examined the Twitter feeds in the U.S. House of Representatives and found that "politicians with extreme ideologies tend to benefit more from their social media adoptions" (50). While Hong's study was focused on a very specific subgroup (members of the House of Representatives), his findings are consistent with what we see with social media more broadly: More emotional, incendiary, and extreme points of view garner more attention and feedback online, thus creating an incentive to generate more such posts and comments.

The voices on social media that are the loudest and offer the most extreme perspectives are often the ones that get amplified (50). The most vocal people include those who are the quickest to launch social media fusillades against people perceived as the "enemy" and to denounce those within their own ranks who fail to sufficiently toe the party line. Put differently, the dominance of social media creates a confluence of factors that push people into expressing more extreme positions. It should come as no surprise that discourse can suffer as a result.

4.2 Online Disinhibition

less restraint

An additional consequence of the lack of nonverbal cues in most social media exchanges is that the feedback that would normally prompt people to exercise restraint in in-person interactions is often absent in online communication. Inhibitions are often far lower online than offline, leading to a greater tendency toward incivility.

As early as 2004, when social media were far less prevalent than they are today, Rider University psychologist Jonathan Suler published a paper titled "The Online Disinhibition Effect." Suler argued that six factors contribute to this effect, which he defined as the way in which "people say and do things in cyberspace that they wouldn't ordinarily say and do in the face-to-face world" (51, p. 321). He noted that the effect can take on two forms. Benign disinhibition promotes the revelation of emotions and wishes, and can also be associated with unusual acts of kindness or generosity. On the other end of the spectrum is what Suler called toxic disinhibition, which includes a greater propensity toward "rude language, harsh criticisms, anger, hatred, even threats" (51, p. 321).

The six contributing factors Suler identified are "dissociative anonymity," "invisibility," "asynchronicity," "solipsistic introjection," "dissociative imagination," and "minimization of status and authority" (51, pp. 322–324). Dissociative anonymity refers to people's ability to separate online interactions from their "in-person lifestyle and identity" (51, pp. 322). Invisibility refers to the fact that people in online interactions generally can't see one another and, more specifically, that it's possible to lurk in ways that others don't even know they're there. Asynchronicity refers to non–real-time interactions—for example, in contrast with in-person conversations, exchanges in online forums often occur in settings in which words transmitted by a speaker are received by the listener with some delay. The lack of opportunity to observe and manage someone's immediate reaction, Suler argued, contributes to disinhibition.

Solipsistic introjection is the alteration of self-boundaries, which Suler described in the following manner: "People may feel that their mind has merged with the mind of the online companion. Reading another person's message might be experienced as a voice within one's head, as if that person's psychological presence and influence have been assimilated or introjected into one's psyche" (51, p. 323). Suler argued that the interaction may be experienced as with oneself, which can feel safer than interacting with others. Dissociative imagination is where "consciously or unconsciously, people may feel that the imaginary characters they 'created' exist in a different space, that a person's online persona along with the online others live in a make-believe dimension, separate and apart from the demands and responsibilities of the real world" (51, p. 323). Finally, minimization of status and authority occurs because the indicators of status and authority that are conveyed through in-person interactions are sometimes absent in online interactions. In their absence, relationships that wouldn't otherwise feel as though they are with peers nonetheless appear as such online. Suler argued that these six factors conspire to alter the way people behave online in a way that can result in a breakdown of the norms of communication.

4.3 Online Call-Out Culture

One of the most visible changes to public discourse in the social media age has been the rise of call-out culture, a term used to describe the use of social media to build a wave of public indignation regarding behavior deemed transgressive. Of course, there is nothing new about airing public criticisms. With social media, however, call-outs can cascade through the online ecosystem in hours, gaining thousands of retweets and other endorsements, often in ways that lack full context.

The indignation is particularly noticeable because, in an era in which so much of public discourse is conducted via social media, the public commentary on an issue can disproportionately amplify the most vociferously expressed views, making it difficult to gauge true sentiment. While disproportionality in public dialog isn't new, it is exaggerated through social media as a result of near-instantaneous dissemination to (and amplification by) very large audiences. People who are offended are a lot more likely than those who are not to take to platforms like Twitter and Facebook. In addition, as *New York Times* columnist David Brooks has written, "these days the social media tail wags the mainstream media dog" (52). The result is that call-out campaigns that start on social media can quickly cross over to mainstream news media, and in both settings the story is largely defined by those who raise the loudest criticism—even if they don't necessarily represent a majority view. Further illuminating these differences, the Hidden Tribes project, which was "launched by More in Common in late 2018 to better understand the forces that drive political polarization and tribalism in the United States today" (53), found, as reported in an April 2019 *New York Times* article, that "48 percent of Democrats on social media"—but a much higher "70 percent of other Democrats"—"say political correctness is a problem in the U.S."[1] (54).

It is also illustrative to consider the results of a 2016 survey in which the Pew Research Center and Elon University's Imagining the Internet Center asked over 1,500 experts to respond to prompts, including "How do you expect social media and digital commentary will evolve in the coming decade?" (55). The responses paint a picture of discourse in the social media age that is both familiar and concerning.

Baratunde Thurston, a fellow at the MIT Media Lab, observed that "we've built a system in which access and connectivity are easy, the cost of publishing is near zero, and accountability and consequences for bad action are difficult to impose or toothless when they do." Internet pioneer Vint Cerf, who is now with Google, wrote that "the combination of bias-reinforcing enclaves and global access to bad actions seems like a toxic mix. It is not clear whether there is a way to counter-balance their socially harmful effects." And according to Michael Kleeman of UCSD, "Increased anonymity coupled with an increase in less-than-informed input, with no responsibility by the actors, has tended and will continue to create less open and honest conversations and more one-sided and negative activities" (55).

Not surprisingly, the features described by the survey respondents reflect what might be called a perfect storm for communication breakdown and online conflagrations. And while it isn't news that online interactions can have an unhealthy dynamic, they set up an environment for call-out culture that has important implications for the beliefs we describe in this book.

Online call-out culture is notable not only for the speed at which it operates, but also for its scale: Within hours, it can focus the ire of thousands of people on someone who has said or done something deemed offensive.

---

[1] According to the *New York Times* article, "'Democrats on social media' means respondents identified as Democratic-leaning voters who said they had posted political content on social media in the last year; 'Democrats off social media' means Democratic-leaning voters who said they had not."

To take one of many examples, consider what happened near the Lincoln Memorial on January 18, 2019, in an encounter including participants in the Indigenous Peoples March and students from Covington Catholic High School who were in Washington to participate in the March for Life. Over a period of hours, a video interpreted by many to show Covington student Nicholas Sandmann mocking Native American elder Nathan Phillips went viral. The dominance of the story on social media quickly drew the attention of establishment media outlets.

The Associated Press published a story (56) with the headline "Students in 'MAGA' hats mock Native American after rally" that was quickly picked up by multiple other news organizations (57). The *New York Times* ran a story titled "Viral Video Shows Boys in 'Make America Great Again' Hats Surrounding Native Elder" (58). The *Guardian*'s story was titled "Outcry after Kentucky students in Maga hats mock Native American veteran," with the subtitle "Teenagers from Covington Catholic High School filmed jeering at Nathan Phillips and chanting 'build that wall'" (59).

In response to the cascading publicity, the Roman Catholic Diocese of Covington and Covington Catholic High School quickly responded that they were launching an investigation and would take "appropriate action, up to and including expulsion." "We extend our deepest apologies to Mr. Phillips," they added. "This behavior is opposed to the Church's teachings on the dignity and respect of the human person" (60).

A few weeks later, after an investigation commissioned by the Covington diocese and Covington Catholic High School was complete, Covington bishop Roger J. Foys released a letter stating that the investigation "has demonstrated that our students did not instigate the incident that occurred at the Lincoln Memorial" (61). In addition, he noted that "the immediate worldwide reaction to the initial video led almost everyone to believe that our students had initiated the incident and the perception of those few minutes of video became reality" (62).

Whatever one thinks of this incident, it is clear that the initial viral video didn't provide the full context. Online call-out culture was used to generate a wave of anger and condemnation, with relatively few voices in the initial hours calling for a pause while more information could be gathered. Once it became clear that the situation was somewhat more complex, the online and establishment media ecosystem began to recalibrate. For example, the *New York Times* added a note at the top of its original story stating that "Interviews and additional video footage have offered a fuller picture of what happened in this encounter, including the context that the Native American man approached the students amid broader tensions outside the Lincoln Memorial" (58). *assuming guilt*

A condemn-first, ask-questions-later online call-out culture is problematic for multiple reasons. First, it leads to rash decisions—in this case, by many news outlets to publish hastily reported news stories, and by the Covington diocese to issue a condemnation that it would walk back a few weeks later. Second, while the Lincoln Memorial incident was so extraordinarily visible that there was plenty of effort devoted to doing proper reporting in the days after the initial stories were published, many incidents that result in social media call-outs don't receive nearly that much attention once the initial wave of social media amplification has waned. In those cases, further information that might clarify the record gets much less visibility from a social media ecosystem that has already turned its attention elsewhere. A third problem with call-out culture is that, as Conor Friedersdorf has observed in the *Atlantic*, public discourse is "dominated not by efforts to persuade or debate anything on the merits, but by attempts to cast, locate, or portray the target of one's opprobrium as out of bounds" (63).

For another example of call-out culture, consider the oft-cited case of Justine Sacco, who as of Friday, December 20, 2013,[2] was senior director of corporate communications for IAC, a major media and internet holding company. Just before boarding a flight that morning at London's Heathrow Airport for a holiday trip to South Africa, Sacco, who is white, sent a highly offensive tweet ("Going to Africa. Hope I don't get AIDS. Just kidding. I'm white!") to her 170 followers (64). Over the next 11 hours while she was in the air without internet access, her tweet went viral. Outrage, often accompanied by calls for her to be fired, multiplied across the Twittersphere. Her tweet was retweeted over 30,000 times, and the hashtag it spawned, #hasjustinelandedyet, was tweeted nearly 100,000 times (65). The next day, IAC announced that Sacco was no longer in their employ, explaining in a statement that "The offensive comment does not reflect the views and values of IAC. We take this issue very seriously, and we have parted ways with the employee in question" (66).

While there are certainly those who view this outcome as a case of much-deserved punishment, it's also possible to find her tweet offensive while simultaneously finding the dynamics of how quickly it led her to become

---

[2] While this example is from 2013, it illustrates a dynamic that still exists today.

both unemployed and a global pariah to be unsettling. Only a day went by from her midmorning tweet from Heathrow to when New York–based IAC "parted ways" with her, and during much of that time, she was on an airplane, completely cut off from and unaware of the career-altering social media conflagration she had sparked.

There's also the interesting question of why she lost her job. It would strain credulity to suggest that it was the content of her tweet alone that led IAC to let her go. If instead of tweeting her statement she had spoken the exact same words to a group of people at a social gathering, she might have received some icy stares or perhaps a verbal rebuke. But even if someone present at the party had informed Sacco's employer of what Sacco had said, it's unlikely that she would have lost her job.

Even after she sent the tweet, the aftermath could have played out differently. If she hadn't been out of contact while in flight, and had instead seen the initial responses to her tweet and issued a prompt apology and deleted the tweet, it's also likely that it wouldn't have generated broad interest. And if the random dynamics of Twitter on that day had been different—if some of the owners of the Twitter accounts that played the largest roles in amplifying her tweet had not been online that day—her tweet might have simply joined the pile of millions of other offensive tweets that draw little or no notice and cause little or no professional consequences to the people who send them. But the combination of circumstances that day made Sacco infamous in a matter of hours. And it's a reasonable supposition that IAC reacted as much to the firestorm of publicity surrounding her tweet as it did to the actual content of her tweet.

4.4 Social Media and Digital Footprints

One of the many consequences of social media is that it makes it easy and fast to publish textual utterances that in an earlier era would more likely have been expressed verbally, if at all. And, social media create a permanent archive that can—at least for public postings—be examined by anyone who cares to look.

The risk posed by a person's digital footprint depends on several factors. The first factor is how visible a person is—or becomes in the future. The second is the content of what the person has said online. Politicians are perhaps the most at risk in this respect, given how high they are on the first

The stakes are higher

factor, as paid and volunteer opposition researchers now routinely scour the internet with the specific goal of finding something incriminating. But opposition research, or something akin to it, isn't limited to political campaigns any more. Digital scrutiny has become the norm when anyone is appointed to a position in the public eye. The searching is often conducted using the power of crowdsourcing, in which large numbers of people will collectively look for a target's potentially problematic online postings, and enthusiastically share nuggets they unearth. This occurs from both sides of the political spectrum.

When the *Atlantic* announced in May 2018 that it had hired the conservative writer Kevin Williamson, internet sleuths on the left quickly found a 2014 tweet in which, referring to punishment for women who get abortions, he wrote, "I have hanging more in mind" (67). A predictable firestorm followed, and shortly afterward Williamson was let go, with the *Atlantic's* editor-in-chief Jeffrey Goldberg writing in a memo to his staff that "I have come to the conclusion that the *Atlantic* is not the best fit for his talents, and so we are parting ways" (68).

When the *New York Times* announced in August 2018 that it had hired Sarah Jeong to its editorial board, internet sleuths on the right got busy. They quickly found a series of tweets including "oh man it's kind of sick how much joy i get out of being cruel to old white men" and "are white people genetically predisposed to burn faster in the sun, thus logically being only fit to live underground like groveling goblins" (69). Again, a firestorm ensued, though in this case the *Times* stood by Jeong, writing that "[h]er journalism and the fact that she is a young Asian woman have made her a subject of frequent online harassment," and that "[f]or a period of time she responded to that harassment by imitating the rhetoric of her harassers. She sees now that this approach only served to feed the vitriol that we too often see on social media"[3] (71).

Among other things, the Williamson and Jeong episodes illustrate that social media opposition research is a bipartisan phenomenon. Williamson was a well-known figure on the right, so there were plenty of people on the left ready to go on the offensive when his new position was announced. Jeong was an established writer whose views were well known to align with the

---

[3] As of August 2019, Jeong was reportedly no longer part of the *New York Times* editorial board (70).

left, so there were plenty of people from the right ready to attack when the *New York Times* hired her.

The lesson from these and many other cases is clear: In a social media era, people's reputations and careers can be shaped by the most offensive things that they have ever expressed on social media. While that observation is obvious, it is nonetheless interesting and relevant to consider the dynamics of how past social media postings become problematic. Often, this occurs when a person moves to a more visible professional position. Consider a person who is strongly aligned with one end of the political spectrum and who regularly tweets things that aren't viewed as particularly problematic to his or her ideological allies, but that would be seen as offensive by people on the other end of the political spectrum. It's possible for years to go by without any negative repercussions. But if the person then gets a public-facing, high-visibility job, the offensive (at least to some) tweets will be dredged up. This clearly creates a set of incentives for behavior modification, because people know that even though they may be posting via social media to a like-minded audience today, tomorrow those same postings may be scrutinized more broadly.

There's a broader lesson here that applies to us all. Who among us, after all, has never written or said something that might be viewed as offensive? If the many examples of ill-advised statements that have gone viral on social media and come back to bite their publishers teach us anything, it's that today's technology landscape has broadened the applicability of a lesson that used to apply only to the most famous and highly visible people: that anything you say can run away from you. It can be stripped of context and retransmitted by people who have never met you, who know little or nothing else about you, who may want to exploit what may be a decontextualized statement or a temporary and uncharacteristic lapse in judgment to advance their own agendas or status or simply for sport, and for whom the public humiliation they are so enthusiastically amplifying may be an end in itself. And all of this can happen in the space of days or even hours.

Technology in general and social media in particular have altered and accelerated how we receive, engage with, and react to information—and misinformation. And they have amplified the level of mob-like dynamics in public discourse. When faced with pressure to act immediately in the face of a growing social media firestorm in response to a controversial position or opinion voiced by one of their employees, many employers (including, in the case of colleges, academic administrators) will respond in ways chiefly driven by their desire to protect their public image and put out the fire—even if that response lacks the examination of nuance and context that might be possible absent a perceived need to take immediate action.

4.5 Social Media and Academic Discourse

Why is all of this particularly relevant to academia? Because social media can act both directly (e.g., through call-out campaigns) and indirectly (through behavior modification aimed at avoiding social media opprobrium) to shape what happens on campus. One reason is that technology has upended how everyone—including the academic researchers we entrust to discover and disseminate new knowledge and the professors and other instructors we entrust to teach college classes—communicates. Another is because academia and the pursuit of knowledge have always been closely linked to broader political, social, and religious currents. Social media provide a new feedback mechanism through which those currents can shape and be shaped by what happens on campus.

A third reason—and one that applies both within academia and outside it—is that public shaming on platforms such as Twitter and Facebook is an extraordinarily effective tool for behavior modification. Individuals who have been targeted by call-out campaigns highlighting real or perceived transgressions will be less likely to do anything in the future that might once again attract online wrath. Even people who have not been targets of call-out campaigns see what happens to those who have, and will modify their behavior as well to avoid becoming targets themselves.

While the social media–induced incentives for behavior modification apply generally, they operate particularly powerfully in academia because college instructors, researchers, and high-level administrators are by definition in the public eye. By virtue of the appointments they hold at their institutions, the classes many of them teach, and their regular participation in conferences, academic publishing, and other forms of professional engagement, they have a platform. The opinions they express will be noticed, at least by a small group of colleagues and students, and, when things go particularly well or particularly poorly, by a much larger audience. And opinions that elicit controversy will be noticed by far more people than historically have paid attention to academia.

Academic researchers are particularly exposed to the vicissitudes of social media not only because they are visible, but because the advancement of knowledge by its very nature requires making assertions that are new and that may be risky. This advancement will at times involve assertions that run counter to the established orthodoxy, that may appear correct (or incorrect) today but, in the future, prove to be incorrect (or correct) in light of new information.

The interplay between social media and the dominant orthodoxy in a field is a particularly important feature of the landscape. Consider an academic researcher who publishes a paper that goes through the traditional peer-review process but that, once published, is viewed as offensive by some members of the broader public who have an interest in the topic. This raises the prospect of social media attacks, with the potential to damage a person's reputation and career. As Jeffrey Flier, a professor and former dean at Harvard Medical School observed, "Increasingly, research on politically charged topics is subject to indiscriminate attack on social media, which in turn can pressure school administrators to subvert established norms regarding the protection of free academic inquiry" (72).

The risk of exposure to this sort of dynamic depends in part on the field. Take, for example, physics. While scientific controversies[4] certainly exist in physics, they generally (though certainly not always) steer well clear of any of the growing number of third rails that now circumscribe academic dialog in other fields. For example, there has been a robust debate within the physics community regarding the proper role of empirical evidence (73). There are strongly held differences of opinion regarding how much experimental confirmation (or at least the possibility of experimental confirmation) should matter when propounding new theories. A physicist who takes one particular side of this debate may experience scorn or a loss of professional respect from physicists on the other side of the debate. But there has traditionally been little risk that taking a position one way or the other would lead a physicist to be the target of more generalized social opprobrium from outside the academy.

Now consider an academic researcher whose focus is on U.S. immigration policy. It's almost impossible to make any sort of detailed, substantive proposal about immigration policy without arguing a position that will be offensive to someone. And it's also the case that the dominant political biases in academia mean that some policy proposals regarding immigration are far

---

[4] We are referring here to controversies regarding the subject matter that is the focus of the field, as distinct from controversies arising, for example, from discrimination *within* the field, which are certainly present in abundance in physics and more broadly in STEM disciplines.

more palatable than others to the majority of other academics. While this sort of conformance pressure is as old as academia itself, when it comes to hot-button topics, today's communications technology environment creates a much higher potential for criticisms to mushroom into a full-blown social media campaign against the researcher. This exerts pressure to shape the types of immigration policies that get articulated. By analogy, the same is true for a long list of other topics.

An additional reason why social media are relevant to academic research is that, while academia has a well-deserved reputation for plodding along at glacial time scale with respect to issues such as hiring and publications, decisions *not* to renew appointments or reactions to publications with arguments deemed offensive can happen much more quickly. Academics live in the same world as everyone else, where an errant tweet or ill-advised comment can sidetrack a reputation or a career. Writing in 2017 of the impact of social media mobs on the intellectual atmosphere in Canada, Jonathan Kay observed in the *National Post* that "the idea that a whole career can fall victim to a single social-media message sent in a moment of anger or frustration—or even a bad joke—has produced an atmosphere of real terror that is compromising the art and intellect of Canada's most creative minds" (74). While this observation cited the environment in Canada, it could just as easily be made with respect to academic discourse in the United States.

What this means is that academics—or at least the subset of them who teach and/or do research on topics involving the potential for saying or publishing something that could place them on the receiving end of a hostile social media campaign—are wittingly or unwittingly adapting to this new environment. This can occur because they are supportive of the constraints that are being placed on academic discourse, or because they oppose those constraints but are unwilling to pay the professional costs involved in saying so. In any event, this adaptation profoundly shapes the areas of inquiry that get pursued, the ideas that get proposed, the papers that get published, the way classes are taught, and the people who get hired and retained.

In essence, the social media ecosystem becomes a participant in academic research, so that before a paper even gets written and submitted to peer review, the ideas in it have often been subjected to an internal vetting by the researcher(s) against the tripwires of the moment as dictated by the loudest voices on social media. The immediacy and intensity of potential and actual responses on social media serve as a strong reinforcement mechanism for the set of three beliefs we have described. This limits research, teaching, and the academic endeavor more broadly.

Social media can interact with academia in other ways as well. Consider the case of University of Mississippi sociology professor James M. Thomas, whose tenure case was almost derailed due to his social media posts, including an October 2018 tweet stating "Don't just interrupt a Senator's meal, y'all. Put your whole damn fingers in their salads. Take their apps and distribute them to the other diners. Bring boxes and take their food home with you on the way out. They don't deserve your civility" (75). Responding to the tweet, University of Mississippi chancellor Jeffrey Vitter said in a statement that "[a] recent social media post by a UM faculty member did not reflect the values articulated by the university, such as respect for the dignity of each individual and civility and fairness. While I passionately support free speech, I condemn statements that encourage acts of aggression" (75). Thomas's social media activity became an issue in his tenure process.

As described by *Insider Higher Ed*, in a May 2019 meeting, "the Board of Trustees of State Institutions of Higher Learning debated his record for two hours in a closed-door session. None of the other dozens of professors up for promotion triggered such a discussion" (76). Thomas received tenure, though, as a statement from the Board of Trustees of State Institutions of Higher Learning noted, it was "with dissent" (77). We cite this example not to endorse Thomas's tweet (we agree with Chancellor Vitter that "statements that encourage acts of aggression" deserve condemnation) but simply to illustrate that the Thomas case is proof that deliberations regarding the award of tenure can be impacted by what a tenure candidate posts on social media.

5

Academic Freedom, with an Asterisk

Academic freedom is closely tied to freedom of expression. Both concepts are rooted in a recognition of the problems that come from censorship. And both are subject to vigorous on-campus debates about their scope. Given these similarities, in considering academic freedom it's helpful to start with the language of formal university academic freedom policies. We then consider a set of case studies that illustrate how, in practice, academic freedom is often significantly narrower than what the lofty language of those formal policies would suggest.

5.1 Academic Freedom, in Theory

Censorship by an academic institution is inconsistent with free inquiry. In other words, academic freedom is only possible when an institution does not impede the free exchange of ideas either in the classroom or in research. Reflecting this understanding, most institutions of higher education, both private and public, have academic freedom policies that expressly circumscribe an institution's right to limit expression and research, and that—in theory—are very broad.

Many colleges have adopted academic freedom policies based on (and often using nearly identical wording to) the *1940 Statement of Principles on Academic Freedom and Tenure* developed by the American Association of University Professors (AAUP). The *1940 Statement* specifies three key aspects of academic freedom:

1. Teachers are entitled to full freedom in research and in the publication of the results, subject to the adequate performance of their other academic duties; but research for pecuniary return should be based upon an understanding with the authorities of the institution.
2. Teachers are entitled to freedom in the classroom in discussing their subject, but they should be careful not to introduce into their teaching

Unassailable Ideas. Ilana Redstone and John Villasenor, Oxford University Press (2020). © Oxford University Press. DOI: 10.1093/oso/9780190078065.001.0001.

controversial matter which has no relation to their subject. Limitations of academic freedom because of religious or other aims of the institution should be clearly stated in writing at the time of the appointment.

3. College and university teachers are citizens, members of a learned profession, and officers of an educational institution. When they speak or write as citizens, they should be free from institutional censorship or discipline, but their special position in the community imposes special obligations. As scholars and educational officers, they should remember that the public may judge their profession and their institution by their utterances. Hence they should at all times be accurate, should exercise appropriate restraint, should show respect for the opinions of others, and should make every effort to indicate that they are not speaking for the institution. (78, p. 14)

Additional context was provided in 1970, when the AAUP endorsed a set of *Interpretative Comments* that are now included as footnotes to the *1940 Statement* (78).

Each of the three principles in the *1940 Statement* is aimed at preventing an institution from engaging in censorship. The first principle calls for "full freedom in research and in the publication of the results." The *Interpretive Comments* clarify that "teacher" in the *1940 Statement* is "understood to include the investigator who is attached to an academic institution without teaching duties" (78, p. 14). In relation to the second principle (giving "teachers" the right to "freedom in the classroom in discussing their subject"), the *Interpretive Comments* noted that:

The intent of this statement is not to discourage what is "controversial." Controversy is at the heart of the free academic inquiry which the entire statement is designed to foster. The passage serves to underscore the need for teachers to avoid persistently intruding material which has no relation to their subject. (78, p. 14)

The recognition that "controversy is at the heart of the free academic inquiry" serves as a particularly important point of reference given the current climate in higher education, which creates strong disincentives to engaging in classroom discussions of sociopolitically controversial issues. In relation to the second principle, the *Interpretative Comments* also stated that "[m]ost church-related institutions no longer need or desire the departure from the principle of academic freedom implied in the 1940 'Statement,' and we do not now endorse such a departure" (78, p. 14). The third principle calls on colleges and universities to respect the free expression rights of "teachers" by avoiding "institutional censorship" (78, p. 14). While this language dates from 1940, it is particularly important in the era of social media in light of the much greater access that university teachers and researchers now have to "speak or write as citizens."

Many public and private universities (see, for example, Duke (79), Tufts (80), the University of Illinois (81), and, as we will discuss later, Marquette University (82)) have policies that reflect the language of the *1940 Statement*. Some universities go even further. UCLA's academic freedom policy, in addition to providing the expected protection for "freedom of inquiry and research, freedom of teaching, and freedom of expression and publication," states that "Members of the faculty are entitled as University employees to the full protections of the Constitution of the United States and of the Constitution of the State of California. These protections are in addition to whatever rights, privileges, and responsibilities attach to the academic freedom of university faculty" (83).

The upshot is that both public and private universities tend to have policies on academic freedom that on their face appear to protect a very broad range of inquiry. That said, when a faculty member engages in controversial expression or research that leads to complaints and then to a disciplinary proceeding, the *actual* scope of an institution's freedom of expression becomes a matter of interpretation. What, for instance, is the effect of the language in the *1940 Statement*—and included in the academic freedom policies of many universities—that faculty members "should exercise appropriate restraint"? What additional unwritten exceptions to an academic freedom policy might a disciplinary committee apply? We will see this when discussing the *McAdams v. Marquette* litigation regarding a professor who was suspended over a blog post. In that case, Marquette provided a long list of caveats that it asserted limited the scope of academic freedom, despite the fact that those caveats were not listed in the text of Marquette's formal academic freedom policy.

The measure of what can be said or published by members of a university community is often based on the extent to which it offends or is viewed as harmful. In the current campus climate, the burden is on the speaker or researcher *not* to offend—with offense potentially judged by the most easily offended person who gets wind of the controversial expression or research.

Unsurprisingly, in relation to controversial issues this leaves a very narrow set of permissible opinions. If a teacher accidentally or intentionally fails to meet that burden and engages in expression that offends, this is viewed as a license to complain to the university and issue a call for disciplinary action.

The contemporary technology environment amplifies this dynamic, because even if an assertion is only offensive to a small percentage of people in a large university, that small percentage can, in absolute numerical terms, still amount to dozens or hundreds of people. People from outside a university and potentially from entirely outside academia can also weigh in to complain about on-campus expression or research they deem offensive. Social media help ensure that complaints are communicated to the very people most likely to agree with the complainant, leading to a feedback cycle that further increases the risks that opinions or research conclusions falling outside of campus-proscribed boundaries will attract attention and protest.

It would defy logic to suggest that this does not impact academic freedom. Faculty members have a natural desire to avoid being targeted by social media–driven calls for disciplinary action over something they say or write. This is the academic freedom elephant in the room, and it plays a far more powerful role in shaping discourse and (in relation to sensitive topics) research than does the text in a university's formal academic freedom policy.

5.2 The Bounds of Academic Freedom

When considering academic freedom in relation to publications, an objection to focusing on the few cases that generate controversy might go as follows: Thousands of academic papers are published by U.S. faculty members each year, and the overwhelming majority of them don't raise any academic freedom questions. So when considering this issue, is it really fair to focus on the tiny subset that do?

The answer is that to understand the scope of a freedom we have to examine its boundaries. By analogy, consider the scope of a different freedom: freedom of expression under the First Amendment of the Constitution. The First Amendment operates in the negative, by stating what the government *can't* do: "Congress shall make no law . . . abridging the freedom of speech." It also operates indirectly. A private citizen can't get prosecuted or otherwise sanctioned by the government for violating the First Amendment. Rather, when the government criminalizes or otherwise takes some action to restrict speech, that often leads to questions regarding whether, in doing so, the government has run afoul of the First Amendment. Court rulings arising from those questions have helped to fill in the contours of the bounds of the right to free expression.

threats

In 1969 in *Brandenburg v. Ohio,* the Supreme Court held that speech that "is directed to inciting or producing imminent lawless action and is likely to incite or produce such action" is outside First Amendment protection (84). Similarly, under the 1969 *Watts v. United States* Supreme Court ruling, "true threats" are a form of unprotected speech (85).

The Supreme Court has also at times issued rulings that identify categories of speech that are *within* the scope of protected speech. In 1989 in *Texas v. Johnson*, the Supreme Court held that a Texas statute (and, therefore, similar statutes in dozens of other states as well) criminalizing desecration of the American flag was unconstitutional. In 2017 in *Matal v. Tam*, the Supreme Court considered the government's denial of a trademark application filed by a band called "The Slants," whose members were Asian American. In denying the application the government had invoked a law preventing the registration of trademarks that "disparage" any "persons, living or dead." The Court ruled against the government, writing that the law in question "offends a bedrock First Amendment principle: Speech may not be banned on the ground that it expresses ideas that offend" (86).

flag

These examples help drive home the point that the boundaries of a freedom are defined at the margins. In fact, it is precisely when the boundaries are tested that the protective power of these freedoms springs into action. We wouldn't need a First Amendment to protect the right to make completely uncontroversial statements such as "I like ice cream." Rather, the power of the First Amendment is that it protects people's right to say and write things that they might otherwise be prohibited from (or punished for) expressing.

This provides a useful framing for considering the scope of academic freedom at universities. By analogy, the scope of that freedom is only truly clarified when it is tested. If we want to understand where the boundaries lie, the fact that the overwhelming majority of academic research and publications raise no academic freedom issue doesn't give us useful information. We know that a paper by a mechanical engineering professor proposing a new way to improve the strength of materials used in constructing bridges isn't likely to run up against academic freedom issues. But papers like those aren't why we have and need protections on academic freedom. We need those protections for the tiny minority of cases where a college teacher or

scope of freedom is tested

researcher says or publishes something that has potential value in academic discourse, but that also generates controversy, opposition, and pressures on the institution (and often from *within* the institution as well) to engage in censorship. If academic freedom can't provide protection in those cases, then it becomes a hollow concept devoid of any real meaning.

For the sake of completeness, it's also worth noting that academic freedom is not designed to protect activities devoid of any possible contribution to the mission of the university and/or that violate well-established ethical norms. If a professor unleashes a tirade of racist invective at a colleague, it would be ludicrous to suggest that this would be protected by academic freedom. Academic freedom is also not designed to protect publications that violate research ethics frameworks. For example, it certainly wouldn't protect a professor who, while receiving money under the table from a pharmaceutical company, publishes a paper concluding that a new drug manufactured by that company is highly effective in curing disease.

5.3   A Broad View of Academic Freedom Is Vital

In considering what academic freedom should protect, it is worth examining the words that make it up. "Academic" refers to activities including teaching, performing research, publishing research results, and participating in broader intellectual engagement through publications such as op-eds aimed at a more general audience. "Freedom," in this context, underscores the importance of leaving members of the university community the full latitude to perform these activities without fear of institutional censorship.

Controversies in academic freedom arise when a faculty member or other member of the university community publishes or says something that runs afoul of current campus norms about what is and is not deemed acceptable to express. Given the contemporary technology environment, those controversies grow rapidly on social media, leading to high censorship pressures. The problem with an approach to academic freedom that gives what amounts to veto power to social media mobs is that it presumes that the social norms underlying the backlash always set the right parameters around permissibility. History teaches us what a risky assumption that is.

To see why, consider a thought experiment. Imagine that it is the 1950s, but with the modification that the same social media technology we have today is in place. Now imagine that a professor in that environment makes a highly visible public statement arguing that same-sex marriage should be permitted and be on equal footing with marriage between a man and a woman. Today a rapidly growing majority of Americans, and an even higher fraction of people in campus communities (and the Supreme Court in *Obergefell v. Hodges*), agree with that position. But given the social climate that was in place in the 1950s, it's easy to see that this would have been immediately met with a storm of social media opposition. Within days, the professor's university would likely have issued a statement saying that the professor's views do not reflect the values of the university. It's likely that no mainstream academic journal would have allowed the professor to publish a paper expounding this view, and his or her future career prospects would have been imperiled.

As this and many other examples that could be constructed illustrate, historically speaking, when it comes to opinions that might generate backlash, the particular set of assumptions that were in place in any particular era don't always stand the test of time. Unless we believe that we have, against all historical precedent, arrived at a moment when the worldview that predominates on campuses is one that has *all* the right answers on *all* sociopolitical issues, we should be cautious about using that worldview as a source of authority on the limits of academic freedom.

A far better approach is to let university teachers and researchers freely voice and publish their opinions and research assertions, including those that people on social media might find offensive. Social media criticism, when it comes, should be *part* of the dialog, but it shouldn't be given the power to *stop* the dialog.

5.4 Dueling Priorities

There is a tension between the prioritization of academic freedom and the three beliefs. This is a particular challenge for university administrators who have an incentive to be perceived as all things to all people, including all students.

To take one example, consider the third belief under which everything is seen through the lens of identity, and under which one should not question identity-based, subjectively defined, claims of harm. If there's a possibility that an individual or group might end up with a grievance resulting from, for instance, a topic discussed in a class, the incentive for the university is to come down on the side of restricting academic freedom.

More broadly, from an institutional perspective, the perceived risks of a backlash from classroom discussions that might lead to identity-based claims of harm can outweigh the perceived risks of avoiding those discussions. As one expert we spoke with noted, the costs (financial and otherwise) for a university to have a permissive free speech and academic freedom policy are higher than the costs associated with having a restrictive policy. By "policy" we do not mean a formal, documented statement from a university that it is going to sacrifice academic freedom in the name of furthering a more harmonious campus environment. Of course, no university would ever issue such a statement. Rather, we are referring to what could be called a *de facto* policy—one that isn't written anywhere, but that nearly all instructors and administrators know and understand.

This allows universities to attempt to have it both ways. When challenged by advocates of academic freedom who accuse universities of being too censorious, they can point to formal policies that, at least in theory, confer enormous latitude to members of the campus community to perform research on and debate controversial topics. But at the same time, everyone knows that to operate near the edges of the academic freedom envelope is to invite protest, and that when the protest comes, the person targeted by the protest should expect at most tepid support from administrators. In light of this climate, it's unsurprising that most members of the campus community avoid testing boundaries, and instead engage in discourse, teaching, and research within a much narrower range than is theoretically permitted by a university's official policies.

This restrictive approach to academic freedom serves to protect institutions by signaling an unwillingness to tolerate transgressions of any kind. For those who do transgress, the penalties can be high. An instructive illustration is the set of events that played out in the mid- to late-2010s with Laura Kipnis, a professor in the School of Communication at Northwestern University. In the view of some at Northwestern, Kipnis's sin was to publish an opinion on Title IX that was at odds with the on-campus orthodoxy. The controversy originated in an essay Kipnis had published in 2015 in the *Chronicle of Higher Education* titled "Sexual Paranoia Strikes Academe." In the essay, she argued that "students' sense of vulnerability on campus was expanding to an unwarranted degree, partly owing to new enforcement policies around Title IX" (87). She also addressed charges of sexual misconduct that had been brought against philosophy professor Peter Ludlow, writing:

In brief: The two had gone to an art exhibit together—an outing initiated by the student—and then to some other exhibits and bars. She says he bought her alcohol and forced her to drink, so much that by the end of the evening she was going in and out of consciousness. He says she drank of her own volition. (She was under legal drinking age; he says he thought she was 22.) She says he made various sexual insinuations, and that she wanted him to drive her home (they'd driven in his car); he says she insisted on sleeping over at his place. She says she woke up in his bed with his arms around her, and that he groped her. He denies making advances and says she made advances, which he deflected. He says they slept on top of the covers, clothed. Neither says they had sex. He says she sent friendly texts in the days after and wanted to meet. She says she attempted suicide two days later, now has PTSD, and has had to take medical leave. (88)

Kipnis's 2015 *Chronicle of Higher Education* essay led to a Title IX complaint against her alleging that publication of certain information in the article constituted retaliation. Thus began what Kipnis referred to as her "Title IX Inquisition," under which, as Kipnis put it, the university was "allowing intellectual disagreement to be redefined as retaliation" (89). In fact, over a period of several years, Kipnis was targeted by multiple Title IX complaints, including in relation to her 2017 book *Unwanted Advances: Sexual Paranoia Comes to Campus*. A September 2017 *New Yorker* article on Kipnis's experience by Harvard professor Jeannie Suk Gerson included a photo of Kipnis with the caption "Students and educators now live in a world where expressing an opinion about sexual harassment can be sincerely perceived as sexual harassment" (87).

One way to reshape what might be perceived as incompatible priorities of academic freedom and concerns over certain claims of harm is to reemphasize the idea that the existence of differing opinions and disagreement has intrinsic value of its own. In other words, debate and dissent are important because they make the university community and society stronger, because they make ideas stronger, and because they help those who engage in (and witness) debate to better contextualize their own views and gain an understanding of the views of others. Conversely, the value of debate and dissent is muted when discourse is too narrowly constrained.

Academic freedom can also be undermined through the implicit silencing of voices that express views that are out of step with the views of a majority of people in an academic department or an academic organization such as a scholarly society. This is apparent through the numerous examples where faculty have used departments and academic organizations as platforms to make statements on political issues. It also runs counter to recommendations made by the Kalven Committee in 1967 (90). The *Kalven Committee Report* (also known by the more formal title *Report on the University's Role in Political and Social Action*) was issued by the University of Chicago after the committee was convened by the university president to prepare "a statement on the University's role in political and social action" (90). As University of Chicago professor Richard Shweder wrote in summarizing the report nearly a half century after its initial publication:

> The University as an institution is cautioned against taking any collective or institutional stance on the social and political issues of the day, in part because there is no intellectually defensible process (including the process of voting and polling members of the community) "by which it can reach a collective position without inhibiting the full freedom of dissent on which it thrives." In other words, the university as an institution refrains from social, political and moral posturing out of respect for the autonomy of its faculty and students, and especially out of respect for those individuals in a disputatious academic community who may embrace an unpopular, minority or politically incorrect point of view. (91)

One example of an academic organization pushing for collective action is told through Shweder's own 2017 experience, which he described in the *Huffington Post* (92). Shweder wrote of the American Anthropological Association's November 2015 vote to move a resolution forward on whether to participate in the movement known as BDS (Boycott, Divest, Sanctions) targeting Israeli universities and academics. As he wrote, BDS proponents within the American Anthropological Association "argue that Israel is a predacious Goliath undeserving of international support. They are energized by the prospect of receiving a corporate branding and seal of approval for their political judgments from a large academic association." During the debate over the resolution, he describes how "[d]issidents who were lined up and waiting to voice their views were suddenly denied access to the microphone by the president of the association and effectively silenced" (92). In the end, the American Anthropological Association's resolution was narrowly defeated.

6

The New Landscape of Tenure

The current climate in higher education has changed tenure in several ways. First, due to social media, obtaining tenure now requires a more careful effort than in the past to steer clear of politically controversial topics, both in research and in public statements. Even small missteps can get amplified on social media, leading to reputational damage that could be problematic in a tenure decision. Second, tenure today doesn't offer the level of security that it once did, again in significant part because of the role of social media. In other words, from the standpoint of faculty members the barriers to obtaining tenure have been raised and from the standpoint of institutions the barriers to removing it have been lowered.

Before getting into specifics, it may be useful to provide a bit of background on tenure itself. As explained by the American Association of University Professors (AAUP), "A tenured appointment is an indefinite appointment that can be terminated only for cause or under extraordinary circumstances such as financial exigency and program discontinuation" (93). AAUP further explains that:

> The principal purpose of tenure is to safeguard academic freedom, which is necessary for all who teach and conduct research in higher education. When faculty members can lose their positions because of their speech, publications, or research findings, they cannot properly fulfill their core responsibilities to advance and transmit knowledge. (93)

and that:

> Education and research benefit society, but society does not benefit when teachers and researchers are controlled by corporations, religious groups, special interest groups, or the government. Free inquiry, free expression, and open dissent are critical for student learning and the advancement of knowledge. Therefore, it is important to have systems in place to protect academic freedom. Tenure serves that purpose. (93)

Unassailable Ideas. Ilana Redstone and John Villasenor, Oxford University Press (2020). © Oxford University Press.
DOI: 10.1093/oso/9780190078065.001.0001.

The existence of tenure is a direct reflection of the fact that academics some-times publish things that other people don't like. Absent this protection, critics might be in a position where they can take steps to get academics fired from their jobs for expressing an unpopular opinion on a controversial topic.

While tenure is often described in terms of how it protects academics, it is also important to recognize the corresponding employment commitment it places on academic institutions, which need to be prepared to keep ten-ured faculty on the payroll for decades. As a result, academic institutions are careful about awarding tenure, as they don't want to be saddled with paying years of salary to an unproductive professor. Given this asymmetry, under which tenured faculty can quit at will but institutions are far more constrained, it makes all the sense in the world that the barriers to obtaining tenure are high.

While there is plenty of variation, in many cases the path to tenure at a college or university begins when an early career scholar is hired just after, or within a few years of, earning a Ph.D. (or a corresponding terminal degree such as a J.D.). The requirements for tenure and the specific steps involved in the tenure process vary across institutions. For example, at institutions where the primary mission is teaching, a faculty member is evaluated primarily on his or her contributions to teaching (and, to a lesser degree, to service to the institution). At research institutions, tenure candidates are evaluated on their research and teaching as well as in relation to their university service.

When it comes time to evaluate the candidate for tenure, a committee of tenured faculty members will evaluate the candidate's record. At research universities, the committee will also seek a number of letters from accom-plished researchers outside the university who are asked to opine on the candidate's contributions to and standing in his or her academic discipline. The committee writes a report containing a recommendation to grant or deny (or potentially defer) tenure, and the case is then subject to a vote by tenured faculty in the candidate's department. From there, the case usually goes to the chair of the department, then to the dean of the school or college, and then often to a university-level committee, and beyond that to the presi-dent of the university.

The point of providing this detail is to illustrate that there are many steps involved, and the process can be derailed at any point. To get tenure, professors have to be doing very good work. But, they also have to make sure that people like them, or, perhaps more importantly, that people don't *dislike* them. As they are rising through the ranks in their pre-tenure years, they only have partial knowledge regarding who is going to weigh in on their tenure case. They know that the tenured members of their department will have a say. But they don't always know who the department chair will be a few years in the future when their case is up for evaluation. They also don't know which researchers from outside the university might be asked to weigh in on their tenure decision, or who might be on the campus-level tenure committee that evaluates their case.

6.1 Why Obtaining Tenure Today Is Different

None of this is new. Processes similar to that just described have been in place for decades. What *is* new is that there is a lot more archived expression now than there was in the past, meaning that there is a higher probability that a prior controversial statement can derail a budding academic career. A few decades ago, no one was tweeting, no one was posting to Instagram, and no one was posting to Facebook. The internet was not yet an easily searchable archive of every public utterance any of us have ever made. Private communications were different as well. People weren't using text messaging to have conversations that often involve the perilous combination of unguarded expression intended only for one person yet conducted over a medium that has a potentially permanent memory.

Professors—and in particular, early career professors who are working their way toward tenure—aren't public figures in the way that politicians are, and most pre-tenure professors aren't subject to a particularly high degree of public scrutiny. But it also wouldn't be accurate to say that social media postings by faculty members don't get noticed, or that they can't potentially cost a faculty member his or her job. And a controversial publication by a pre-tenure professor will likely get noticed, with people using social media to broadcast and amplify their criticisms.

The tenure decision is a particular point of vulnerability because it is a process specifically engineered to require a thumbs-up or thumbs-down decision on future employment. In other words, the tenure decision is intentionally constructed around the very idea of career vulnerability, since the real possibility of denial is central to the entire process.

The last thing a tenure-track professor wants or needs is to do or say anything, or conduct and publish any research, that will motivate people to oppose a positive tenure decision. The surest way to accomplish this goal is to steer clear of both research and social media activity that might stir up opposition. This incentive to self-censor applies to topics well outside a professor's field of work. Consider a tenure-track physics professor who wants to minimize the odds of running into a tenure problem. Even though his or her research raises no politically controversial issues, he or she would still be well advised not to tweet opinions on unrelated issues that risk offending some of the people who might be involved in the tenure decision. Keeping one's head down and sticking only to physics is a safer course of action.

Not surprisingly, the self-censorship incentive is particularly strong when a professor's work itself is on a topic that generates strong political views. It would be career suicide for a researcher on immigration policy to publish a series of papers advocating approaches that are viewed negatively by most of his or her colleagues or by a significant number of social media users. In short, while tenure has always been in part a popularity contest (or, at least, a contest to avoid *unpopularity*), far more people are watching than in the past. Given this environment, it is a natural and unfortunate consequence that a larger number of researchers are likely to shape their research to 1) match the narratives most favored by the people who will be evaluating them and 2) avoid narratives that could bring negative attention to their work.

Tenure doesn't provide a guarantee of permanent job employment. For instance, no one would find fault with a university that fires a tenured professor proven to have embezzled funds from his or her academic department. Rather, tenure protects academic freedom. As a result, when a verbal or written statement by a tenured professor leads to disciplinary proceedings and the threat to revoke tenure, the core question is whether the expression in question is protected by academic freedom. In the social media era, conceptions of the proper limits of academic freedom have narrowed. If a tenured professor says something offensive that leads to significant protest, institutions are unlikely to offer a vigorous defense of academic freedom.

6.2 The McAdams Case

Consider the case of Professor John McAdams, who was suspended and nearly lost his tenure at Marquette University due to a blog post, and only regained his right to teach after seeking recourse through the court system. The chain of events that led to McAdams's suspension started in an undergraduate *Theory of Ethics* class that he wasn't even teaching. The graduate student instructor of that class was discussing the philosopher John Rawls, and agreed with the suggestion by one of the students that same-sex marriage was consistent with Rawls's Equal Liberty Principle. She also reportedly suggested that any student who did not agree with this conclusion could speak with her after the class.

Unsurprisingly, one of the undergraduate students took her up on this suggestion. In an exchange that the undergraduate student surreptitiously recorded, he expressed his opposition to same-sex marriage. After some disagreement between the student instructor and the undergraduate student over whether this opinion was homophobic, the student instructor told the student that "in this class homophobic comments, racist comments, and sexist comments will not be tolerated. If you don't like that you are more than free to drop this class" (94).

The undergraduate student then went to McAdams, who on November 9, 2014 published a post about the incident on his personal blog. In the post McAdams mentioned the graduate student instructor by name and opined that the instructor "was just using a tactic typical among liberals now. Opinions with which they disagree are not merely wrong, and are not to be argued against on their merits, but are deemed 'offensive' and need to be shut up" (95).

The blog post led to a strong reaction at Marquette, including a letter to a campus publication signed by a number of department chairs "deplor[ing] the recent treatment of a philosophy graduate student instructor by political science professor John McAdams on his Marquette Warrior blog." The authors also wrote that "McAdams's actions—which have been reported in local and national media outlets—have harmed the personal reputation of a young scholar as well as the academic reputation of Marquette University. They have negatively affected campus climate, especially as it relates to gender and sexual orientation. And they have led members of the Marquette community to alter their behavior out of fear of becoming the subject of one of his attacks" (96).

The blog post also led to disciplinary proceedings, and on December 16, 2014, Dean Richard Holz told Professor McAdams in a letter that McAdams was being relieved of his teaching duties. Then, on January 30, 2015, Dean Holz informed McAdams that "I wish to advise you that Marquette University is commencing the process to revoke your tenure to dismiss you from the faculty." Dean Holz wrote that "As a result of your unilateral, dishonorable and irresponsible decision to publicize the name of our graduate student, and your decision to publish information that was false and materially misleading about her and your University colleagues, that student received a series of hate-filled and despicable e-mails" and that "Instead of being an example of academic excellence and competence as a tenured, senior faculty member, your inaccurate, misleading and superficial Internet story lacked any measure of the due diligence we expect from beginning students." Dean Holz concluded that "Therefore, in accord with Section 307.03 [of the Marquette Faculty Statutes], we are commencing as of this date the procedures for revoking your tenure and dismissing you from the faculty" (97).

McAdams's case was referred to the Marquette Faculty Hearing Committee (FHC), an "advisory body whose membership consists solely of University faculty members" (98). In January 2016, the FHC issued its report, concluding that:

> the University has established neither a sufficiently egregious failure to meet professional standards nor a sufficiently grave lack of fitness to justify the sanction of dismissal. Instead, the Committee concludes that only a lesser penalty than dismissal is warranted. The Committee thus recommends that Dr. McAdams be suspended, without pay but with benefits, for a period of no less than one but no more than two semesters. (99)

In a March 16, 2016 letter to McAdams, Marquette president Michael Lovell wrote that he had "decided to accept your fellow faculty members' recommendation to suspend you without pay" (100). In addition, Lovell informed McAdams that his reinstatement was "conditioned upon you delivering a written statement to the President's Office by April 4, 2016," that would be shared with the graduate student instructor and that was to contain "acceptance of the unanimous judgment of the peers who served on the Faculty Hearing Committee" and "acknowledgement that your November 9, 2014, blog post was reckless and incompatible with the mission and values of Marquette University and you express deep regret for the harm suffered by our former graduate student and instructor" (101).

McAdams refused to submit the letter, and in May 2016 sued Marquette for breach of contract. After the Circuit Court for Milwaukee County issued a May 2017 decision granting summary judgment in favor of Marquette, McAdams appealed to the Wisconsin Supreme Court, which issued a 4–2 ruling in his favor in July 2018. The court wrote that:

The undisputed facts show that the University breached its contract with Dr. McAdams when it suspended him for engaging in activity protected by the contract's guarantee of academic freedom. Therefore, we reverse the circuit court and remand this cause with instructions to enter judgment in favor of Dr. McAdams, conduct further proceedings to determine damages (which shall include back pay), and order the University to immediately reinstate Dr. McAdams with unimpaired rank, tenure, compensation, and benefits. (102)

In one of the most important paragraphs of the ruling, the court addressed the risks in weighing down academic freedom with too many caveats:

The University posited that educational institutions assume academic freedom is just one value that must be balanced against "other values core to their mission." Some of those values, it says, include the obligation to "take care not to cause harm, directly or indirectly, to members of the university community," "to respect the dignity of others and to acknowledge their right to express differing opinions," to "safeguard[] the conditions for the community to exist," to "ensur[e] colleagues feel free to explore undeveloped ideas," and to carry out "the concept of cura personalis," which involves working and caring "for all aspects of the lives of the members of the institution." These are worthy aspirations, and they reflect well on the University. But they contain insufficiently certain standards by which a professor's compliance may be measured. Setting the doctrine of academic freedom adrift amongst these competing values would deprive the doctrine of its instructive power; it would provide faculty members with little to no guidance on what it covers. (103)

Among the many problems with Marquette's position was that by providing such a long list of caveats, the university placed itself in the position of being able to argue that essentially *any* controversial statement can fall outside the protection of academic freedom. Take, for example, Marquette's assertion that "academic freedom is just one value that must be balanced against" the obligation "to respect the dignity of others." It's difficult to express an opinion on a controversial issue without creating the risk that someone will feel that his or her dignity isn't respected. A proponent of abortion rights might believe the abortion opponents don't respect her dignity. An opponent of abortion rights might believe that proponents don't respect her dignity or that of an unborn child. Analogous examples could be given in relation to any number of topics, including affirmative action, same-sex marriage, immigration policy, Title IX, religious freedom, and so on.

Academic freedom that excludes expression that, as judged by college administrators and faculty disciplinary committees, does not "respect the dignity of others" has a completely arbitrary scope, and can be narrowed at whim to exclude nearly anything that a vocal constituency deems offensive. Stated another way, it allows the process of deciding when expression falls outside the protections of academic freedom to be a results-driven exercise where the goal of finding a faculty member in violation can always be attained by simply narrowing the boundaries to the point of excluding the expression in question.

We emphasize that in making these points, we are in no way endorsing or agreeing with McAdams's actions or opinions. Rather, we are illustrating an issue of process and culture that, while specific to Marquette in this particular case, could easily have occurred at many other U.S. universities. And, it is a process and culture that stands ready to penalize faculty—including tenured professors—who express opinions that fail to align with the current campus orthodoxy.

To see why, consider a thought experiment in which the opinions expressed in the Marquette case were reversed. More specifically, imagine that while teaching a class, a graduate student instructor had invoked a philosophical framework to support *opposition* to same-sex marriage. Suppose that a student in the class who disagreed strongly with that view went to see her after class and recorded a subsequent conversation in which the instructor stated that views in favor of the *right to* same-sex marriage shouldn't be expressed in class.

Now suppose that the student who made the recording had brought it to a professor who then published a blog post naming the graduate student instructor and complaining that it was inappropriate for the instructor to prevent the student from voicing support for same-sex marriage in class. Would a group of over half a dozen department chairs have excoriated the professor in a letter to the university newspaper? Would the professor have been suspended without pay, ordered to write an apology letter, and subjected to disciplinary proceedings aimed at revoking his or her tenure? It strains credulity to suggest that any of these consequences would have occurred.

This thought experiment helps clarify that McAdams was likely not just punished for the fact that he published the name of a student instructor, but rather the fact he published the name of a student instructor *and* he added commentary that not only criticized her but also clearly placed himself outside the political mainstream of the campus while simultaneously confirming the student instructor as solidly within it.

And what about the potential criticism that this thought experiment is premised on an improper attempt to assert symmetry between support for same-sex marriage rights on the one hand and opposition to such rights on the other? After all, it could be argued (correctly, in our view) that opposition to same-sex marriage is discriminatory in a way that support is not. But that is not the point of highlighting this example. The point is that if tenure can be formally called into question the moment that a professor is accused of failing "to respect the dignity of others" in a blog post, then its protections are thin indeed.

6.3 Eroding Academic Freedom

Earlier, we discussed the implicit tensions that can arise between the three beliefs and academic freedom. In that setting, the tension is assumed based on the apparent incompatibility of the two ideas. As we have noted, in attempting to justify its handling of the McAdams case, Marquette argued that academic freedom must be balanced against "other values core to their mission," including the obligation to "take care not to cause harm, directly or indirectly, to members of the university community" and to "to respect the dignity of others and to acknowledge their right to express differing opinions," to "safeguard[] the conditions for the community to exist," to "ensur[e] colleagues feel free to explore undeveloped ideas" (104).

The subjectivity inherent in assessing harm turns this test into a particularly potent attack on academic freedom. When a large group of students in a classroom setting is exposed to a discussion with the potential to cause discomfort, it is the students within the group who have the lowest threshold for declaring that harm has occurred who will drive the dialog, as they are the ones most likely to call for punishment of the instructor.

Thus, in actual practice, academic freedom in the classroom can be limited by the people with the most expansive views of harm. Once universities have adopted a view of tenure as something that must be "balanced" against other factors such as "values core to" a university's mission, that sets the stage for arbitrary declarations of what is and is not a core value—declarations that directly undermine the strength of tenure. The inevitable result is that the practical scope of academic freedom is far narrower than would be suggested by the lofty academic freedom policy statements that many universities have on their websites.

Yet another factor is the slippery slope that arises from the feedback loop that occurs as academic freedom disputes play out. When there is a controversy involving academic freedom, college administrators have strong incentives to favor—or at the very least appease—the complainants. An administrator who issues statements and takes actions viewed as sympathetic to the complainants will see his or her social and professional standing increase both on campus and on social media. By contrast, an administrator who takes the unpopular position of offering too strong a defense of the accused professor and insufficient sympathy for those levying the complaints will not only suffer a loss of standing but may also become a target of social media ire. An additional factor is that many administrators aspire to higher office. They know that one of the surest ways to torpedo their chances of advancement is to be publicly identified as being on the "wrong" side of an academic freedom controversy involving a socially contentious issue.

When faced with the choice of offering sympathy to people who claim to be offended or to a professor accused of generating offense, the career-enhancing path for an administrator (and for other faculty) is to side with the complainant. An alternative option for administrators is to stake out a middle ground by issuing pronouncements that avoid saying anything substantive. Under this approach, an administrator might issue a statement expressing concern that the complainants feel aggrieved while also dropping in some boilerplate language about the importance of academic freedom—in some cases accompanied by a sort of "however" clause that telegraphs a willingness to agree that the expression in question is harmful to the campus community.

Through this dynamic, which is visible to all members of the community of the college in question, there is a *de facto* readjustment of the bounds of academic freedom that occurs whether or not there is any formal investigation, and, if there is an investigation, regardless of its outcome. The expression in question gets classified as unprotected, and everyone—faculty, administrators, and students—recalibrates their expectations accordingly. Notably, this process always operates in one direction; it never operates to *expand* academic freedom. Over time, the inevitable result is that academic freedom is undermined.

6.4 Academic Freedom and Tenured Professors

In the popular conception, obtaining tenure is often viewed as an endpoint. But in the arc of a decades-long academic career, it's often much closer to the beginning. While there are plenty of exceptions, many assistant professors are initially hired when they are in their late 20s, as soon as or shortly after they earn a Ph.D. This means that they will be in their 30s when they receive tenure. For many, the majority of their careers will be spent after this milestone, not before it.

Tenure does indeed provide some measure of protection from getting fired, but in a post-tenure career that can easily span 30 years or more, most professors aspire to do more than simply avoid this outcome. Those who hold the title of associate professor—the rank most commonly given upon the grant of tenure—want to earn a further promotion to the title of "full" professor. Professors at all levels go through regular personnel review processes that include salary advancements. Professors want their institutions to assign them as instructors for classes they like teaching as opposed to classes that are considered a burden. Some professors want to rise through the administrative ranks and become department chairs, deans, and university provosts or presidents.

Professors also generally want the flexibility to be able to move to a different university that might offer them better professional or personal opportunities. The upshot is that tenured professors are in these respects just like people in many other professions: Their prospects for advancement are very much dependent on how they are perceived both internally and externally, including whether they have steered clear of bringing controversy or other unwanted attention to their organization.

Any professor, tenured or not, who has published or said anything that has generated a social media backlash has injured his or her future career opportunities. Regardless of its eventual resolution, the fact that the backlash occurred at all makes it much harder to rise internally to a position of greater responsibility (such as a department chair or dean) or to obtain an offer of employment at a different university.

Even those tenured professors who have no aspirations to advance to higher faculty ranks, obtain a university executive position, or make a lateral move to a different institution have strong incentives to avoid academic freedom controversies. Very few faculty want to pay the professional, financial, social, and emotional costs that accompany being caught up a situation like McAdams's.

So, when we speak of threats to tenure, we are not suggesting that tenure itself is in danger of being formally abolished (at least not directly, though the massive move toward adjuncts has the effect of reducing the fraction of teaching performed by tenured faculty). Rather, we are noting that the strength of tenure protection has been weakened. The fact that in the end McAdams was not fired is not, in our view, a sign that the protections of tenure have not yielded in the face of pressures arising from the current social environment.

Neither do we find it to be much of a consolation that the number of tenured professors who find themselves in disciplinary proceedings arising from academic freedom issues is extremely small. The numbers are small because the incentives involved in hiring and promotion to tenure favor people unlikely to challenge the limits of academic freedom. And, they are small because the relatively low percentage of faculty who, despite these incentives, might nonetheless be inclined to contemplate engaging in expression that risks offending students or faculty will think twice, and rightly so given the tepid protections that their university administrations are likely provide.

6.5 The Abrams Case

Even in the absence of any formal disciplinary proceeding, academic freedom disputes can still have a chilling effect. An illustrative example can be found in relation to an October 2018 *New York Times* op-ed by Sarah Lawrence College professor Samuel J. Abrams. In the op-ed, Abrams described the results of a national survey he had conducted on the political affiliation of college faculty. He also criticized the Sarah Lawrence administration for, as he described it, "organizing many overtly progressive events—programs with names like 'Stay Healthy, Stay Woke,' 'Microaggressions' and 'Understanding White Privilege'—without offering any programming that offered a meaningful ideological alternative" (105). After the op-ed was published, there was a backlash at Sarah Lawrence that included, among other things, vandalism of Abrams's office door and an emergency student senate meeting (106). After Abrams asked Sarah Lawrence president Cristle Collins Judd to condemn the vandalism, Judd reportedly issued a broadly distributed e-mail that stopped well short of full-throated support for Abrams's right to express his views (something that is even more ironic given that the *New York Times* op-ed was largely devoted to relaying data acquired in a survey).

In an interview with *Reason* conducted shortly after the op-ed's publication, Abrams recounted a phone conversation with President Judd in which, as Abrams described it, "she said I had created a hostile work environment" (106). On November 6, President Judd published a statement referencing remarks she had made at an event the prior evening, including "First, and unequivocally, academic freedom is a fundamental principle at Sarah Lawrence College. That means that as a member of our faculty, Professor Abrams has every right, and the full support of the College, to pursue and publish this work," "Those who disagree with the published opinion have every right to respond and even to protest the views expressed in the piece," and "As a diverse and inclusive community, we are governed by principles of mutual respect. That means that no one has the right to remove or destroy personal property and replace it with messages of intimidation, as occurred on Professor Abrams' door the evening following the opinion piece's publication" (107).

In March 2019, about four months after the publication of the op-ed, the main on-campus newspaper published a list of demands from the Diaspora Coalition, a student group created "to address the pain of marginalized students as well as to advise the administration on how to best address this pain" (108). Most of the demands were unrelated to Abrams, but one of the them directly implicated his status as a tenured faculty member: "We demand that Samuel Abrams' position at the College be put up to tenure review to a panel of the Diaspora Coalition and at least three faculty members of color. In addition, the College must issue a statement condemning the harm that Abrams has caused to the college community, specifically queer, Black, and female students, whilst apologizing for its refusal to protect marginalized students wounded by his op-ed and the ignorant dialogue that followed" (108).

As quoted in an *Inside Higher Ed* article published a few days later, Abrams said in an e-mail interview that "the college administration should make clear to the students that they have no intention of acceding to this outlandish demand. Students who want to air their own perspectives through writings, discussions or meetings on campus should always be encouraged. But to call for punishment in response to an op-ed runs roughshod over the principles of free inquiry that should govern any campus." He also criticized the administration's response, telling *Inside Higher Ed* that the administration had missed a "chance to take the lead and serve as an national example in terms of how to have civil debates and disagreement and discuss facts and how they differ from opinions" and that "sadly, the school did not come out strongly on academic freedom and free speech, and this behavior runs against the core value of the college itself" (109).

In a March 12 statement, President Judd wrote that "During the morning, in the afternoon, and again this morning, I met with members of the Diaspora Coalition and with elected members of Student Senate to express how seriously I take these issues and my willingness to engage in meaningful dialogue about them." In relation to Abrams, she wrote that "while recognizing and acknowledging the urgency of many of the concerns expressed in the [Diaspora Coalition] document, I must also reference the inappropriateness of demands related to the work and tenure of one of our faculty members" (110).

On the one hand, the Abrams case can be held out as an example of academic freedom being protected when a faculty member expresses views that fail to line up with the prevailing on-campus narrative. In fall 2018 the Sarah Lawrence administration did, though not as quickly as some would have preferred, publicly affirm Abram's right to publish his op-ed. And when the Diaspora Coalition published its list of demands in March 2019, the administration quickly responded, and included in its response the statement that the call to review Abrams's tenure was inappropriate. But the very fact that the Abrams op-ed generated the level of controversy that it did is an indicator of the practical (as opposed to theoretical) narrow scope of academic freedom, both at Sarah Lawrence and well beyond.

In combination, these factors create a powerful set of incentives to avoid crossing any of the many red lines that define permissible on-campus debate. In many respects, those incentives are no less powerful and pervasive after a positive tenure decision than before it. What tenured faculty do and don't say and write is shaped accordingly.

6.6 Mandated "Diversity" Statements

Another increasingly common feature of the higher education landscape is the requirement to include a diversity statement as part of an application for a faculty position and/or for promotion within a college or university. Campuses with requirements along these lines include UCLA ("all ladder rank faculty searches must now require each candidate to submit an EDI [equity, diversity, and inclusion] statement as a distinct component of their application") (111), UCSD ("All candidates applying for faculty appointments at UC San Diego are required to submit a personal statement on their contributions to diversity") (112), UC Berkeley ("the Contributions to Diversity Statement should describe your past experience and activities, and future plans to advance diversity, equity and inclusion") (113), Oregon State University ("contributions to equity, inclusion, and diversity should be clearly identified in the position description so that they can be evaluated in promotion and tenure decisions") (114), and Pomona College ("At Pomona, this [diversity, equity, and inclusion] statement is one of the four components most critical in our evaluation of candidates") (115). Even when there is no campus-wide applicant diversity statement requirement in place, such a pre-condition is often imposed at the level of an academic department or school.

UCLA's approach is instructive. Since the 2018–2019 academic year, all applicants to UCLA tenure-track and tenured faculty positions have been required to include an EDI statement. Starting in the 2019–2020 academic year, all tenure-track and tenured faculty already at UCLA were required to include an EDI statement each time they go through an internal promotion process. A June 2018 UCLA document provides examples of activities that would be relevant to include in an EDI statement. These activities are divided into the four categories of teaching, research, professional activity, and university and public service, and include the following examples:

Teaching:
- "Teaching at a minority-serving institution"
- "Record of success advising women and minority graduate students"
- "Developing effective teaching strategies for the educational advancement of students from under-represented groups"

Research
- "Studying patterns of participation and advancement of women and minorities in fields where they are underrepresented"
- "Studying socio-cultural issues confronting underrepresented students in college preparation curricula"

Professional Activity
- "Engagement in activity designed to remove barriers and to increase participation by groups historically under-represented in higher education"

University and Public Service

- "Participation in service that applies up-to-date knowledge to problems, issues, and concerns of groups historically underrepresented in higher education"
- "Presentations or performances for under-represented communities" (116)

All of the above are worthy endeavors. But they collectively constitute a filter that, ironically given the topic at hand, is biased: In the hiring and promotion process, it favors candidates who are studying topics that happen to line up well with diversity-related issues. Consider an applicant for a faculty position who is completing doctoral research with a focus on increasing the opportunities for K-12 girls to be exposed to STEM subjects. Such a person can earn a high diversity statement score just through the simple act of describing his or her research. There is no need for the applicant to do anything extracurricular to ensure that he or she has something substantive to say on this portion of the application.

Now consider a newly graduated mathematics Ph.D. who is looking for a mathematics faculty position. Let's assume that her work is uniformly regarded as groundbreaking, and that her peers and mentors are in universal agreement that she is one of the world's brightest young mathematicians, and is likely destined for a decades-long career of important mathematical breakthroughs. But let's also assume that she hasn't done any of the things listed above as examples that could be listed in an EDI statement. She hasn't studied "socio-cultural issues confronting underrepresented students in college preparation curricula;" she hasn't developed "effective teaching strategies for the educational advancement of students from under-represented groups;" she hasn't engaged "in activity designed to remove barriers and to increase participation by groups historically under-represented in higher education;" and she hasn't participated "in service that applies up-to-date knowledge to problems, issues, and concerns of groups historically under-represented in higher education" (116).

What she has done, over the course of her doctoral research, is publish paper after groundbreaking paper to advance her field of mathematics. And, let's suppose that she has demonstrated that she is an excellent teacher as well. Are the best interests of society or a university really served by placing this person at a substantial *disadvantage* in the faculty application process because she hasn't done any of the things that the university wants to see in a diversity statement? Clearly, the answer is no.

profs have to be able to teach to diverse backgrounds tho.

Of course, as diversity statement requirements for faculty position applications become more widely adopted, aspiring faculty members will naturally react analogously to the way many high school students have long done when told that college admissions officers want to see lots of extracurricular activities: They will make calculated decisions to engage in activities for the express purpose of enhancing their applications. For the many Ph.D. students who are pursuing research on topics that don't directly lend themselves to discussion in a diversity statement, this will mean duly engaging in activities designed to bolster what they can say. Some of them will find diversity-related activities that were originally motivated by resume-building to in fact be highly engaging and rewarding and in the end will be grateful for the professional pressure that spurred their involvement. But some of them will simply be going through the motions, engaging in diversity-related activities not out of any personal passion or interest, but for purely utilitarian reasons.

An additional challenge to mandated diversity statements, as observed by Jeffrey Flier, is that:

> the key terms—diversity, equity, and inclusion—are rarely defined with specificity, and their meaning has been subtly shifting. That's a serious problem, especially if diversity efforts are to be a criterion for faculty evaluation. The term "equity," for instance, can imply equality of opportunity or equality of outcome—two quite different things with distinct policy implications. The concept of "inclusion" might imply the welcoming of diverse groups and perspectives, or it might involve the avoidance of microaggressions and the creation of safe spaces—two controversial goals. The lack of definitional clarity of key terms creates confusion, suspicion, and disagreement. (117)

We would argue that although, as Flier indicates, there are multiple possible interpretations of these terms, interpretations that are in line with the set of beliefs are given higher priority. That means, for example, that "diversity" refers to the axes of identity that include race, gender, sexual orientation, and gender expression—and not to diversity of perspectives or political views. Thus, while the definitions are indeed potentially ambiguous, they are interpreted by most people on campus in a manner that's consistent with all three beliefs.

There is also a broader consequence of the trend toward diversity statements that involves questions of social engineering. To the extent that diversity statement requirements become more common in faculty applications, universities are engaging in a form of social engineering that says, in effect, that to be a person who is qualified to hold a faculty position, you must have a demonstrated track record of contributing to diversity and a future plan to continue to do so. It is possible to be a strong believer in the value of diversity while also posing the question of why this topic in particular is the one that warrants this sort of social engineering of future faculty members. After all, without in any way discounting the value of diversity, it's possible to identify any number of other worthy topics for which universities are not applying similar filters.

Take, for example, charity. There's a strong case to be made that part of being a good citizen and role model is engaging in charity. Why then are universities not requiring "charity statements" in which prospective (or current) faculty members outline the efforts they have undertaken to engage in charitable endeavors? Or what about community engagement? People who devote time and effort to better their communities are vital to the health of any society. So why do university hiring committees not ask for "community engagement" statements that would allow a faculty applicant who has been a consistent and passionate participant in his or her community for years to shine? And so on. The answer, of course, is that the third belief (the insistence on seeing everything through the lens of identity) imposes a hierarchy that places promotion of diversity above other worthy endeavors such as community engagement and charitable work. Mandated "diversity statements" are a way to signal fealty to this prioritization, both for the faculty within a university who argue to adopt the mandate and for the applicants who get the message that what they write in relation to diversity may be at least as important to the outcome of their application as their accomplishments and future plans in relation to research and teaching.

The point, again, is not to downplay the importance of diversity. We are a vastly better society today because of the profoundly important work that has been done in recent decades to improve the climate in relation to diversity, and there is much work yet left to do. The question is rather whether, in relation to faculty applications and promotions (including tenure decisions), the mandate that candidates must focus on this particular issue over various other laudable issues is merited.

[handwritten margin note: because charity has nothing to do w/ being a good teacher]

Is the ideal outcome to end up 10 years from now with university faculties in which every single faculty member is continuously engaged in some form of compelled diversity-related activity? Or, with respect to endeavors that can improve our universities and our society, are we perhaps better off letting people pursue their passions, giving support and encouragement to those who wish to make diversity a focus of their efforts, while also supporting and valuing the work of those who wish to find other ways to enhance their communities? Our belief is that the latter will lead to a healthier, more balanced higher education system and society.

7

Social media and the Publication Process

7.1 How Publishing Normally Works

Academic research matters a great deal. Knowledge produced through scholarship plays multiple roles in society, ranging from the creation of new opportunities for businesses and economic growth, to improving our understanding of society and the challenges we face, to technological and medical advancements that better our quality of life. These tangible functions are in addition to the value of knowledge for its own sake.

Moreover, the process of research itself plays an important role in student learning. While one of the ways research makes its way into the classroom is through textbooks, it is also the case that scholars with active research agendas of their own or who are familiar with the current research of others can bring the new knowledge into the classroom in something closer to real time. This chapter provides a description, in general terms, of how the research production process works.

In the context of academia, many faculty view an active research agenda as a core professional responsibility, though there are many variations across disciplines, institutions, and type of faculty appointment. Institutions with a teaching orientation anticipate less research output from their faculty than those with a focus on both research and teaching.

Research output can take multiple forms. The most traditional is a publication in a peer-reviewed academic journal. "Peer-reviewed" means that prior to publication, an editor of the journal sends the submitted manuscript to several reviewers who are experts in the field but who were not directly involved in the work described. Based on the feedback from the reviewers, the editor can accept the manuscript for publication, reject it, or ask the authors to make revisions and then resubmit the manuscript for an additional round of review.

In most fields, authors are prohibited from submitting the same manuscript simultaneously to two different journals.[1] That said, if a manuscript

---

[1] Law is an exception. In law, it is routine for authors to simultaneously submit the same manuscript to multiple law reviews, with the hope of creating what amounts to a competition among law reviews. In the end, of course, the manuscript can only be published in one venue.

Unassailable Ideas. Ilana Redstone and John Villasenor, Oxford University Press (2020). © Oxford University Press.
DOI: 10.1093/oso/9780190078065.001.0001.

is rejected by one journal, the authors are free to then submit it to a second journal. The publication process can take a long time from start to finish. It is not uncommon for several years to elapse from the original submission of a manuscript to its actual publication.

Another possible venue for publishing research is through a peer-reviewed conference proceeding. This occurs when an academic conference is accompanied by a publication containing papers describing the work that participants presented at the conference. While a peer-review process is used in this case as well, the time scales for conference publications are often shorter, with initial submissions of manuscripts typically occurring some number of months before the conference. Some conferences are extremely competitive, with acceptance rates significantly lower than those found at some well-regarded journals. There are also conferences (and journals) where the peer-review process involves a much lower hurdle, and the acceptance rates are very high.

It is also possible to publish in venues other than traditional peer-reviewed academic research journals. These can range from respected non-academic journals that publish articles with a fairly analytical focus (e.g., *Foreign Affairs*), to magazines that serve a wide but relatively academically focused audience (e.g., *Scientific American*), to news sites that reach extremely broad audiences.

In general, non-academic publications are given less weight when evaluating the contribution of a faculty member's research, though how much less weight depends on the nature of the publication. An op-ed would get no credit as a scholarly publication. A lengthy article in *Foreign Affairs* would be viewed as substantially more scholarly, though it would still not be considered to be as scholarly as a paper in a well-regarded peer-reviewed research journal. A notable exception to the rule that only peer-reviewed publications can get "full credit" as scholarly publications is in the field of law, where most scholarship occurs through publication in student-edited law reviews, many of which are extremely well regarded even though they are not peer-reviewed in the same manner as publications in many other disciplines.

Books are another common way to publish scholarship. There is enormous variation in the types of books that are published by faculty members. Some are extremely scholarly and can provide as much of a contribution to knowledge as do multiple journal papers, and are acknowledged as such in the author's evaluation and promotion process. Others are less so, but can still play an important role in research dissemination.

Researchers can supplement traditional academic publications with other forms of publication aimed at reaching larger audiences. A scientist, after publishing a series of peer-reviewed articles that receive wide notice and acclaim, may be invited by a prestigious non-academic publication such as *Scientific American* to write an article explaining his or her research results to a broader audience. Faculty members also can engage with the public regarding their research through publication of op-eds, articles written for popular online news sites, personal blogs, and social media. While these sorts of engagements can help disseminate research, they are generally evaluated as distinct from the original publication of the research in a more academic context. An early career tenure-track faculty member who is prolific in publishing groundbreaking, peer-reviewed articles but never publishes op-eds or blog posts will almost certainly be granted tenure, while an early career faculty member who only publishes op-eds and blog posts but never publishes in traditional academic venues will almost certainly be denied it.

Finally, this discussion about peer-reviewed publications of articles in academic journals applies to most but not all fields. In some fields, scholarly output is measured differently. Professors with a focus on areas such as screenwriting, music composition, or fiction writing are evaluated on their output in those respective areas. The upshot is that academic scholarship takes many different forms.

In part because of the numerous possible variants, there have long been discussions of how to evaluate research productivity. Disagreements occur over the relative weight of journal articles versus books versus conference proceedings. For instance, how many articles count as much as one book? How should a prestigious conference acceptance be weighed against a lower-prestige journal publication? Or, how are articles counted in a field, like English, in which books are a very common form of creative output? These are all real questions that departments and disciplines have to address. And while the complexity of this landscape creates many points of potential divergence, there has traditionally been a common and shared understanding knowledge production (and in some fields, production of creative works) is a key goal of research.

The three beliefs have created a situation where certain ideas, claims, and questions are protected from criticism, and therefore from open inquiry. Academic publications that present ideas running counter to these beliefs are

certain beliefs as protected from criticism

subject to what is in essence an extra round of social media–driven review that starts *after* a paper has already successfully navigated the traditional peer-review process and been published. As the examples we will provide illustrate, this dynamic acts as a form of censorship that can impact a journal's handling of the paper in question, both before and after publication. The very existence of post-publication social media review acts to shape the behavior of researchers and journal editors.   *" social media review"*

7.2 The Littman Case

In 2018, Lisa Littman was an assistant professor in the Department of Behavioral and Social Sciences within the School of Public Health at Brown University, with research interests that included gender dysphoria, which "denotes persistent discomfort with one's biologic sex or assigned gender" (118, p. 217).

On August 16, 2018, Littman published a paper in the peer-refereed journal *PLOS ONE* in which she described what she termed "rapid-onset gender dysphoria," writing:

> Rapid-onset gender dysphoria (ROGD) describes a phenomenon where the development of gender dysphoria is observed to begin suddenly during or after puberty in an adolescent or young adult who would not have met criteria for gender dysphoria in childhood. ROGD appears to represent an entity that is distinct from the gender dysphoria observed in individuals who have previously been described as transgender. The worsening of mental well-being and parent–child relationships and behaviors that isolate AYAs [adolescent and young adults] from their parents, families, non-transgender friends and mainstream sources of information are particularly concerning. More research is needed to better understand this phenomenon, its implications and scope. (119, see S1 file)

On August 22, Brown published a lengthy press release promoting Littman's paper. The press release, which has since been removed by Brown but was archived externally (120) before its removal, noted that "This month, a Brown University researcher published the first study to empirically describe teens and young adults who did not have symptoms of gender dysphoria during childhood but who were observed by their parents to rapidly develop gender dysphoria symptoms over days, weeks or months during or after puberty."

Littman's study was perceived by some as increasing the potential for harm to a vulnerable population and, as such, in the days after its publication, her methodology and conclusions were attacked on social media and through longer articles (see, for instance, 121,122). Littman had run up against the belief about the primacy of identity, particularly one's right to self-directed identity. After all, her work could be interpreted by some to suggest that parents with adolescent children fitting the description in her study would be justified in questioning whether their children's dysphoria was genuine. On August 27, *PLOS ONE* responded to the criticism, saying in a statement that:

> *PLOS ONE* is aware of the reader concerns raised on the study's content and methodology. We take all concerns raised about publications in the journal very seriously, and are following up on these per our policy and COPE guidelines. As part of our follow up we will seek further expert assessment on the study's methodology and analyses. We will provide a further update once we have completed our assessment and discussions. (123)

Brown removed the original August 22 press release from its website and, on August 27 and 28, replaced the contents of the link that formerly contained the press release with both a statement from Brown University and a letter from Bess Marcus, dean of the Brown University School of Public Health (124). Brown added an additional statement to the site on September 5. The August 27 Brown University statement explained that "In light of questions raised about research design and data collection related to Lisa Littman's study on 'rapid-onset gender dysphoria,' Brown determined that removing the article from news distribution is the most responsible course of action." Marcus's August 28 letter stated, among other things, that:

> Independent of the University's removal of the article because of concerns about research methodology, the School of Public Health has heard from Brown community members expressing concerns that the conclusions of the study could be used to discredit efforts to support transgender youth and invalidate the perspectives of members of the transgender community.

and that:

> The spirit of free inquiry and scholarly debate is central to academic ex-
> cellence. At the same time, we believe firmly that it is also incumbent on
> public health researchers to listen to multiple perspectives and to recognize
> and articulate the limitations of their work. This process includes acknowl-
> edging and considering the perspectives of those who criticize our research
> methods and conclusions and working to improve future research to ad-
> dress these limitations and better serve public health. There is an added
> obligation for vigilance in research design and analysis any time there are
> implications for the health of the communities at the center of research and
> study. (124)

It's also important to note that while pullbacks at Brown and *PLOS ONE*
were celebrated by those who had attacked the paper, they also occasioned
a growing chorus of concern. A petition defending Littman's study quickly
gained over 4,000 signatures (125).

In March 2019, *PLOS ONE* published a revised version of Littman's paper,
along with a "Notice of republication" stating that:

> After publication of this article, questions were raised that prompted the
> journal to conduct a post-publication reassessment of the article, involving
> senior members of the journal's editorial team, two Academic Editors, a
> statistics reviewer, and an external expert reviewer. The post-publication
> review identified issues that needed to be addressed to ensure the article
> meets PLOS ONE's publication criteria. (126)

In addition to publishing the revised article, *PLOS ONE* published an extensive "Correction Notice" authored by *PLOS ONE* editors as well as a "formal
comment" on Littman's paper authored by Angelo Brandelli Costa, a faculty member of the Psychology Graduate Program of the Pontifical Catholic
University of Rio Grande do Sul in Brazil (127).

So, what went wrong here? The short answer is: a lot. As an initial matter,
PLOS ONE's assertion that "the post-publication review identified issues that
needed to be addressed to ensure the article meets *PLOS ONE*'s publication
criteria" is ironic. Through the act of publishing Littman's *original* paper in
2018, *PLOS ONE* deemed it publication-worthy. Yet *PLOS ONE*'s March
2019 "Notice of republication" implied otherwise.

PLOS ONE's statement that "a post-publication reassessment of the article" was performed after "questions were raised" points out another problem: A sufficiently loud social media campaign can cause a respected journal to open "a post-publication reassessment" of a paper, adding a very substantive additional layer of review—and one that is apparently preferentially applied to papers that reach ideologically controversial conclusions.

Littman explained in an interview with *Quillette* that the post-publication reassessment "included input from three senior members of the *PLOS ONE* editorial staff, a statistical reviewer, two academic editors, and an external expert reviewer" (128). This is a dramatically higher level of attention than is normally provided in peer review of an academic paper. Littman also said:

> Not to put too fine a point on it, but the message of these critics is that research using parent reports, targeted recruitment and online, anonymous surveys is unacceptable for my study, but not at all problematic when used in studies where the findings support their desired narrative. But, that's not how science works: You can't judge the strength of a methodology by the results it produces, you must judge the results by the strength of the methodology that produced them. (128)

[handwritten margin note: method > results]

Littman also stated that the paper and resulting controversy had caused her to lose her consulting contract with the Rhode Island Department of Health, where she had been working "on a variety of public-health projects mostly related to the health of pregnant women (immunizations, smoking cessation, oral health, premature births)"—all topics that are unrelated to the subject of her *PLOS ONE* paper (128).

In addition to the publication process concerns raised by *PLOS ONE*'s handling of the Littman case, there are multiple academic freedom concerns raised by Brown University's actions. First, Brown moved precipitously, taking action well before it was possible to know with any certainty whether Littman's methods were flawed in the ways that some critics suggested. It was not credible, during the limited time span (under two weeks) that elapsed from the date of the paper's publication to the date when Brown pulled the press release and issued its initial statement and the letter from School of Public Health dean Bess Marcus, for anyone to conclude with certainty that Littman's conclusions were *not* correct. Thus, while academic freedom clearly doesn't include the right to publish provably faulty research, Littman's paper could not have been shown to be in that category when Brown backpedaled.

Second, Brown's actions are particularly concerning in light of the lofty principles the university articulates regarding academic freedom: "Academic freedom is essential to the function of education and to the pursuit of scholarship in universities. Therefore, Brown University, mindful of its historic commitment to scholarship and to the free exchange of ideas, affirms that faculty and students alike shall enjoy full freedom in their teaching, learning, and research" (129). Is a professor whose own dean and university issue statements calling her recently published paper into question enjoying "full freedom" in research? It's hard to make a serious argument that she is.

Third, Brown's actions created enormous potential future harm to Littman's career. Her reputation was undermined by Brown's willingness to lend credence to criticisms of her methodology in the absence of any scholarly determination that her methodology was indeed flawed. It's important to emphasize that Brown's retreat occurred when there had been no formal finding against Littman regarding a failure to adhere to academic standards. The only thing that had happened by August 27 is that objections had been raised to her paper, and the journal that published it, *PLOS ONE*, had stated that it would investigate. The fact that Brown acted *before* waiting for the results of *PLOS ONE*'s investigation suggests that Brown was reacting not to the results of any formal academic review but rather to feedback received through mechanisms entirely outside the normal paper publication process.

Fourth, Brown's September 5 statement asserted that "This is not about academic freedom" and "This is about academic standards." Brown further stated that "As a research institution, we feel we must ensure that work that is featured on the University website conforms to the highest academic standards. Given the concerns raised about research design and methods, the most responsible course of action was to stop publicizing the work published in this particular instance. We would have done this regardless of the topic of the article" (124).

The assertion that "We would have done this regardless of the topic of the article" is an interesting logical construct that, upon a bit of analysis, actually *increases* the concern raised by this series of events. Brown's stated reason for acting was "concerns raised about research design and methods." Those "concerns" included tweets, articles at sites such as Medium, and (according to Marcus's letter) feedback from unnamed "Brown community members." This dynamic could play out in relation to *any* publication on *any* controversial topic. What this means, in essence, is that the years-long process of performing research, writing a paper, documenting the results, and seeing that paper through the peer-review and publication process can be second-guessed in a matter of days by the Twittersphere—with that second-guessing then leading to actions by high-ranking administrators at the researcher's own institution. By definition, a paper on a controversial topic will lead to complaints by those who oppose the positions that are articulated. These days, that opposition will be expressed and propagated largely through social media. Brown's statement that "We would have done this regardless of the topic of the article" therefore suggests a veto-by-Twitter approach that applies generally. And we suspect it's not limited just to Brown.

Few researchers want to experience what Littman did. There is one very easy way to ensure this doesn't happen: Avoid publishing papers with assertions that could lead to a social media backlash. Many researchers are undoubtedly making this choice. That's only something to celebrate if all of the undiscovered knowledge in the world involves conclusions that would meet with approval on the Twittersphere.

7.3 The Tuvel Case

In spring 2017, Rebecca Tuvel, an assistant professor of philosophy at Rhodes College in Memphis, TN, published a peer-reviewed article titled "In Defense of Transracialism" in *Hypatia*, a feminist philosophy journal. Tuvel argued that:

> considerations that support transgenderism extend to transracialism. Given this parity, since we should accept transgender individuals' decisions to change sexes, we should also accept transracial individuals' decisions to change race . . . I conclude that if some individuals genuinely feel like or identify as a member of a race other than the one assigned to them at birth—so strongly to the point of seeking a transition to the other race—we should accept their decision to change races." (130, p. 264)

The article led to a wave of criticism on Facebook and Twitter and to the drafting and online posting of a highly critical "Open letter to Hypatia." While the open letter was gathering signatures, but before it had been formally submitted to *Hypatia*, a group of the journal's associate editors posted an apology on Facebook. "We, the members of *Hypatia*'s Board of Associate Editors," the post read in part, "extend our profound apology to our friends and colleagues in feminist philosophy, especially transfeminists, queer feminists and feminists of color, for the harms that the publication of the article on transracialism has caused." They continued, "Perhaps most fundamentally, to compare ethically the lived experience of trans people (from a distinctly external perspective) primarily to a single example of a white person claiming to have adopted a Black identity creates an equivalency that fails to recognize the history of racial appropriation, while also associating trans people with racial appropriation." The most salient offense that Tuvel made was to suggest an equivalence in the hierarchy of identity-based claims to harm (131).

On May 2, the "Open letter to Hypatia," which had by that time gathered over 800 signatures, was formally submitted to *Hypatia*. Addressed to editor Sally Scholz "and the broader Hypatia community," it asserted that the "article falls short of scholarly standards" and urged *Hypatia* to "immediately acknowledge the severity of these concerns," to retract the article, and (among other things) "issue a statement taking responsibility for the failures of judgment associated with publishing this article" (132).

 In a May 6 statement, Scholz defended the decision to publish the paper, writing that "I firmly believe, and this belief will not waver, that it is utterly inappropriate for editors to repudiate an article they have accepted for publication (barring issues of plagiarism or falsification of data). In this respect, editors must stand behind the authors of accepted papers. That is where I stand. Professor Tuvel's paper went through the peer review process and was accepted by the reviewers and by me" (133). A few weeks later, on May 18, the board of directors of *Hypatia* issued a statement backing Scholz: "We endorse her assessment that, barring discovery of misconduct or plagiarism, the decision to publish stands . . . The Board also recognizes Professor Tuvel for her work and condemns any ad hominem and personal attacks that may have been directed against her. As a scholarly publication, *Hypatia* supports our authors and appreciates their contributions to advancing understanding of contemporary social issues" (133). The board also wrote that it "acknowledges the intensity of experience and convictions around matters of intersectionality, especially in the world of academic philosophy, which has an egregious history of treatment of women of color feminists and feminists from other marginalized social positions," and that "Going forward, with consultation amongst those who perform various roles for our organization, *Hypatia* will review its governance structure, procedures, and policies, aiming to continue to improve its inclusiveness and respect for marginalized voices in a manner consistent with the continuation of *Hypatia* as a scholarly enterprise committed to feminist values."

Unsurprisingly, this did not put an end to the controversy. In July 2017, *Hypatia* editor Scholz and *Hypatia Online Reviews* editor Shelley Wilcox resigned, with the board of directors stating that "As the board ultimately responsible for the well-being of the journal, we find it necessary at this time to take emergency measures to restore the academic integrity of the journal and shepherd it through a transition period to a new editorial team." Also in July, eight of *Hypatia*'s associate editors stepped down, writing in a resignation letter that "on Monday, July 17 the nonprofit board gave us an ultimatum of either resigning by noon on July 19 or they would suspend the journal's governance documents and, thus, the authority of the Board of Associate Editors. . . . their unilateral decision is a de facto suspension of *Hypatia*'s governance documents and a firing of us" (134).

So what is to be made of this? In one very narrow sense, the Tuvel controversy had an outcome that preserved Tuvel's right to publish in the sense that, despite the combination of social media–driven demands for a retraction and a repudiation of the paper by many of *Hypatia*'s associate editors, the journal's editor and board of directors stood by the paper. But this came at a steep price.   *injury → can't they sue?*

Writing in May 2017, even before the July resignations of Scholz, Wilcox, and many of the associate editors, Texas A&M University philosophy professor José Luis Bermúdez published an op-ed in *Inside Higher Ed* stating that the "behavior of the open letter signatories and the anonymous editorial board members has already led to clear and identifiable injury and loss, and will continue to do so." One injured party, he noted, is "Tuvel, whose academic reputation has been publicly dragged through the mud and who has been personally vilified. As a former dean, I can only imagine the problems that this episode will cause for her tenure case and future career prospects." He also cited the reputational harm to *Hypatia*: "It is hard to see how this journal can retain academic credibility, after its editorial board has publicly repudiated its own peer reviewers and reviewing practices." He also noted the harms to the broader philosophy community, commenting on "the chilling effect within the discipline of seeing a vulnerable member of the community publicly shamed by a group that will avoid accountability (unless the legal system intervenes)" (135).

While Tuvel's paper was not depublished, the costs—to Tuvel, to the *Hypatia* editor Scholz, and to the journal's reputation—were so severe that they are certain to shape future research and publication decisions not only within philosophy but also well beyond. For academics without the protection of tenure, a group that includes not only tenure-track assistant professors but also non–tenure-track adjuncts, the incentives are clear: If you want to retain or obtain a university position, publishing a paper that gets you embroiled in this sort of controversy is very unlikely to be a career-enhancing move. A far safer path is simply to avoid writing a paper on a topic likely to generate a social media backlash. For journal editors, the incentives are also clear: Accepting and then standing behind papers like Tuvel's puts your editorial position at risk. And for journal boards of directors, the reputational costs of controversy create a strong incentive to avoid it.

We emphasize that we take no position regarding the scholarly contribution of Tuvel's paper. However, the whole *point* of peer review and oversight by an editor is to perform that assessment and reach a decision regarding whether or not a paper merits publication. Once that determination is made, if the resulting decision is to accept the paper, the academic enterprise should be robust enough so that a social media backlash doesn't generate anywhere near the level of carnage that occurred at *Hypatia*. If Tuvel's paper is viewed as offensive or flawed, other scholars should feel free to write and submit their own articles explaining why. That is exactly the sort of robust discourse that allows academic disciplines to move forward. Instead, the reaction to Tuvel's paper will chill academic examinations of questions that go well beyond those Tuvel addressed.

7.4 The Gilley Case

An unfortunate but inevitable consequence of the current environment is that when an academic paper is deemed sufficiently offensive, some critics will resort to threats of physical violence in order to force it to be depublished. To explore this further, consider the set of events that followed the September 2017 publication of an article by Portland State University professor Bruce Gilley titled "The Case for Colonialism" in the journal *Third World Quarterly*. We cite this example not because we agree with the premise of Gilley's publication (we don't), but because the reaction to it illustrates how threats of violence can shape editorial decisions.

In the article, Gilley asserted that "for the last 100 years, Western colonialism has had a bad name. It is high time to question this orthodoxy."

"Western colonialism," he continued, "was, as a general rule, both objectively beneficial and subjectively legitimate in most of the places it was found" (136).

Unsurprisingly, a backlash ensued. Vijay Prashad, a professor at Trinity College in Connecticut and a member of *Third World Quarterly*'s editorial board, tweeted, "I told the managing editor that if @thirdworldq does not retract this essay, I will resign from the editorial board" (137). Two online petitions calling on *Third World Quarterly* to retract the article were launched and quickly gathered thousands of signatures.

About ten days after the original publication, *Third World Quarterly* editor-in-chief Shahid Qadir issued a statement defending the publication. As described in an article in *Inside Higher Ed*, Qadir stated that in publishing this article "we are not endorsing its procolonial views" but are instead "presenting it to be debated within the field and academy" (138).

On September 19, a group of over a dozen members of the journal's editorial board resigned, writing in the accompanying letter that "We are deeply disappointed by the unacceptable process around the publication of Bruce Gilley's Viewpoint essay, 'The case for colonialism,' which was published in *Third World Quarterly* without any consultation with the Editorial Board" (139).

A few days later, the article was withdrawn. In its place, the publisher provided the following statement, attributing the withdrawal to threats of violence received by the editor:

> This Viewpoint essay has been withdrawn at the request of the academic journal editor, and in agreement with the author of the essay. Following a number of complaints, Taylor & Francis conducted a thorough investigation into the peer review process on this article. Whilst this clearly demonstrated the essay had undergone double-blind peer review, in line with the journal's editorial policy, the journal editor has subsequently received serious and credible threats of personal violence. These threats are linked to the publication of this essay. As the publisher, we must take this seriously. Taylor & Francis has a strong and supportive duty of care to all our academic editorial teams, and this is why we are withdrawing this essay. (136)

Of course, the people who signed the petitions calling for the article to be retracted have free expression rights, as do the people who tweeted that it should never have been published, and the editorial board members who resigned. All of those actions can be understood as the response that might be expected to a controversial article. But the fact that the final disposition of the article was determined by threats of violence against the journal editor should be disturbing to everyone, including staunch opponents of the article.

Why? Because, as the adage goes, if threats of violence are used to silence views we don't like, it's only a matter of time before they will be used to silence views we *do* like. And while the use of threats of violence to attempt to silence expression, is, unfortunately, not unheard of outside of academic publication circles, the Gilley incident is surely one of the first in the social media age that was centered around a publication in an academic journal. It marks a disturbing evolution in how controversial publications get addressed.

Unfortunately, there's no easy solution. We can't expect journal editors to simply shrug off credible threats of violence. But that leads to a situation where anyone with access to the internet who is willing to anonymously threaten violence to a journal editor can potentially wield veto power over an academic publication. Surely that isn't something to be celebrated.

8

Challenges to open inquiry

One of the most important components of free inquiry is the willingness to engage with alternative explanations to observed outcomes or patterns. This is not a new observation. As University of Chicago philosopher Allan Bloom wrote in his 1987 book *The Closing of the American Mind*:

> Freedom of the mind requires not only, or not even especially, the absence of legal constraints but the presence of alternative thoughts. The most successful tyranny is not the one that uses force to assure uniformity but the one that removes awareness of other possibilities, that makes it seem inconceivable that other ways are viable, that removes the sense that there is an outside. (11, p. 249)

Knowledge grows when conventional wisdom can be challenged, extended, modified, updated, and, in some cases, proven to be completely wrong. Examples of conventional scientific wisdom being upended abound.

Galileo was famously punished for his insistence that the sun, and not the Earth, was at the center of the solar system. Or to take another example, during a period of hundreds of years beginning in the Middle Ages, many European medical experts believed in the miasma theory of disease, under which "diseases were caused by the presence in the air of a miasma, a poisonous vapour in which were suspended particles of decaying matter that was characterised by its foul smell" (140). It was not until the mid-19th century that miasma theory fell out of favor, replaced by the recognition that disease transmission was attributable to germs.

In the 1920s, Edwin Hubble questioned the belief, then held by many astronomers, that the universe was limited to our own galaxy. He showed that there are actually many galaxies (141), and then went on to show that the universe is expanding (142). Until relatively late in the 20th century, the assumption in the medical establishment was that duodenal and gastric ulcers

Unassailable Ideas. Ilana Redstone and John Villasenor, Oxford University Press (2020). © Oxford University Press.
DOI: 10.1093/oso/9780190078065.001.0001.

were primarily attributable to stress. Drs. Barry Marshall and Robin Warren won a Nobel Prize for, as described in the official press release from the Nobel Assembly at Karolinska Institutet, doing work that "challenged prevailing dogmas" through their discovery of the bacterium *Helicobacter pylori* and its role as a primary cause of ulcers.

Supposed "truths" can be heavily influenced by the dominant sociopolitical climate. When the American Psychiatric Association (APA) published the first edition of its *Diagnostic and Statistical Manual of Mental Disorders* (DSM-I) in 1952, it listed "homosexuality" as a "sociopathic personality disturbance." The second edition, DSM-II, was published in 1968 and listed homosexuality as a "sexual deviation." After a contentious debate and vote by APA members in 1973, homosexuality was reclassified as "sexual orientation disturbance." This was followed, in 1980, by its association with a new category, "Ego Dystonic Homosexuality," included in the DSM-III. Finally, with the publication of DSM-III-R in 1987, "Ego Dystonic Homosexuality" was removed, and being gay was no longer pathologized in the DSM (source for all citations in this paragraph: (143)).

This evolution furnishes an important reminder of the value of humility. In the 1950s and 1960s, many eminent psychiatrists considered it an unshakable truth that being gay was pathological, and would have scoffed at suggestions to the contrary. We know today that they were wrong. This doesn't mean that all socially informed beliefs we hold today are wrong, but it does mean that we should think twice before assuming that all of them must be right. In fact, if history is any guide, some percentage of the "truths" we hold today will in fact be understood to be wrong in the future. It would have been ludicrous for someone in the 1950s to claim that the widely accepted consensus of that era reflected a final and perfect understanding of complex social issues. It is just as ludicrous to make that claim today about the present consensus on current contentious issues.

If we accept that proposition, then of logical necessity, moving toward a fuller understanding of complex social issues requires that we view them with a wide aperture, including being willing to engage with, criticize, and either accept or reject hypotheses that may be out of step with our current worldview. If, by contrast, we are so beholden to our worldview that we fall all over ourselves in an attempt to find evidence supporting it, we will undermine our ability to arrive at more informed perspectives.

8.1   Gender and the Workplace: Academic Inconsistency

The issue of gender and the workplace provides an interesting example of some of the inconsistencies of the current academic climate. If asked, most people in academia today would agree with the assertion that there are no differences between men and women that impact their ability to perform in the workplace. Consistent with this view, they would find an assertion that men are better than women at any of the skills needed to succeed in business to be offensive, and rightly so.

Yet, at the same time, it is very much in vogue to publish (and approvingly cite) studies purporting to show that women are better than men at a professionally relevant skill. While it might be tempting to overlook this inconsistency because of the long history of workplace discrimination against women, making a coherent argument requires asserting either that there are gender-based differences that matter or there aren't. Put another way, this inconsistency illustrates what amounts to an exception attached to the second belief. The second belief holds that that group differences are due entirely to discrimination. But, despite this belief, it seems to be permissible to publish results that specifically argue *against* equality if they do so in a way that inverts historical discriminatory hierarchies. For example, it is acceptable in academia to assert that women outperform men when it comes to business acumen.

In December 2017, *Harvard Business Review* (HBR) published an article titled "Women Respond Better Than Men to Competitive Pressure" (144). In the article, HBR cited the research of Dr. Alex Krumer of the University of St. Gallen, who arrived at this conclusion based on studying 8,200 games from Grand Slam tennis matches. The HBR article also featured a pullout quote based on Krumer's earlier research, stating that "Men are more affected by psychological momentum than women are."

A July 2016 article in *Investor's Business Daily* (IBD) stated that "Several studies back up that claim that women investing in stocks are better at it than men" (145). The IBD article cited separate studies from Fidelity, Warwick Business School, and a team of academics at University of Sydney and University of New South Wales, all of which indicated that women outperformed men in investing. The IBD article also quoted Bankrate chief financial analyst Greg McBride, who said that "studies have shown men tend to be much more risk takers, when it comes to investing, to their own detriment because they trade too much" and "women tend to generate better returns because they don't trade as often and tend to hang in there" (145).

There are many more examples like this. In September 2016, the Washington, DC-based Urban Institute published a report titled "Women Are Better than Men at Paying Their Mortgages" (146). A January 2018 BBC article titled "Women really are stronger than men, according to study" opened with the sentence: "Women really are the stronger sex" (147). In November 2017, a CNET article titled "Women are better in tech than men, says a report" stated that "A report from the Metropolitan Policy Program at the Brookings Institution measured men's and women's digital scores, and found that women had stronger skills than men do" (148).

Now imagine if the genders in some of the statements quoted above were reversed. Would HBR have dared to publish an article titled "Men Respond Better Than Women to Competitive Pressure"? Would IBD have quoted a finance industry expert who asserted that "studies have shown women tend to be much more risk takers, when it comes to investing, to their own detriment because they trade too much" or "men tend to generate better returns because they don't trade as often and tend to hang in there"? Would CNET have published an article titled "Men are better in tech than women, says a report"? Of course not.

When the genders are reversed, we find these statements offensive, and rightly so given the long history of discrimination against women in so many areas. And, given the context of historical and continuing bias against women in the workplace, it can be heartwarming—and feel like a small act of atonement—to read about studies that purport to show, for example, that women make better investment decisions than men.

But as a matter of logic, we can't have it both ways. In other words, if we are willing to grant plausibility to academic studies that purport to identify gender-based differences in professional skills that tilt in favor of women, then in the name of consistency—and as uncomfortable as it might make us—we should also be willing to consider studies that might suggest differences that tilt the opposite way. On the other hand, if we are going to reject any assertions that there might be some business-relevant skills at which, for whatever set of reasons, men tend to be better at, consistency demands that we take the same approach when presented with assertions that women have superior business-relevant skills to men.

In making these points, we are not arguing that men are inferior or superior to women at managing debts, making investment decisions, or any other professionally relevant skill. Rather we are pointing out the logical in-consistency in the academic discourse on this issue. Ironically, part of the motivation to approvingly cite "Women are better than men at . . ." research results may lie in the same sort of assumptions about gender-specific traits that people readily condemn in other contexts.

Consider risk aversion. Without any further context, many people would find the claim that women are more risk averse to be offensive, as it might be deemed to connote a lower likelihood of female success in the many busi-ness endeavors that inherently involve risk. Yet when the claim is made that because women are more risk averse, they are better than men at investing, the same people who find the "better than men at investing" portion of this assertion to be refreshing do not seem to mind that it is based on a separate claim (that women are more risk averse) that has often been presented as a negative attribute.

Given this context, consider again the assertion that we used to open this section: "There are no differences between men and women that impact their relative performance or participation in the workplace." And we can ask whether, in the current academic climate, this is 1) a fact or 2) a debatable supposition.

We now see that the answer is: It depends. Academic studies claiming that women are better than men at a professionally relevant skill are met with nods of agreement and approval. Of logical necessity this means that those providing the approval cannot consider the statement "There are no differences between men and women that impact their relative performance or participation in the workplace" to be a fact. Yet many of those same people would invoke that statement as fact in order to counter an assertion that men were better than women at a professionally relevant skill.

The existence of this contradiction may seem unremarkable or even laud-able to those steeped in the beliefs that govern academic discourse. But viewed objectively, it is illogical. And it illustrates how the goal of dispassionate anal-ysis and open inquiry can be impeded by incentives that favor hypotheses and conclusions that resonate with the dominant on-campus views.

8.2 Limits on Objective Research

In the current climate, it can be hard to perform objective research on topics that raise the possibility of findings that might run afoul of the three beliefs.

Consider a researcher who wants to investigate whether the notably higher average SAT scores of Asian American high school students relative to all other groups is ascribable to factors other than discrimination.

This could generate hypotheses that touch on questions with important social and policy implications. However, asking such questions is perilous, as it risks pushing back against the second belief, which holds that differences in group outcomes are due exclusively to discrimination (or its corollary, privilege). As a result, any publication on Asian American SAT performance that does not use a discrimination-centered narrative in its analysis would likely stir controversy.

The belief that differences in group outcomes are due entirely to discrimination carries with it an unspoken fear that the *absence* of group differences could be wielded by those who might argue against the power of discrimination to shape outcomes. Thus, any finding suggesting that discrimination *isn't* present in a sufficiently significant way to constitute an impediment to the group in question runs counter to the narrative required by the second belief.   *asian americans*

The work of Arthur Sakamoto, a professor of sociology at Texas A&M, provides an illustrative example of how papers that don't elevate the role of discrimination in discussing group differences can encounter difficulty getting published. Sakamoto has argued that attention to Asian Americans, particularly in the field of sociology, is severely limited precisely because Asian Americans don't fit the paradigm according to which majority group members are the oppressors and minority group members are the oppressed. In a 2017 podcast, he said that:

> I've been submitting to the *American Sociological Review* on Asian Americans for the past 25 years and apparently there's no data good enough for the ASR to convince the reviewers that Asian Americans have reached parity with respect to whites. Every single one gets rejected. What happens is when the paper doesn't conform to the conventional wisdom, the methodological standards are raised. But when you argue that there's discrimination against Asians, the methodological standards are relaxed. (149)

Not only are there disincentives in place when it comes to advancing certain findings and explanations that run counter to the three beliefs, but there are also disincentives to criticizing certain ideas that are consistent with the three beliefs. Since criticism plays an important role in providing feedback on research and therefore in making the resulting conclusions stronger, its absence is detrimental to the advancement of knowledge.

It is easy to imagine how this dynamic impacts the peer-review process. As noted earlier, when an academic paper is submitted to a peer-reviewed journal for publication, the journal editor seeks feedback from expert reviewers. Reviewer identities are (in theory at least) not known to the paper author(s). But the editor knows who is reviewing the submission. This means that the reviewers are engaging in a non-anonymous form of in-group communication. It follows that reviewers will often filter their potential criticisms in order to avoid providing feedback that might impact their standing with the journal editor, and therefore potentially more broadly within their field. As an inevitable consequence, this lowers the barrier to publication for papers making assertions that reviewers are less willing to criticize. And it raises the barrier for papers making assertions running counter to the three beliefs.

A journal may be more willing to accept a paper at odds with one of the beliefs if it is accompanied by a simultaneously published rebuttal that has the effect of assuring readers of the journal's continued fealty to the belief in question. For instance, earlier in this book we noted that the elevation of sensitivity to microaggressions and associated claims of harm are protected by the third belief, since giving primacy to identity also means that identity-based claims of harm are not to be questioned. In 2017, Emory University psychology professor Scott Lilienfield published a paper (150) in which he not only raised concerns about the ambiguous definition of microaggressions, but also explored the question of whether the claims of the resulting harms might be at least partly attributable to self-selection.

To minimize the potential for generating offense in light of these claims, special accommodations were made. Lilienfeld's paper, "Micro-aggressions: Strong Claims, Inadequate Evidence," was published alongside other commentaries assuring readers of the theoretical and conceptual value and importance of academic research on microaggressions. (151). If Lilienfield's study had been published unaccompanied by these commentaries, it might well have generated an immediate backlash. However, by placing it in a context that specifically paid homage to the narrative consistent with the three beliefs, the potential for backlash was reduced. The upshot is that in the rare exception where someone is willing to defy the norm and publish a paper in a mainstream academic journal with assertions that don't line up with the dominant narrative, the path to publication can be smoothed

I disagree → commentary/ discourse is the goal, no?

by surrounding the paper by countervailing voices questioning and contextualizing the conclusions.

8.3 Evaluating Research Quality

The first of the three beliefs is that any action taken to undermine traditional frameworks or power structures is automatically deemed good. One of the many consequences of this belief is that traditional ways of evaluating academic research, and even traditional ways of acquiring and conceptualizing knowledge, can be viewed as suspect. This raises the issue of how academic research is assessed. While emphasis in the popular imagination is often placed on the *fact* of publishing (as reflected in the "publish or perish" adage), within academia it is just as important to gauge the *quality* of what is published.

Given the high degree of specialization in most academic fields, it can be hard even for people within the same academic department to read and confidently evaluate the published work of their colleagues. This is a key reason why for academic hiring and for major promotions (such as the granting of tenure), colleges seek letters of reference from outside experts who work in the candidate's area of research. In addition, the quality of a candidate's research (for hiring and for major and minor internal promotions) is often assessed using metrics such as the number of publications and through quantitative measures of their impact.

Any attempt to quantify research output is imperfect. Counting the number of papers produced by an academic researcher provides no indication of paper quality. To avoid relying solely on publication count, colleges also try to assess impact. For articles published in academic journals, citation counts (i.e., the number of times the article is cited in future academic publications) are often used.

In addition to attempting to measure the quality of individual papers, academics have also devised metrics aimed at assessing the quality of journals. Journals are often evaluated using their impact factor, which can be defined as "the average number of citations received per article published in that journal during the 2 preceding years"[1] (153). All else being equal, a

---

[1] For a more formal definition, see Eugene Garfield's 2006 commentary in the *Journal of the American Medical Association* stating that "A journal's impact factor is based on 2 elements: the numerator, which is the number of citations in the current year to items published in the previous 2 years, and the denominator, which is the number of substantive articles and reviews published in the same 2 years." See (152).

widely cited article appearing in a journal with a high impact factor will be given more weight in hiring and promotion decisions than an article with few citations and/or published in a journal with a low impact factor. For academic books, potential indicators of quality include not only the critical reception the book receives, but also the reputation of the academic press, the number of sales, and (when sufficient time has passed) the number of citations.

All of these metrics are imperfect. Consider a visionary paper that might have its greatest influence (and therefore generate the most citations) multiple years after its original publication. This can mean that many promotion cycles elapse before the value of the paper is recognized. The same phenomenon can limit the utility of metrics for evaluating journal quality. When journal impact factors use a look-back period of only two years, there is no credit given to visionary articles that might have their greatest influence (and therefore generate the most citations) years later.

Despite these flaws, citations and the reputation of the journal or academic presses in which a researcher publishes are widely recognized indicators of the importance of scholarship. While there are plenty of exceptions, publications that constitute a major contribution to knowledge will generally find their way to journals or academic presses with good reputations, and will tend to garner a significant number of citations. In addition, journals that consistently publish highly impactful papers will find that reflected in their reputations. This is why, for instance, it's usually a safe bet that an article published in a top journal such as *Nature* or *Science* has been carefully reviewed and is presenting important new information that advances the state of knowledge in a particular field.

But most journals don't have the stature or selectivity of *Nature* or *Science*. As the number of academic journals has proliferated, so too have concerns about the screening process through which journals accept or reject papers. For every accusation that a particular journal is too lax in its publication standards, there is a defender who argues that the accusers simply don't understand the value of the publications they are criticizing. This is a challenge that can occur in relation to any academic discipline, not only those that focus on topics that are closest to the three beliefs we have discussed.

It is a challenge that is particularly fraught when debate about research is constrained by the tripwires that arise in relation to the three

Sokal

beliefs we have discussed. This is why the 2018 "Sokal Squared" hoax received so much attention. The "Sokal Squared" designation is a nod to NYU physicist Alan Sokal's 1996 hoax article asserting that "physical 'reality,' no less than social 'reality,' is at bottom a social and linguistic construct" (154).

The Sokal Squared hoax occurred two decades later and refers to a project by James Lindsay, Peter Boghossian, and Helen Pluckrose, who crafted 20 hoax papers and submitted them to journals in what they referred to as "grievance studies" fields (referred to as such due to what the Sokal Squared authors called "their common goal of problematizing aspects of culture in minute detail in order to attempt diagnoses of power imbalances and oppression rooted in identity") (155).

When the hoax was revealed in fall 2018, four papers had been published, three had been accepted but not yet published, six had been rejected, and seven were still under review (155). Two of the most notable published papers included one that rewrote a section of *Mein Kampf* from a feminist perspective and another titled "Human Reaction to Rape Culture and Queer Performativity at Urban Dog Parks in Portland, Oregon."

Not surprisingly, people tended to view the Sokal Squared hoax through the lens that validated their prior opinions. Those defending the journals that accepted the Sokal Squared papers asserted that the hoax proved nothing about those fields more broadly, and that the problem was not the journals but that the project was done in bad faith. Those who supported the Sokal Squared authors argued that the hoax revealed an alarming level of ideological bias in these fields. As the hoax authors wrote, "this does show that there is something to be concerned about within certain fields within the humanities which are encouraging of this kind of 'scholarship.' We shouldn't have been able to get any papers this terrible published in reputable journals, let alone seven" (155).

At the very least, Sokal Squared illustrated that peer review can sometimes be a pretty low hurdle. This ties to the broader issue of relativism in academia, under which any criticism that a paper or a journal is of low quality can be countered by an accusation that the problem lies with the critic's flawed judgment, and not with the paper or journal. The three beliefs further complicate this dynamic by attaching a social penalty to criticism that may be viewed as unsupportive of the worldview they reflect.

Sokal Squared Hoax

Relativism is tied to the first belief (that any action taken to undermine traditional frameworks is automatically deemed good) in other ways as well. Under the first belief, it becomes reasonable to ask, for instance, why science should be privileged as a way of knowing. Consider the scientific method, which prioritizes objectivity and replicability through a process of observation, measurement, experimentation, and the testing of hypotheses.

But under a relativist approach, that entire framework becomes suspect. As Marcel Kuntz wrote in a 2012 paper titled "The Postmodern Assault on Science," "If all truths are equal, who cares what science has to say?" (156). Kuntz also observed:

> If there is no universal truth, as postmodern philosophy claims, then each social or political group should have the right to the reality that best suits them. What, then, are the consequences of applying postmodernist thinking when it comes to science? (156, p. 886)

Relativism can undermine how knowledge accumulates, because it creates a lower willingness to engage with questions like: Is it replicable? Can it be confirmed or disconfirmed? And as relativism has gained more traction in academia, so has a willingness to question or even reject the scientific approach to knowledge discovery. This rejection is also sometimes accompanied by the claim that science is *inherently* racist (which is a different claim than the observation, which we would agree with, that science has often been *practiced* in ways that are racist).

Science + Math are racist

8.4 Assertions That Science and Math Are Racist

Recent years have seen a growing number of academic publications calling for an identity-based reframing of how we see science and mathematics. This can be viewed as a reflection of the third belief, which makes identity the prism through which all aspects of academia are understood. Consider a paper titled "Unveiling Privilege to Broaden Participation," authored by senior research scientist Rachel E. Scherr and research associate professor Amy D. Robertson (both in the Seattle Pacific University physics department) and published in October 2017 in *The Physics Teacher* (157). In the paper, Scherr and Robertson wrote (quoting in part from another paper, and then adding additional commentary in brackets) that physics is "laden with masculine [and we would add, White] connotations" and asserted that "conceptualizing Nature as governed by laws can suggest that it is ruled by a lawmaker, who is often implicitly conceptualized as a male authority." Consistent with the third belief, this framing places identity at the center of the analysis (157, p. 395).

Yet, there is nothing at all wrong with "conceptualizing Nature as governed by laws." In fact, entire disciplines such as physics and chemistry are premised on the belief that such laws exist and that our understanding of the world and ability to improve the human condition can be advanced by discovering them. Put another way, without that belief, much of science would grind to a halt.

Scherr and Robertson's claim that recognizing that there are laws of nature "can suggest that it is ruled by a lawmaker" brings us into the realm of religion. Many people do indeed believe that a "lawmaker" rules nature, but it is their right to hold such beliefs, and it can't be credibly asserted in the 21st century that religion is a large-scale impediment to physics teaching or research in the United States. The final part of the phrase quoted above states that the "lawmaker" who rules nature "is often implicitly conceptualized as a male authority." Again, we are in the realm of religion. There is certainly plenty of merit to questions about the role of "male authority" in religion, but those questions belong to theology, not to 21st-century physics.

Scherr and Robertson also tied science to European colonialism, writing "[h]istorically, the questions that science has addressed have disproportionately advantaged White people, motivated by colonial expansion (to improve land and sea travel, mine ores, manufacture and farm for the benefit of Europeans living in Europe and in colonies)" (157, p. 395). Ironically, this statement itself is arguably Eurocentric. Historically, all sorts of civilizations, many of them neither white nor European, have used science to further their ambitions. Long before the European colonial era, the Chinese invented the compass and used it to achieve extraordinary feats of navigation; the Aztecs, Olmecs, and Mayans invented rubber (158) and used it for shoes and glue (159), people in what is now Tanzania had developed complex iron smelting technologies and were making steel (160), and indigenous Australians had invented the boomerang for use in hunting (161). Human ingenuity is universal, as is the desire to apply that ingenuity to enable greater scientific understanding and access to the technological breakthroughs that often follow.

Scherr and Robertson closed their paper by writing "If our aim is, in part, to disrupt White and/or male privilege within physics, we need to be willing to open up the space of what counts as physics." In response to objections raised to their paper, Scherr wrote in the January 2018 edition of *The Physics Teacher* that "I do not share your concern that physics will be weakened by admitting social theories into the study of physics" (162, p. 396).

There is certainly value in exploring, both historically and today, the interaction between physics and the social sciences. Consideration of the role of social theories in shaping physics research and teaching is a worthy part of that exploration. But we will impede knowledge discovery if we require that the actual practice of physics itself—for example, the work at the frontiers of particle physics—be conceived and performed through the lens of social theories.

To take another example, consider a 2013 article in the *Journal of Urban Mathematics Education* by Rochelle Gutiérrez, a professor of mathematics education at the University of Illinois at Urbana-Champaign (163). Gutiérrez expressed concern that "we continue to view mathematics as truth, not social phenomena," adding that "similar to whiteness, mathematics holds unearned privilege in society." She also explicitly distinguished her work from previous work that she characterized as arguing that education "operates as White institutional space." By contrast, she wrote, "I am arguing that mathematics itself operates as whiteness" (163, p. 10).

In a 2018 publication (164) Gutiérrez addressed this topic again, asserting that "[t]hings cannot be known objectively; they must be known subjectively" (164, p. 20). Gutiérrez also wrote that:

> School mathematics curricula emphasizing terms like Pythagorean theorem and pi perpetuate a perception that mathematics was largely developed by Greeks and other Europeans. Perhaps more importantly, mathematics operates with unearned privilege in society, just like Whiteness. (164, p. 17)

and that

> We treat mathematics as if it is a natural reflection of the universe. When we identify mathematics in the world around us (e.g., Fibonacci sequences in pinecones, fractals in snowflakes), we convince ourselves that mathematics occurs outside of human influence. (164, p. 18)

But here's the thing: Mathematics *is* a natural reflection of the universe. Take pi, the ratio of the circumference of a circle to its diameter. Pi is a number that occurs "outside of human influence." It is possible to know it objectively—and today, to extraordinary precision, we do. Whether we measure pi or not, and whether we refer to it using a letter from the Greek alphabet or using some other symbol or not at all, it exists, and it is not merely a social phenomenon. The fact that circles have a fixed ratio of circumference to diameter and that the ratio is slightly larger than 3 was no doubt discovered and rediscovered countless times by countless different societies. Today, in the United States and much of the rest of the world we happen to call that ratio pi. But the ratio existed long before humans emerged as a species and will exist long after we are gone.

When we discover mathematical truths, when we give those truths names and symbols, and when we analyze what they mean and how they can be used, we inevitably see those truths in part through a broader contextual lens. Social science can be an invaluable tool to help to explain this phenomenon. But, in our view, it is incorrect to assert that underlying mathematical truths themselves are objectively unknowable, or that they exist only because of human influence.

9

Classroom Consequences

Knowledge production happens mainly through research, but an important mechanism for knowledge *dissemination* to students occurs in the classroom. The classroom experience plays a central role in one of the key goals of a college education: to teach students how to engage thoughtfully, creatively, and critically with complex, nuanced topics.

Yet, evidence indicates that students do not feel that their classroom discussions are as open as they should be, despite the fact that openness is a necessary precondition for intellectual growth. The May 2019 report "Free Expression on College Campuses" published by the Knight Foundation/ College Pulse noted that "More than two-thirds (68 percent) of college students say their campus climate precludes students from expressing their true opinions because their classmates might find them offensive" (165, p. 11). If the goal is an environment that fosters independent and critical thinking in the classroom, we have a long way to go.

The learning experience for students, particularly in courses that address potentially controversial topics such as race and gender, is constrained in several ways. First, frank discussion is frequently a casualty of the pressures associated with adhering to the three beliefs. Second, even in the absence of a single complainant about self-censorship, the learning process is not accomplishing its goals.

This is partly because what's taught in a given class is a function of both the knowledge base and the dominant operating assumptions in the discipline more broadly. In some fields, like sociology or social psychology, the process of "capturing" by the three beliefs occurred over time and appears to have deepened, inspiring discipline-specific treatises on the topic (see, for instance, 166, 167). And, as we've seen earlier in the book, the three beliefs are increasingly being applied to previously unaffected fields, such as mathematics and physics.

In making these points, we are not criticizing any specific discipline. There is excellent scholarship occurring in all academic fields. Rather, our

Unassailable Ideas. Ilana Redstone and John Villasenor, Oxford University Press (2020). © Oxford University Press.
DOI: 10.1093/oso/9780190078065.001.0001.

observation is that there is a range regarding the extent to which the beliefs we have discussed have shaped what is taught within different topic areas. In sociology and social psychology the influence is very strong. By contrast, in mathematics and physics it is present but only at the periphery, and in engineering it has so far been largely absent—though perhaps that will soon change.

An additional challenge is that like many other people, college instructors tend, whether consciously or not, to express views that align with their own politics. Not everyone believes that this leads instructors to promote their own ideological perspective. For instance, in a May 2016 op-ed in the *Los Angeles Times*, Colby College sociology professor Neil Gross acknowledged that "liberals predominate on faculties," but then asserted that "just because most professors are liberal doesn't mean the average student is being force-fed liberal ideology." He also wrote:

> The vast majority of professors focus on teaching students the subject matter of their fields as well as basic skills such as analytical reading, writing and critical thinking. If current events do come up in classroom discussions, the usual pattern is for professors to promote what they see as open conversation. (168)

Of course, one challenge is that what an admittedly predominantly liberal (or conservative) group of people "see as open conversation" is unlikely to be as open as they imagine. Or, put another way, if we had two groups of people—one liberal and one conservative—both independently facilitating classroom conversations about current events and both aiming to do so in what they saw as an "open" manner, there would often be differences across the types of discussions that result. Unconscious bias, which is so readily recognized in other domains, is certainly a factor in this context as well. Despite these challenges, we think it is well worth the effort to promote a culture in which faculty strive to foster open conversations in their classrooms. One important step in this process is to recognize the ways in which classroom teaching is falling short of this objective.

To illustrate this issue, and more broadly the issue of how the three beliefs we have identified can play out in the current instructional environment, we can draw off of the home discipline—sociology—of one of the authors, although the relevance is much broader. Sociology, along with anthropology and social psychology, is considered to be one of the most captured disciplines with respect to the ways in which its members see the world. This influence is visible in courses from the undergraduate introductory level through the doctoral level. Beginning at the introductory level, students in sociology are taught three major theoretical foundations: symbolic interactionism, functionalism, and conflict theory.

Symbolic interactionism emphasizes the importance of subjective meanings and ways of communicating that happen through the use of symbols and language. Functionalism is based in the view that all aspects of society can be understood in the context of the functions they serve. However, today, both pale in their influence to the third: conflict theory. As assistant professor of sociology at the University of Alabama in Huntsville Richard Simon described:

> Conflict theory is one of the major paradigms used by sociologists to make sense of the social world. All sociology that takes as its object of study the processes by which social groups compete with each other for scarce resources such as power, wealth, and status, or the inequalities that result from these competitions, falls within the conflict paradigm.

Simon continued:

> Conflict theory impels us to recognize that every dimension of social structure can be conceptualized in terms of winners and losers, and social conflict often causes disastrous and tragic consequences for the losers in the social struggle. People are tortured, mutilated, and incinerated as a consequence of social conflict; they are also shunned, humiliated, exploited, and otherwise systematically shortchanged by the social structures they take part in. (169)

that's a jump.

?   One might further describe conflict theory as a way to see the world as a series of struggles between oppressor and oppressed that unfold within tyrannical hierarchies.

The problem isn't that conflict theory is taught; the problem is that it is often presented in university sociology classes as the only way to see the world. As a foundational theory, it is generally introduced toward the beginning of the semester so that the material that follows can be used to demonstrate its application. This approach reinforces the worldview communicated in the early weeks. As a result, the learning experience for students is profoundly affected by the dominance of a singular perspective.

More generally, an instructor's belief that there is open conversation admitting a wide range of perspectives in the classroom does not mean that is, in fact, occurring. To the contrary, the beliefs that we described earlier are just as much present in the discussions that take place in a classroom as they are elsewhere on campus. It is possible to have a robust debate within the confines of the three core beliefs we have articulated and to as a result *think* that the discussion has been truly open, while in reality it may only have been open within a very limited aperture.

9.1 The Shepherd Case

An instructive way to examine ideological filtering in the classroom is to examine cases where the boundaries are challenged. In November 2017, Lindsay Shepherd, a graduate student and teaching assistant at Wilfrid Laurier University in Waterloo, Ontario, showed video clips of a segment of *The Agenda with Steve Paikin*, a current-affairs show in Canada. (While our focus is generally on campus climate issues in the United States, a similar dynamic has played out in Canadian universities.) In the clips, the host was discussing a range of topics on gender pronoun usage with Jordan Peterson, a psychology professor at the University of Toronto who has emerged as a polarizing figure in relation to issues such as free speech and identity politics on campus.

During the class, an active debate ensued with both supporters and critics of Peterson's views represented. After the class, a student complaint asserted that the discussion had created an environment that was offensive to trans students. Shortly thereafter, Shepherd was called to a meeting including her supervisor and the head of her academic program in which she was reprimanded. Shepherd recorded the meeting, during which she was told she had created a "toxic climate" in the classroom (170).

After the recording became public, Wilfrid Laurier University's president and vice-chancellor Deborah MacLatchy said she was "shocked" by Shepherd's treatment and that "It's not who we are as a university and it doesn't represent what we stand for at Laurier" (171). In an open letter to Shepherd published on the university's website, she wrote, "I'm writing to make an apology on behalf of the university. Through the media, we have now had the opportunity to hear the full recording of the meeting that took place at Wilfrid Laurier University. After listening to this recording, an apology is in order. The conversation I heard does not reflect the values and practices to which Laurier aspires. I am sorry it occurred in the way that it did and I regret the impact it had on Lindsay Shepherd" (172).

But suppose Shepherd had never made and publicized the recording? Suppose that, without having a recording to support her claims, she had complained about the meeting to university administrators? It's easy to imagine an outcome in which the university would never have issued any sort of formal apology or even admitted that Shepherd had been wrongly treated. In other words, it is reasonable to ask whether the university apologized primarily because Shepherd suffered repercussions for showing the Peterson video in class and facilitating the ensuing discussion, or because Shepherd was able to use audio to *publicly prove* that she suffered repercussions for doing so.

While Shepherd's experience is alarming, situations rising to the same level of visibility are few and far between. This might suggest that concerns over classroom climates are overblown. But is that really the right conclusion? Or is the relative lack of incidents like Shepherd's in fact more a reflection of a combination of self-censorship and the dominance of the set of beliefs among people who teach in disciplines that involve consideration of topics that could raise controversy?

As we explained in the chapter on tenure, the incentives relating to hiring and the award of tenure (and to the hiring of teaching assistants) tend to strongly favor people who will remain within the boundaries set by the beliefs. When instructors teach classes, they will endeavor to do so within those boundaries, and the likelihood of in-class discussions that could lead to a complaint is low. But what about the minority of university instructors who do not fit this mold?

These are instructors who, absent any pressures to the contrary, would facilitate in-class discussions that would consider perspectives that are outside those deemed permissible by the set of beliefs. Such instructors have two options: They can allow those perspectives to be presented and debated and in doing so know that they are risking student complaints and possible consequences to their own careers. Or they can self-censor and choose to teach within the same boundaries followed by their more ideologically conforming colleagues.

9.2 Self-Censorship

How much of this self-censorship is occurring? Among instructors, due to the lack of survey data, we don't have quantitative evidence. But there is compelling evidence in the form of surveys that have asked *students* about self-censorship. A Foundation for Individual Rights in Education (FIRE) survey conducted in early 2017 found that 30 percent of respondents "have self-censored in class because they thought their words might be considered offensive to their peers" (173). The FIRE survey also observed notable differences by political affiliation, finding that "Very liberal students are 14 percentage points more likely to feel comfortable expressing their opinions in the classroom than their very conservative peers." The Heterodox Academy's Campus Expression Survey, also using data collected in 2017, found that "32% of conservatives (vs. 8% of liberals) were very reluctant to discuss politics in the classroom," "29% of conservatives (vs. 8% of liberals) were very reluctant to discuss gender in the classroom," and "30% of conservatives (vs. 15% of liberals) were very reluctant to discuss race in the classroom" (174). And as we noted earlier, the Knight Foundation/College Pulse survey published in May 2019 reported that "More than two-thirds (68 percent) of college students say their campus climate precludes students from expressing their true opinions because their classmates might find them offensive" (165, p. 11).

As these data suggest, there's a lot of self-censorship among students, and there is a notable difference in the responses with respect to political affiliation. But what about instructors? Instructors in a university classroom setting have an even stronger incentive to self-censor than students. Unlike students, instructors are in charge of the classroom and are therefore viewed as accountable for what occurs there. If a classroom debate occurs on a topic that some students find offensive, it is the instructor, not the students, who will be held responsible. At Wilfrid Laurier University this is why Shepherd, and not the students in her class who defended the views that other students found offensive, received a reprimand.

In addition, all else being equal, an instructor who is the subject of a complaint that an offensive issue was discussed in class is more exposed than a student who, during that discussion, voices a position on that issue that another student deems offensive. Once the complaint against the instructor is lodged, an entire apparatus swings into motion to hold the instructor responsible. In the current climate, bolstered by the third rule, if a student claims *but what happens when the other side is QAnon supporters?*

to have been offended during a classroom discussion, the complaint itself can lead to the automatic conclusion that the instructor has done something wrong. Instructors on college campuses are expected to conduct their classes in a manner that ensures that no one is ever offended, in a climate where the bounds of what is considered offensive continue to expand.

The potential consequences of a complaint are a strong incentive to avoid controversial in-class discussions in the first place. A formal complaint that an in-class discussion was offensive will often lead to engagement by multiple levels of the administrative hierarchy. No instructor wants a dressing down by a department chair or dean—the same people who wield enormous power over the instructor's promotions and (for those without tenure) continued employment. Given these considerations, instructors who would otherwise want to broaden the dialog in their classrooms to include perspectives outside those permitted by the set of beliefs have strong incentives not to do so.

Beginning with introductory classes, particularly those that stand to touch on controversial topics, the boundaries of permissible discourse are constricted and enforced. As we've described, this occurs through the way the beliefs have narrowed the core material that is taught and through the looming threat of penalties for an instructor when the boundaries are challenged. These factors combine to create a learning experience that doesn't stray from the accepted narrow parameters, to the detriment of both students and instructors.

9.3 Viewpoint Diversity in the Classroom

What is lost when the classroom experience is constrained by the three beliefs we've described? In answering that question, it is helpful to consider some perspectives that emerged when viewpoint diversity in the classroom is explicitly encouraged. During the spring 2019 semester, one of the authors (Redstone) taught two courses at the University of Illinois at Urbana-Champaign in which a wide range of views were welcomed. The first was a course on viewpoint diversity called *Bigots and Snowflakes: Living in a World Where Everyone Else is Wrong*. The second was a more traditional sociology course on *Social Problems*, but, in contrast with what occurs in most sociology departments, it was taught from a heterodox political perspective. From this experience, which included student discussions in which they described the climate in other classes they had taken, two features became clear.

First, *when viewpoint diversity is absent, the classroom environment is negatively affected*. When, as so often occurs in many social science classes, instructors teach in a manner directly or indirectly conveying that their personal views represent unquestionable truths, they convey the message that there's only one acceptable position, regardless of the claims they make to the contrary. In one class, a student described another course in which the professor had asked, rhetorically, "Who here thinks Trump's border wall is a good idea?" Students were not prohibited in any direct sense from answering in the affirmative, yet the message of the correct response was clearly conveyed from the instructor.

An alternative, and preferable, way to discuss border security would have been through a conversation acknowledging its complexities—including the fact that almost no one thinks that there should be no physical barrier at all anywhere on the U.S./Mexico border. In framing the issue through a "yes" or "no" question of whether President Trump's border wall was a good idea, an opportunity to engage in a complex and important topic—and one on which reasonable people can have a diversity of views—was lost.

Second, *when viewpoint diversity is absent, the ability to think critically is affected*. Consider a widely viewed January 2019 Gillette advertisement that was designed to provoke discussion about masculinity and stereotypical "male" behavior (175). After the students in the *Social Problems* class at the University of Illinois were shown the advertisement, they were asked what they thought was positive about it. They gave thoughtful answers, including the messages to men and boys that it's okay to show emotion and that fighting is not the best way to solve problems.

Then the question was posed as to what might be objectionable about the advertisement. After a few quiet moments, a couple of hands went up. The consensus was that people who are consciously or unconsciously afraid of letting go of old gender norms might object to the advertisement. Yes, students were told, some viewers might have objections on that basis. But are there any other potential objections? The students greeted this question with silence. At this point, the instructor offered the following: Without in any way excusing harassment, is it potentially objectionable to suggest that masculinity itself is inherently toxic and pathological? Not a single student seemed familiar with the notion.

The challenges of creating a classroom environment open to a diverse range of perspectives are exacerbated by instructors' own potentially inaccurate perceptions of their teaching. In late February 2019, Redstone gave a talk in the University of Illinois Department of Sociology and noted that instructors in the field often present only a singular perspective in the classroom. One of faculty members in attendance objected to this characterization, stating that he didn't appreciate being implicitly described in that (inaccurate, in his view) manner. When this comment was relayed (without attribution) to the students in the *Bigots and Snowflakes* class, one student responded that he didn't think that what the faculty member was saying was possible. The student remarked that he'd taken a lot of sociology classes and that, in his experience, they are all taught from a narrow perspective. In spite of the single faculty member's objection, the scope of the problem suggests that even instructors who *think* they are incorporating multiple viewpoints may not be doing it to the extent they think they are.

9.4 Teaching Evaluations and Diversity

As they should, colleges generally provide students with the opportunity at the end of an academic semester to submit an evaluation of the course and instructor. Typical evaluation forms ask students to rate the course, the instructor, the workload, and other aspects of the class and teaching. In general, course evaluations are viewed by college administrations as useful though imperfect. They are useful because they provide students with a formal mechanism to voice feedback about the class, and they contain helpful information about the strengths and weaknesses of instructors. They are imperfect in the sense that there is only a partial correlation between high evaluation scores and a good class or instructor. For example, an excellent, committed instructor who expects a lot from his or her students might pay a price in lower evaluation scores from students who would have preferred a lighter workload.

Course evaluations also figure prominently in promotion cases for tenure-track and tenured faculty. At research universities, tenure-track and tenured faculty are judged on teaching, research, and service to the institution and to the broader profession. While there is some variation among and within institutions regarding the relative priority given to research and teaching contributions when making promotion decisions, teaching quality matters everywhere. Simply put, a faculty member who is a consistently poor teacher will experience challenges in professional advancement.

At colleges where the primary focus is on teaching alone as opposed to being split between teaching and research, teaching effectiveness plays an even greater role in professional advancement. And for adjunct instructors, whether at large research universities or smaller colleges focused exclusively on undergraduate education, teaching evaluations are at the center of rehiring decisions. The upshot is that teaching evaluations are a key input to decisions regarding hiring and professional advancement across the entire higher education ecosystem. Adjuncts, tenure-track junior faculty, and tenured faculty all have an incentive to build a strong teaching record.

Thus, the issue of what gets asked in teaching evaluations is of high importance. This is particularly relevant if teaching evaluations are revised to ask not only the traditional questions about the overall quality of the course and instructor, but also questions specifically addressing diversity or bias. For example, an evaluation form used by Villanova University included a multiple-choice question asking whether the instructor "demonstrates cultural awareness." The response options were "strongly agree," "agree," "neutral," "disagree," and "strongly disagree." Using the same set of response options, the evaluation form also asked whether the instructor "creates an environment free of bias based on individual differences or social identities." In addition, the form included a free-response portion with the prompt: "Please use this space to comment on the instructor's sensitivity to the diversity of students in the class (for example, biological sex, disability, gender identity, national origin, political viewpoint, race/ethnicity, religious beliefs, sexual orientation, socioeconomic status, etc.)" (176).

As is always the case with surveys, much depends on how questions are phrased. When asked whether the class was "free of" something negative ("bias based on individual differences or social identities"), a respondent is more likely think of negative experiences when answering the question. By contrast, if the question had been structured to ask whether the course "created a positive environment in relation to individual differences or social identities," a larger number of students would likely respond with "strongly agree" or "agree."

Asking the students to rate the "instructor's sensitivity" in relation to a long list of characteristics such as religious beliefs and national origin is also potentially problematic if the subject matter of the class of necessity requires exploring any topic involving the complex policy, legal, or broader societal questions that can reasonably relate to these characteristics. Consider, for example, an instructor who moderates an in-class discussion regarding immigration policy in which some students voice opinions that other students find offensive. How is an instructor who is trying to maximize her "sensitivity" score supposed to facilitate such a discussion? There might be a first group of students in the class who would consider the instructor insensitive if she does not publicly endorse the side they agree with. Yet in the same class there could be a second group of students who would be offended if the instructor publicly sides with the first group of students. To avoid this sort of no-win situation, an instructor has an incentive to completely avoid covering any topic that might lead to expression of divergent views in the classroom.

Stated another way, using the teaching evaluation process to invite students to cite instances of perceived instructor failures to meet student definitions of sensitivity and cultural awareness pushes instructors to favor anodyne teaching styles. Inviting students to comment on a list of ways that an instructor may have offended them broadcasts a set of priorities regarding areas in which instructors had better tread very carefully. But that prioritization raises concerns.

For example, consider a professor who belittles a student based on his or her weight. That is clearly a terrible thing to do, and something for which a professor should absolutely be held to account. Yet "weight" was not on the list of potentially sensitive topics in the Villanova teaching evaluation question, while "political viewpoint" is—despite the fact that it is clearly more harmful to belittle people based on their weight than on their political viewpoint. This illustrates the challenge of trying to make a list of ways in which an instructor might be "insensitive." In raising this example, we are not arguing that instructors should be *insensitive* about, for example, national origin. And we recognize that the list (biological sex, disability, gender identity, national origin, etc.) in the Villanova question is presented as *exemplary*, meaning that there are other attributes that could lie within the scope of this question yet not be explicitly listed. Nonetheless, the choice of which attributes to include and exclude from the exemplary list sends a message that will inevitably shape the types of answers that students will provide.

It is also interesting to consider the institutional response to criticisms of including questions about bias in teaching evaluations. On March 29, 2019, Villanova professors Colleen A. Sheehan and James Matthew Wilson published an op-ed in the *Wall Street Journal* asserting that "however well-intentioned, the new assessment of faculty 'sensitivity' and 'bias' will harm Villanova's mission to provide a liberal education. Professors will now have a powerful incentive to avoid discussion of anything that might be deemed offensive or insensitive to the various social identities and political viewpoints listed" (177).

This generated a backlash at Villanova. Among the responses was an April 1 letter addressed to "Members of the Villanova Community" from Villanova's president, Rev. Peter M. Donohue stating that "the questions referenced from Villanova's Course and Teacher Survey are not used for evaluating faculty. Rather, the questions are designed to enable our faculty to understand how their students perceive their interactions so they can create an unbiased learning environment for students from diverse backgrounds, social identities and political beliefs" (178).

Given that they are included on Villanova's "Course and Teacher Survey," we're skeptical of assertions that the student responses won't be used in evaluating faculty. More realistically, negative consequences seem possible for instructors who receive low scores from students evaluating their cultural awareness, freedom from bias, and sensitivity. And, it is easy to imagine that instructors who receive consistently high marks on these metrics might be recognized accordingly when their teaching evaluations are evaluated as part of the regular academic promotion process.

9.5 The Community College Classroom

Community colleges are an enormously important part of the American higher education ecosystem. The issues we have described can also arise on community college campuses, though there are important differences. According to the Columbia University Community College Research Center, in the fall of 2017, there were 5.8 million students enrolled in public, two-year colleges in the United States, with about 2.1 million full-time students and 3.7 million part-time students (179). In total, the number of community college students is approximately half of the enrolment at four-year institutions (180).

The socioeconomic and racial/ethnic profile of community colleges students differs considerably from students at four-year institutions. According to the College Board, in the fall of 2014, 22 percent of students at public two-year institutions were Hispanic, compared to 9 percent at private nonprofit four-year or 13 percent at public four-year institutions. In addition, 14 percent of students enrolled at public two-year institutions were Black, compared to 11 percent at public four-year and 11 percent at private nonprofit four-year institutions (181). In addition, Hispanic and Black undergraduates are more likely than white undergraduates to be in two-year colleges. As the Community College Research Center (CCRC) at Columbia University notes, "In fall 2017, 44 percent of Hispanic undergraduates were enrolled at community colleges, while 35 percent of black students and 31 percent of white students were at community colleges" (179). There are important socioeconomic differences as well. CCRC writes that "An analysis of Education Longitudinal Study (ELS: 2002-06) data shows that 44 percent of low-income students (those with family incomes of less than $25,000 per year) attend community colleges as their first college after high school, compared with only 15 percent of high-income students" (179).

While recent data are sparse, a survey conducted over a decade ago suggested that faculty political leanings are more diverse at community colleges than at four-year liberal arts colleges. The study, conducted in 2006 and described in a February 2017 *Inside Higher Ed* article, indicated that 19 percent of community college faculty considered themselves conservative, relative to 3.9 percent of faculty at four-year liberal arts colleges. Similarly, at community colleges, 37 percent of faculty identified as liberals, compared to 61 percent at four-year liberal arts colleges (182). Of course, not all four-year colleges are "liberal arts" colleges. But many are, giving weight to a hypothesis that if a new survey on this issue were conducted today, it would show that faculty at four-year colleges (whether liberal arts or otherwise) are less diverse in their political affiliations than faculty at community colleges.

In any case, among faculty the beliefs we have articulated appear to have a less complete hold on community college campuses than on the campuses of four-year institutions. That also appears to be true among community college students, who tend on average to be less walled off from the world outside campus than students at four-year colleges. Most community college students are commuters. Students therefore leave campus when their classes are over rather than staying in on-campus or campus-adjacent housing. In addition, many community college students have substantial job commitments, leaving less time for the types of extracurricular engagement that is possible for many students enrolled at four-year institutions (some of whom also have substantial non–school-related commitments). An additional factor is that community colleges, in no small part because of their greater financial accessibility, do a better job of actually reflecting the communities in which they are situated. This is manifested in greater (relative to four-year colleges) diversity racially, ethnically, socioeconomically, and, we would hypothesize, in terms of viewpoint diversity.

That said, the climate at community colleges may be moving in a similar direction to that at four-year colleges. While we are not aware of any recent large-scale, multi-institution campus climate survey of community college students, information based on single institutions suggests anecdotally that this may be the case. A study conducted in 2018 at Linn-Benton Community College in Oregon (183) indicated that 45 percent of white students and 37 percent of Hispanic students feel somewhat or very reluctant discussing politics in class. This is in spite of a fairly politically balanced student body in which 27 percent are independent, 27 percent are Democrats, and 24 percent are Republicans.

Another sign is the modification of community college curricula to include diversity requirements (which, as generally taught, reflect the third belief, which places primacy on identity). For instance, Wenatchee Valley Community College is a two-year institution in Washington that, as of fall 2018, instituted a diversity requirement that includes the following six standards: "Understanding Discrimination and Racism," "Self-reflection of Personal Identities and Biases," Global or International Issues and Impact on U.S. Culture," "Identity Development and Intersectionality," "Systemic Discrimination and Oppression," and "Analysis of Public Policy and Its Effect on Diverse Populations" (184).

While it's difficult to know how widespread such requirements are, Wenatchee is clearly not alone. Other community colleges with diversity requirements include Everett Community College in Washington (185), Anne Arundel Community College in Maryland (186), and the Community College of Philadelphia in Pennsylvania (187).

To be clear, the problem isn't that such requirements exist. What matters is whether these topics are taught in a manner that allows a full exploration of a diverse range of perspectives. The trend toward diversity requirements at community colleges suggests that they may be increasingly operating under the same set of beliefs as four-year institutions, with all of the associated resulting challenges that we have described.

10

The Key Role of Adjuncts

Academic freedom is particularly tenuous for the growing number of college teachers who hold positions that are neither tenured nor on the tenure track. Various titles are used to describe these positions, including adjunct professor, visiting professor, professor of practice, professor in residence, acting professor, and lecturer. There is wide variation in the job duties, qualifications for appointment, and appointment procedures associated with the preceding titles. For simplicity we will use the term "adjunct" to describe any college instructor who does not have, and is not on a formal track to receive, security of employment through the tenure system.[1]

There are tremendous variations regarding the length of service and level of involvement that adjuncts have with colleges. An adjunct might be hired for a period of only a few months to teach a single course. Alternatively, an adjunct might be hired sporadically over a period of years, teaching one or two courses at a time during some semesters, and not at all during others. It is also common for adjuncts to teach simultaneously at multiple colleges, piecing together multiple part-time jobs with the goal of constructing the equivalent in compensation terms, at least temporarily, of full-time employment.

In some cases, an adjunct might be a full-time employee of a college, teaching as many as four or more courses simultaneously for a continuous period that might span years. Some people in what we are calling the adjunct category have contracts that might span multiple years, and can have responsibilities similar to those of tenured professors, including performing research as well as teaching. However, even an adjunct with a multiyear contract is less protected than a professor with tenure, who benefits from what amounts to a contract that at least in theory confers a right to permanent employment.

---

[1] There are some cases in which university instructors who are not tenured professors can nonetheless have security of employment. To take one example, the University of California system has a "Lecturer with Security of Employment" job title. However, the large majority of people who hold titles such as lecturer, adjunct professor, professor of practice, etc., do not have employment security.

Unassailable Ideas. Ilana Redstone and John Villasenor, Oxford University Press (2020). © Oxford University Press.
DOI: 10.1093/oso/9780190078065.001.0001.

The common theme across all adjuncts is that they do not have the long-term security conferred by tenure. As Adam Kissell wrote in a commentary on the Foundation for Individual Rights in Education (FIRE) website in 2008, "Adjunct contracts often make no mention of academic freedom, but the contracts often do remind instructors that their schools can fire them at any time, for any reason, or simply refuse to rehire them once a contract is up" (188). Thus, while a tenured professor is supposed to have security of employment, adjunct positions are designed by colleges with the specific intent of *avoiding* the need to guarantee employment.

From the standpoint of colleges, access to an adjunct workforce offers the ability to easily adjust the number of teachers up or down in response to changes in institutional priorities and student course demands. An additional feature of this part of the university ecosystem is that it can be exploitative, particularly in fields where there are fewer employment options outside of academia. As a result, adjuncts are often paid very poorly and in many cases lack access to benefits such as health insurance. What adjuncts (quite rightly) view as exploitative, colleges tend to view as financially efficient. This increases the financial incentive for universities to rely on them for teaching.

Today, adjuncts constitute a much higher fraction of college teachers than in the past. As Chad Gregory Evans observed in a 2018 doctoral thesis at the University of Pennsylvania, the fraction of "tenure-ineligible" faculty grew under one-quarter in the 1960s to almost two-thirds in 2009 (189). A 2013 report from the American Association of University Professors concluded that "Using a broad definition of faculty that includes graduate-student employees as well as full- and part-time instructors regardless of title, the AAUP has calculated that by 2009—the latest year [at the time of the AAUP publication] for which national data are available—75.6 percent of US faculty appointments were off the tenure track" (190).

10.1 Academic Freedom and Adjuncts:
A Longstanding Concern

Concerns about academic freedom for adjuncts are not new. Back in 1999, a *Chronicle of Higher Education* article titled "To Many Adjunct Professors, Academic Freedom is a Myth" noted that "As the ranks of part-timers swell, they lament how easily colleges can dump them" (191).

A 2001 law review publication by Georgetown law professor J. Peter Byrne on "Academic Freedom of Part-Time Faculty" explained that:

> The tenuousness of the adjunct's contractual claim against the University and her frequent invisibility to peers create persistent risk of violations of academic freedom. The adjunct professor's supervisor can simply decide not to renew the adjunct contract because in that supervisor's opinion the course is not needed or can be taught better by another. Thus, the faculty member can be separated with no or some anodyne reason informally given by a single person. Thus, it is easy for the supervisor to dump someone who criticized a colleague's work in class or argued for social policy against the interests of a school benefactor. Even when this discretion is exercised with appropriate regard for the values of academic freedom, as no doubt it generally is, the structure itself *ex ante* will encourage faculty to avoid controversy. (192, p. 587)

AAUP has been sounding the alarm for decades about the challenges faced by adjuncts. A 1981 AAUP publication, "The Status of Part-Time Faculty," observed that "the presence of large numbers of faculty serving 'at will' can have a chilling effect on general conditions of academic freedom at the institution as well as on academic quality" (193, p. 80).

As the ranks of adjuncts have grown, so too have the questions regarding what the lack of academic freedom for adjuncts means to higher education more broadly. One of the most thorough recent examinations of this issue comes from Jan Clausen and Eva-Maria Swidler in a 2013 paper titled "Academic Freedom from Below: Toward an Adjunct-Centered Struggle" published in the *AAUP Journal of Academic Freedom*. Clausen and Swidler provide a stark assessment of how important this question is: "From a perspective that views academic freedom as the sum of the freedoms of individual faculty members, we may ask: if three-quarters of higher education faculty today are contingent, is it meaningful any longer to talk of academic freedom as a ruling principle in higher education?" (194). In the conclusion of the paper, they write:

> Academia is an arena of civil society that directly engages most people, thereby exerting a huge cultural force. Adjuncts and other contingents are not only three-quarters of the college and university faculty but are overwhelmingly the teachers of the required classes, the introductory courses,

the largest and fullest sections, the lower-level classes that those who never graduate attend nonetheless. Adjuncts fundamentally *are* the college experience for many students. For those who care about college faculty, those who care about the future of the academy and its ability to live up to its own stated ideals, but most of all those who care about what higher education can contribute to the public good, we adjuncts and our realities must become the center of the fight for academic freedom. (194, p. 20)

10.2 The Jensen Case

As we have noted, when it comes to academic freedom, adjuncts are particularly vulnerable because in many cases they are employed under contracts that only last for limited periods, often as short as the duration of the current semester. This means that they are working under circumstances in which they will only be rehired if the college where they are teaching makes an affirmative decision to offer a new contract. Given this arrangement, when an adjunct isn't rehired after a contract expires, it can be difficult to know why. Was it because the teaching needs of the college changed? Was it because the adjunct was an ineffective teacher? Was it due to student complaints, and if so, were those complaints sufficient to justify a decision not to rehire? Was it because, in casual conversation with other faculty members, the adjunct expressed opinions the other faculty deemed problematic? Often, it is impossible to know.

The incentives facing adjuncts are clear: If they want to maximize their chances of getting a new contract after their current one expires, they need to steer clear of doing or saying anything controversial. This means teaching in a way that minimizes the risk of complaints. For example, when teaching a complex issue that touches on one of the many current cultural flashpoints (race, gender, etc.), an adjunct aiming to minimize career risk might reasonably decide to avoid assigning reading materials or conveying opinions (including opinions of people other than themselves) that might offend. And, the boundaries are set by the most easily offended student in the room, as even a single complaint could lead a department chair to decide that future offerings of the class should be taught by someone else.

Consider the case of Mike Jensen, who in September 2015 was teaching an undergraduate writing course at the University of Northern Colorado. Jensen asked his students to read Greg Lukianoff and Jonathan Haidt's

Atlantic article on "The Coddling of the American Mind" and engaged in a classroom discussion regarding transgender rights (195). During the discussion, assertions were made that at least one student found offensive. A few days later, the student submitted a "Bias Response Incident" documents report (196). Following the complaint, Jensen was called in to meet with the university's head of human resources, Marshall Parks. In summarizing the meeting in notes added to the case file, Parks wrote the following: (Jensen's name is redacted in the public version of the Bias Response Incident, though in 2016 Jensen himself went public with the information that he had been the subject of the complaint) (197):

> [Jensen] provided me with a copy of an article from The Atlantic that he shared with all 4 sections [of his class]. [Jensen] described the purpose of the article as spurring conversations on difficult topics that could be interesting to write on. He then asked the class to come up with examples of difficult topics. He said a number of controversial topics came up: gay marriage, abortion, global warming etc., and he provided examples of what people who hold differing positions on those topics might say. He said that transgender topics came up in two of the four sections and he laid out opinions on that topic the same way he had in other topics—he never gave any personal opinions on any of the topics, only opposing perspectives on the topics. He also stated that he shared with the class early in the semester to communicate to him if there are topics that students find uncomfortable and he would be respectful of those concerns.
>
> We then reviewed some of the documents [a staff member of the school's Community Standards and Conflict Resolution office] had shared with me on understanding transgender identity. [Jensen] was fairly informed on the subject and did not share with me any personal opinion on the topic. I advised him not to revisit transgender issues in his classroom to avoid the students [sic] expressed concerns. He then asked what to do if the topic is again brought up by another student. I told him to avoid stating opinions (his or others) on the topic as he had previously when he was working from the Atlantic article. He felt this was workable as the topic had not come back up in any of the sections and they had moved past the general discussion on how to identify interesting topics to write on as the semester has progressed.
>
> I found [Jensen] helpful and cooperative and he was clear with me that the intent of the discussion was to be thought provoking and not in any way his personal opinions on any of the topics discussed. He asked if he need

[sic] to reach out to the student and I said that at this point, the student has asked to remain anonymous, therefore it would not be possible. (196)

While the tone of Parks's description is collegial, it nonetheless contains an explicit instruction to censor: Jensen was instructed to avoid bringing up the topic of "transgender issues" entirely, and, if the topic was nonetheless raised by a student, to avoid stating any opinions at all, including opinions of others. In short, an entire topic had been declared off limits—an ironic outcome in the context of university education, which, at least in theory, is aimed in part at teaching students how to engage with and analyze complex topics on which there are a diverging range of views.

The events noted above occurred in the fall 2015 semester. Jensen was not invited back to teach in the spring 2016 semester, though the public record does not identify a reason why. By early 2016, concerns about the University of Northern Colorado's Bias Response Team had attracted broader attention, including from FIRE (198). After public records requests resulted in the publication of the report about the Jensen case (but not his name, as it had been redacted in the publicly released documents) (199), Jensen came forward to identify himself (197). In an article in the *Greely Tribune*, he said, "In my view, it's absolutely nuts in an educational setting to say, 'You can't talk about these things.' It's the absolute opposite of what academia is supposed to be about" (197). Jensen also revealed that he had surreptitiously recorded his conversation with Marks, an act permitted by law in Colorado, which is a one-party-consent state.

In September 2016, University of Northern Colorado president Kay Norton gave a State of the University speech in which she stated with respect to the Bias Response Team program that "we will no longer have a separate process for bias-related concerns" (200). But for Mike Jensen, the damage to his teaching opportunities at the University of Northern Colorado was already done. Nearly two years later, a May 2018 *Wall Street Journal* article on bias response teams noted the Jensen incident and stated that "Mr. Jensen says he hasn't been invited back to teach since the semester when he was reported" (201).

So was Jensen not invited back to teach as a result of the September 2015 classroom discussion and subsequent run-in with the university's bias response program? The public record doesn't provide a definitive answer. The spring 2016 semester that immediately followed the fall 2015 incident began before the Jensen incident had become public. To the extent that the

University of Northern Colorado's decision not to rehire Jensen in spring 2016 was tied to being caught up in the bias response system, it would have been based on events that were known at that time to the university administration but not more generally. By summer 2016, however, it was in the news. And, as we have noted, Jensen was not invited to teach at the University of Northern Colorado in fall 2016 or in any subsequent semester through at least spring 2018.

10.3 Why Adjuncts Lie Low

Adjunct instructors should be free to ask students to engage with complex and potentially controversial topics in their classes. But the Jensen case illustrates why doing so can be so perilous. If a single student files a complaint that a classroom discussion caused discomfort, the campus bureaucracy swings into action to address it. In terms of the adjunct's prospects for being rehired after the current contract ends, the issue of whether the complaint has merit becomes secondary, as its existence is by definition a problem for the university administration. And, as an inevitable consequence, the complaint is a problem for the instructor whose classroom discussions led to it.

Adjuncts teach because they enjoy teaching and, for many of them, because they depend financially on the income it provides. The temporary, one-semester-at-a-time nature of many adjunct contracts creates a set of incentives not to run afoul of college administrations, which in turn requires avoiding introducing any classroom material or discussions that might lead to a student complaint. In addition, when colleges create "bias response" teams and the associated administrative and bureaucratic infrastructure for collecting and acting on bias complaints, they are essentially inviting students to actively seek out classroom (and other on-campus) situations they deem offensive. The result is an environment in which an adjunct who wants to continue to teach will tread very carefully, with the goal of ensuring that even the most easily offended student doesn't hear or read anything that might spur the filing of a bias complaint.

Another reason this result is ironic and unfortunate is that it blunts the teaching effectiveness of adjuncts, who add enormously to the intellectual vitality of a college. Adjuncts are often better teachers than full-time tenured professors, in part because in contrast with professors who often devote significant time to research, adjuncts often have teaching as their *only* focus. An adjunct whose only engagement with the college is through teaching will be judged on that basis alone. Thus, there are very few longtime adjuncts who are not committed to the job of teaching. In addition, many adjuncts are professional practitioners in fields such as law, business, medicine, music, etc., and bring to the classroom invaluable perspectives from outside academia that many professors lack.

And, in addition to being committed, effective teachers, adjuncts have an outsize role in shaping the undergraduate classroom experience. As Clausen and Swidler observed in the 2013 AAUP paper cited earlier in the chapter, adjuncts "are overwhelmingly the teachers of the required classes, the introductory courses, the largest and fullest sections" (194, p. 20). In short, adjuncts bring immense value to higher education. It is unfortunate that their continued employment is contingent on teaching in a way that pressures them to avoid classroom discussions of topics that might be deemed controversial.

A final point is that the notoriously low salaries paid to adjuncts are in part connected to the question of academic freedom, in the sense that both are consequences of the market. The imbalance between the number of people who want to teach as adjuncts and the number of available spots places colleges in a position where they have enormous leverage over adjuncts. One consequence of this is low pay. Another is that colleges view adjuncts as expendable and easily replaceable. If one adjunct brings up a topic in class that leads to a student complaint, there will be many other potential adjuncts waiting in the wings to teach future offerings of the class.

10.4 Academic Freedom and Adjuncts

So, what can be done to improve academic freedom for adjuncts? One of the first solutions that might come to mind is to expand tenure so that it also covers them. For a host of reasons, this is realistic in only a few narrow circumstances. For example, the University of California offers the titles of "Lecturer with the Potential for Security of Employment" (LPSOE) and "Lecturer with Security of Employment" (LSOE) (202). These titles are used for "appointees . . . whose primary responsibility is teaching and teaching-related tasks and secondary responsibility is professional and/or scholarly achievement and activity" (202, p. 1). However, the majority of people holding the "lecturer" (or equivalent) title in U.S. colleges do not have either potential or actual security of employment.

Most adjuncts, at the University of California and elsewhere, have teaching assignments that can vary significantly over the course of time. It would be financially impractical to expect any university to be required to offer permanent employment to lecturers who are only expected to teach for a short period of time, or only sporadically. As a result, for most adjuncts, tenure—or its equivalent through "security of employment" in the manner of the titles discussed in the previous paragraph—is not a suitable solution to the challenge of how to provide academic freedom.

Another possible solution would be to draft and adopt college-wide policies that explicitly confer academic freedom rights to adjuncts. These policies could identify the existence of such rights, and could further strengthen them by requiring that contracts used for hiring adjuncts contain a clause providing an explicit guarantee of academic freedom. While this would certainly be an improvement over the current system, it would have its limitations due to the sporadic nature of many adjunct appointments. In other words, in contrast with a tenured professor who (at least in theory) can only be subjected to an involuntary separation from the college after a lengthy process and a finding of significant wrongdoing, adjunct positions are temporary by design.

There is a long list of completely legitimate reasons why an adjunct who teaches during one semester might not be asked to return to teach in the next semester. Against this backdrop, it becomes extremely challenging to enforce protections for academic freedom, since it would be very difficult to disentangle a legitimate decision to not rehire from one arising from a violation of contractually guaranteed academic freedom rights. Even in cases where there was a "smoking gun" tying the decision to not rehire the adjunct to a clear violation of academic freedom, the burden to pursue the grievance would fall to the adjunct, who might not have the requisite time and financial resources to see the grievance process through to its conclusion.

And victory, even if it were obtained, would be limited in scope. A tenured professor who successfully contests an attempt at termination over an academic freedom issue is rewarded with the prospect of years of further employment—a result that justifies a significant expenditure of time and expense. An adjunct who wins an analogous battle is rewarded with a return to the pool of eligible adjuncts, which may or may not result in a contract for future work. In addition, colleges, like most organizations, are not particularly enthusiastic to enter into new contractual relationships with people who have filed grievances in the past. A department chair faced with the choice of 1) rehiring an adjunct who has previously filed and prevailed in a formal academic freedom complaint or 2) an adjunct who is an equally good teacher but who has never been involved in any grievance against the college will often choose the adjunct with the "clean" record. The fact that making the choice on this basis would itself be an attack on academic freedom would be irrelevant in a practical sense, since it would often be nearly impossible for the disfavored adjunct to show why he or she was passed over in the rehiring process.

Regardless of any good intentions that a college might have in attempting to draft policies to put adjuncts on more equal footing with tenure-track and tenured professors in terms of academic freedom, the tenuous nature of adjunct appointments is incompatible with strong academic freedom protections. This is an area of substantial asymmetry between teaching and research. Research is generally led by tenure-track and tenured professors who have explicit guarantees of academic freedom written into the policies of their colleges. This means that, at least on paper, there is a foundation for using those guarantees to combat instances when pressures from inside or outside the college are used to attempt to undermine research integrity and autonomy. Teaching is a different story. Not only is much of college teaching performed by adjuncts who in practice have few academic freedom protections, but even if such protections were given a broader role, the nature of adjunct positions would make them more difficult to enforce.

11

Counterarguments

This is a book about the need in academia for free inquiry and open discourse, and the subtle and not-so-subtle ways in which the absence of these traits is problematic. Relatedly, we believe that the lack of sufficient viewpoint diversity on campus arises as a direct consequence of the set of three beliefs that constrain campus discourse. Not everyone will agree with the assertions we make in this book. In this section, we identify and respond to some potential counterarguments.

11.1 Counterargument 1: There Is No Problem

The number of cases in which research or teaching activities lead to academic freedom controversies is very small. This can lead to the counterargument that the "problems" we are identifying in fact do not exist in any substantive way. To explore this, it is instructive to consider some commentary on campus free speech, a topic that is related to but differentiable from the broader issues of free inquiry and open discourse we have been addressing in this book.

Zack Beauchamp wrote for *Vox* regarding data from Georgetown University's Free Speech Project that:

> The Free Speech Project's researchers had cataloged more than 90 incidents since 2016 that fit their criteria for a person's free speech rights being threatened. Of those 90, about two-thirds took place on college campuses. These incidents range from a speaker being disinvited to a faculty member being fired over allegedly offensive comments to a student-run play being canceled over concerns it would offend.
>
> The raw numbers here should already raise questions about the so-called political correctness epidemic. According to the Department of Education, there are 4,583 colleges and universities in the United States (including two- and four-year institutions). The fact that there were roughly only

Unassailable Ideas. Ilana Redstone and John Villasenor, Oxford University Press (2020). © Oxford University Press.
DOI: 10.1093/oso/9780190078065.001.0001.

60 incidents in the past two years suggests that free speech crises are extremely rare events and don't define university life in the way that critics suggest. (203)

Colby College English professor Aaron Hanlon made a related argument in a March 2018 piece published at NBC News when he wrote:

As new and better data on the attitudes of young people toward free speech becomes available, the argument that college students are increasingly against free speech becomes harder and harder to sustain. There will always be anecdotal examples of overzealous and even reactionary young people, but the idea that such beliefs have overtaken a generation is overblown. (204)

① Response: testing boundaries is key

Our response to these points is twofold. First, as we've observed elsewhere in this book, the only way to understand the nature of boundaries is to examine what happens when someone pushes at their edges. With respect to the issue of speech, it is true that both the absolute number and the relative frequency of disinvitations and shutdowns as a fraction of total speaker invitations at universities don't constitute an obvious crisis.

But that isn't the end of the story. While there is evidence that the frequency of such instances grew over the decade or so up to about 2017, at which point it slowed down (205), that doesn't necessarily mean the climate has become more tolerant. The drop in incidents may indicate that some students who would have otherwise invited speakers viewed as likely to attract protest instead decided not to do so because the costs (both literal and figurative) became too high.

② Second and more fundamentally, regardless of the interpretation of the trends, using speaker disinvitations and other forms of disruption as metrics to assess whether there are indeed broader challenges to academic inquiry and campus discourse would be insufficient. And to be fair to the authors of the pieces cited above, neither of them makes that broader argument in those pieces; we raise this point because the data they cite could potentially be used to support such a position. Our thesis is that much of what occurs in academia is circumscribed by a series of assumptions that are held in place through social pressure to self-censor, increasingly applied with the assistance of social media. And as we've discussed, many of these consequences

social media, social pressure

arise in the classroom and in research, and thus would not be captured in tallies of shutdowns or speaker disinvitations.

11.2   Counterargument 2: The Three Beliefs Properly Constrain Dialog

Under this counterargument, the ideas that have been deemed unfit for discussion under the three beliefs are *properly* excluded from discussion. Thus, this counterargument holds that the three beliefs serve as a much-needed mechanism to purge from dialog perspectives that are not only unworthy of consideration, but that can also be harmful if articulated.

To put this in context, it's helpful to visualize a first circle outside of which sit ideas that have, over time, been exiled. Now imagine a considerably smaller second concentric circle inside the first one. The space for academic discourse to operate is now confined within the smaller of the two. In between these two concentric circles lie potentially useful perspectives that are nonetheless often considered impermissible to discuss on campus.

The three beliefs, reinforced through social media, have defined the limits of the inner circle. This is an ideologically motivated delineation that has narrowed the range of ideas, questions, and opinions that can be expressed without penalty. With the passage of time, the inner circle has been redrawn (and nearly always in a manner to shrink it) due to a variety of factors, including a growing list of social and political views that are deemed unacceptable to discuss on campus.

To take a concrete example, consider the debate over race-conscious university admissions policies carried out as part of a broader effort to meet affirmative action goals. There are thoughtful people who support such policies, and thoughtful people who oppose them. But while expressions of support for race-conscious admissions can be made without social penalty, on-campus expressions of opposition to such policies are often viewed as being outside the bounds of permissible discussion. Inevitably, this mutes the debate, starving it of perspectives that would be useful for everyone with an interest in this topic to hear, even if they don't agree. After all, people who are undecided on race-conscious admissions benefit from hearing it argued from a multiplicity of perspectives. And people who either support or oppose race-conscious admissions will have their views strengthened—or perhaps

essentially: can't have it both ways

↳ makes me think of RAV.

have their minds changed—if they meaningfully engage with people who hold opposing views.

More broadly, this example illustrates one of the key points underlying the argument in favor of broader viewpoint diversity: More viewpoint diversity does not mean that *all* of the ideas that would be admitted into academic discourse if the circle of acceptable on-campus expression were expanded are good. Some of the ideas would be useless, or worse. But that alone is not a reason to assume there is no value in considering alternative perspectives.

11.3 Counterargument 3: Campuses Already Have Sufficient Viewpoint Diversity

This counterargument is reflected through caveats like claims of "I support free enquiry, but . . ." Or, it can be made through assertions that increased viewpoint diversity is an impractical ideal. Indeed, Zack Beauchamp, the author of the *Vox* article cited earlier in this chapter, wrote in a follow-up piece that "In a vacuum, the notion of promoting 'viewpoint diversity' is laudable. But we aren't operating in a vacuum." He then cites an example "where Republican legislators are using allegations of a campus free speech crisis and liberal bias among the academy to further efforts to crack down on individual freedom," continuing, "In Wisconsin, the strictest of these states, rules drafted by the state university's board of regents allow students to be expelled if they are found to have disrupted the speech of other students three times" (206). We would agree that this is a draconian and ineffectual response. Nor would we support, for instance, legislation to limit the teaching of social justice in the classroom, as a 2017 bill proposed in the Arizona state legislature would have done (207). Such measures simply replace one overly restrictive environment with another.

More broadly, the counterargument that campuses already have sufficient viewpoint diversity arises from the claim that campuses are communities in which there are frequent, varied disagreements across a range of topics. These disagreements are sometimes cited as evidence of an environment that confers academic freedom. However, it is possible to have a wide range of opinions expressed on topics on which the three core beliefs offer few constraints. This should not be mistakenly used to conclude there is no value at all to a broader range of perspectives.

In other words, someone could argue that there is no need for more viewpoint diversity simply because they don't see it as lacking in the first place. After all, doesn't the contentious nature of many on-campus discussions prove that viewpoint diversity is alive and well? Here, we echo a point we made in the section on knowledge dissemination: It is possible to have a robust debate within the confines of the three core beliefs we have articulated and to as a result *think* that the discussion has been truly open, while in reality it may only have been open within the very limited aperture permitted by the beliefs.

wish they would spend more time on this
don't totally get response to vacuum point.

12

Beyond academia

Up to this point, we've focused on the ways in which the three beliefs and their reinforcement through social media shape academia. We have described the ways in which teaching is circumscribed, how research is limited in the types of questions that are asked and which results are publishable, and how academia recognizes the value of diversity but not of viewpoint diversity. The broader impact on discourse of the climate we describe isn't limited to academia.

While campuses both influence and are influenced by broader society, this dynamic is impacted by a key asymmetry: While thousands of new graduates move every year from the campus to the workforce, far fewer people leave the workforce annually to become students and take up residence in and around campuses. As a result, over time, campus culture tends to exert more influence on workforce culture than the other way around. Sociologists have described universities as a hub "connecting some of the most prominent institutional sectors of modern societies: the labor market and the larger economy, the professions and the sciences, the philanthropic sector, the family, and the nation-state" (208, p. 135).

The repeated infusion of new graduates into the workforce brings a long list of benefits to the companies they join. New graduates tend to be hard-working, energetic, creative, and highly motivated, and as a result they play an important role in the overall economy. They also bring with them worldviews shaped by having spent multiple years on college campuses— something that is in many ways positive, but can also raise concerns when it involves a low tolerance for perspectives not aligning with their own.

Given this context, we explore several non-campus settings. First, we consider the technology sector, which counts many relatively recent college graduates among its employees, and has a culture that is shaped accordingly. We then consider society at large, beyond the technology sector.

Unassailable Ideas. Ilana Redstone and John Villasenor, Oxford University Press (2020). © Oxford University Press.
DOI: 10.1093/oso/9780190078065.001.0001.

12.1 The Technology Sector

The technology sector is in some ways an extension of the American campus. Workers in technology companies in Silicon Valley and beyond tend to be young and politically progressive. Many of them work in companies that provide (prior to, and perhaps after, the Covid-19 pandemic) onsite meals, recreational opportunities, and a variety of other services similar to those offered on college campuses. Collectively, these factors have made the social climate at many technology companies similar to that found on campus. And, many of the same social pressures that operate on campus to conform to a dominant narrative are also found in technology companies.

Google example

12.1.1 Prohibited Assertions

In July 2017, James Damore, who at the time was an employee at Google, wrote a 10-page memo titled "Google's Ideological Echo Chamber" (209). In the document, Damore outlined his thoughts in response to a solicitation of feedback regarding Google's diversity policies. Most controversially, Damore's summary of his points stated that "Differences in distributions of traits between men and women may in part explain why we don't have 50% representation of women in tech and leadership."

This was not the type of feedback Google was hoping for. Damore's memo was made public on August 5, 2017, and led to a backlash that resulted in his firing a few days later for violating the company's code of conduct.

In an e-mail regarding Moore's firing, Google CEO Sundar Pichai wrote:

> First, let me say that we strongly support the right of Googlers to express themselves, and much of what was in that memo is fair to debate, regardless of whether a vast majority of Googlers disagree with it. However, portions of the memo violate our Code of Conduct and cross the line by advancing harmful gender stereotypes in our workplace. Our job is to build great products for users that make a difference in their lives. To suggest a group of our colleagues have traits that make them less biologically suited to that work is offensive and not OK. It is contrary to our basic values and our Code of Conduct, which expects "each Googler to do their utmost to create a workplace culture that is free of harassment, intimidation, bias and unlawful discrimination." (210)

In short, Damore was fired at least in part for suggesting that men and women differ in ways that might contribute to differences in the sex distribution of engineers. To be clear: We are not endorsing what Damore wrote. We are observing that the *reaction* to what he wrote illustrates what can happen when forbidden opinions are voiced in Silicon Valley, a close cousin of academia. In response to the backlash, Damore added a reply to his memo saying, "I value diversity and inclusion, am not denying that sexism exists, and don't endorse using stereotypes." However, for Damore's Google career this was too little, too late.

The story was covered in many major news outlets and generated strongly polarized reactions in Silicon Valley, in academia, and beyond. Those who supported the decision to fire Damore often raised arguments parallel to those invoked in a January 2018 *Guardian* opinion piece titled "James Damore is wrong. It's fine to discriminate against bigots and bullies" (211). In that article, the author wrote that "Damore joins a dull retinue of bad actors asking whether, if it's wrong to judge people because of their gender or the colour of their skin, is it not also wrong to judge people because they happen to have certain 'unorthodox' ideas about social Darwinism? The answer is no, and Damore was fired" (211).

Given that Damore was fired for what he wrote, it's clear that a cultural framework to counter his assertions through debate and discussion as opposed to through dismissal was not present in the Google context. As a result, people at Google who might not have immediately rejected Damore's assertions (and we can be sure that there were and still are such people)—and who might have found the counterarguments to his assertions far more convincing—never got a chance to hear those counterarguments.

12.1.2 Facebook Employees and the Kavanaugh Nomination

The dynamics in the technology sector relating to limitations on the range of acceptable opinions were also in evidence in a series of events that played out in September 2018 in relation to the nomination of then-DC Circuit judge Brett Kavanaugh to the Supreme Court. Joel Kaplan, Facebook's vice president for global public policy, was photographed seated behind Kavanaugh during his confirmation hearings before the Senate Judiciary Committee. As described in a *New York Times* article, after a growing number of Facebook employees voiced their concern regarding Kaplan's presence at the hearing, he sent a note to his staff explaining that "I have known Brett and Ashley Kavanaugh for 20 years. They are my and my wife Laura's closest friends in D.C. I was in their wedding; he was in ours. Our kids have grown up together." He also wrote: "I want to apologize . . . I recognize this moment is a deeply painful one—internally and externally" (212).

Things got even more complicated when another longtime Facebook employee, Andrew Bosworth, wrote a comment viewed as too supportive of Kaplan in an internal Facebook forum. Again as described in the *New York Times* article, Bosworth wrote that "[i]f you need to change teams, companies or careers to make sure your day-to-day life matches your passions, we will be sad to see you go, but we will understand," and that "[w]e will support you with any path you choose. But it is your responsibility to choose a path, not that of the company you work for" (212). Bosworth, too, then came under pressure within Facebook and issued an apology:

> I spoke at a time when I should be listening and that was a big mistake. I'm grateful to employees who shared feedback and very sorry that my actions caused employees pain and frustration when what they needed was better support and understanding from leadership. (212)

The chorus of apologies also included a statement from Facebook itself, with a spokesperson saying, "Our leadership team recognizes that they've made mistakes handling the events of the last week and we're grateful for all the feedback from our employees" (213). Facebook also held a town hall meeting to provide an opportunity for employees to air their views. The irony of Silicon Valley's we-support-diverse-views-*but* . . . culture was summed up well in a *Wall Street Journal* article describing the meeting:

> Facebook Inc. Chief Executive Officer Mark Zuckerberg told a packed room of employees Friday that the company should embrace diverse views, but he expressed frustration that a senior executive had attended Judge Brett Kavanaugh's highly politicized hearing last week, according to a person familiar with the remarks. (214)

Yet another irony of this situation is that Kaplan was reportedly hired in part specifically to help add political diversity to a Washington staff viewed as overly left-leaning (215). A key argument raised in criticizing Kaplan was that, as a high-ranking executive, his mere presence was an unacceptable implied endorsement of Kavanaugh. One problem with this argument is that it would not have been applied in reverse. If, instead of sitting behind Kavanaugh at the hearing, Kaplan had been photographed standing on a Capitol Hill street with people who were demonstrating *against* Kavanaugh, there likely would not have been a large group of Facebook employees who voiced outrage, and there likely would not have been a town hall meeting where Mark Zuckerberg expressed frustration at Kaplan's actions.

Just as would be the case on campus, the rules that applied to views on the Kavanaugh nomination were clear: It was considered unacceptable for Kaplan to signal support by sitting silently behind Kavanaugh during the hearing, despite their status as close friends. Kaplan was not given the latitude to act in his personal capacity, quite apart from his role at Facebook. This contrasts with more latitude to claim a separation of the personal from the professional that can accompany support for positions that are in line with the dominant views inside technology companies.

For example, in a 2017 interview published by *Business Insider*, a Google employee explained that

> I was really involved in the Women's March in January. I built an app with a non-Google friend to help women organize transportation and accommo- dation down in DC. I did interviews with the *New York Times*. I did a ton of press. And I did all of it as Lauren, not Lauren from Google. I was so careful about that because I was like, as Googlers, we don't take a political stance. That's not how this works. We've been told all along we can't speak on behalf of Google politically. That not's what we do. (216)

If Kaplan had used similar language to defend his appearance at the Kavanaugh hearing—for example, if he had said, "I did this as Joel Kaplan, not as Joel Kaplan from Facebook"—that would likely have done little to ap- pease the Facebook employees who had mobilized against him.

Of course, the analogy between Kaplan at Facebook and Lauren (her last name was not published in the *Business Insider* article) at Google isn't per- fect. While Lauren was a product designer, Kaplan was an executive with a job (vice president for global public policy) specifically requiring ex- ternal engagement and visibility. He was therefore more in the public eye and more likely to have his behavior scrutinized. But the contrasts between these two examples are nonetheless notable. Yet another contrast is that while Kaplan was criticized both by employees and by his company, in Lauren's case political engagement led to an invitation to speak to an audience of 70,000 people at a weekly Google all-hands meeting (216). Even when employees claim to be acting only in their personal capacity, technology companies are more likely to amplify and elevate views that reflect one of the three beliefs, and that will therefore resonate with a large fraction of employees.

12.1.3 Pressures to Self-Censor

As the Damore and Kaplan episodes illustrate, suppression of opinions deemed problematic is an integral part of Silicon Valley culture. It is possible to find Damore's views offensive and to have opposed the Kavanaugh nomination while still being concerned about the dynamics that led to Damore's firing and to the cascade of apologies from Kaplan and others at Facebook. For example, if you believe (as we do) that gender and innate mathematical potential are uncorrelated, then the best way to convince people who think otherwise to change their minds is to let them voice their opinions—and then to rebut them. By contrast, censorship (or the threat of censorship) doesn't change any minds; it simply causes people who might have otherwise been open to reconsidering their views to stay quiet and harden their opinions.

For technology company employees, the lesson from these and similar episodes is that even when management claims to be encouraging the expression of diverse views, there are unwritten limits to what can be expressed. In an environment where all employees are one ill-advised comment or e-mail message away from being fired for a "code of conduct" violation, the career-preserving approach is to self-censor to avoid expressing any views that might offend coworkers and lead to the inevitable calls for disciplinary action. One of the multiple consequences of this climate is that the opportunity for debate and education on any number of important issues is lost. For technology company executives, the Kavanaugh nomination furnishes an additional lesson: Like a politician running for a highly visible political office, you can be judged as much (or more) by the friends you keep outside of work as by anything you do at work.

12.2 Society at Large

Does this climate also exist outside of academia and outside of the technology sector? We explore this question through a set of examples that show that the same pressures that govern on-campus discourse also exert a strong influence in areas as diverse as the young adult publishing industry, discussions of the #MeToo movement, and congressional politics.

12.2.1 Identity Politics in Young Adult Fiction

A pair of head-spinning examples of the identity politics–driven meltdown in the world of young adult fiction publishing can be found in cancellation of books by Kosoko Jackson and (separately) Amélie Wen Zhao. Both of these cases illustrate the power of the third belief (i.e., in the primacy of identity and identity-based claims of harm) to shape public discourse.

In early 2019 Jackson was about to publish his debut novel, called *A Place for Wolves*. The novel was set in 1990s Kosovo and followed the relationship between two American teenage boys. Although early signs pointed to the book's potential for success (including multiple starred reviews and a designation as a Kids' Indie Next pick (217)), a lengthy negative review was posted by Tamera Cook on Goodreads in February 2019 (218). As described in a subsequent *Slate* article, Cook "objected to the book's use of a recent genocide as a backdrop to romance, the way some early fans fetishized it as a 'cute gay love story,' that it was not written by a Muslim, that it 'centers' privileged Americans, and that the villain is an ethnic Albanian, among other concerns" (219).

This review led to a rapidly mushrooming social media backlash, and then to Jackson himself canceling the book. In a statement published on his website (as described by a February 28 article at *Publishers Weekly*), he wrote, "While dealing with the hurt my debut has caused and coming up with a plan of action of how to fix the pain I've caused with my words, my site is currently under maintenance. I'll have an update soon. Thanks for your patience and for those who I hurt with my words, especially the Muslim readers, teens, and community members, I'm sorry" (220).

This outcome was particularly ironic given Jackson's own previous work as a "sensitivity reader" for various publishers—a job involving reading manuscripts and highlighting potentially problematic content (219). And, to add another layer of irony, Jackson had been vocal in the past about his support for the #Ownvoices movement (which emphasizes the tie between a writer's identity and his or her legitimacy in writing about a topic). In 2018 he tweeted that "Stories about the civil rights movement should be written by Black people. Stories of suffrage should be written by women. Ergo, stories about boys during horrific and life changing times, like the AIDS EPIDEMIC, should be written by gay men" (221). In sum, the backlash against Jackson illustrates the perils of an environment in which those who contribute today to a culture with ever stricter rules about who can write about what can easily become its targets tomorrow. And, it illustrates the power of a social media mob to exercise veto power over publication decisions that should more properly be made by publishers, editors, and authors.

While one might be tempted to dismiss the Jackson case as an isolated incident, a similar social media campaign had driven young adult fiction author Amélie Wen Zhao to withdraw her debut novel just weeks earlier. In January 2019, Zhao announced her intention to pull her forthcoming book, *Blood Heir*, over concerns about cultural appropriation and the book's portrayal of slavery. As described in a *New York Times* article on the cancellation, the book:

> takes place in a fictional Cyrilian empire where a group of powerful people called Affinites are feared and enslaved, drew on real-world issues, including "the demonization of the Other and this experience of not belonging" . . . Some readers criticized what they viewed as racial stereotypes and careless borrowing from other cultural traditions: the novel features a diverse cast—including "a tawny-skinned minority of a Russian-esque princess; a disowned and dishonored Asian-esque assassin; an is-lander/Caribbean-esque child warrior; a Middle-Eastern-esque soldier," according to Ms. Zhao's description of the novel on her website. (222)

In her January 30, 2019, statement posted on Twitter, Zhao noted her "multicultural upbringing" and that "I wrote Blood Heir from my immediate cultural perspective." She also added that "I am so sorry for the pain this has caused" and that "I have decided to ask my publisher not to publish Blood Heir at this time, and they have agreed" (223). A few months later, in April 2019, Zhao announced that she planned to publish the book after all, but only after making additional revisions. As described in a *New York Times* article:

After Zhao decided she wanted to release the book, she and her publisher sought feedback from scholars and sensitivity readers in an effort to resolve any ambiguity around the type of indentured labor depicted. They had academics from different multicultural backgrounds, as well as one who studies human trafficking in Asia, evaluate the text, and Zhao added new material and made changes based on their comments. They had additional sensitivity readers vet the book for racial and other stereotypes. (224)

12.2.2 Discussions Regarding #MeToo

Discussions of the #MeToo movement are another area in which tripwires abound. An illustrative example can be found in a late 2017 interview in which actor Matt Damon said that the #MeToo movement involved a "spectrum of behavior" (225). He also observed that there's an important difference between groping and rape, adding that "both of those behaviors need to be confronted and eradicated without question, but they shouldn't be conflated" (226).

In the days following the initial broadcast of the Damon interview, there was a social media backlash as well as news stories in the traditional media with titles including "Matt Damon draws backlash for comments on sexual harassment and assault" on the *ABC News* website (227), and "Matt Damon Draws Rebukes for Comments on the #MeToo Movement" in the *New York Times* (228). A few weeks later in an appearance on the *Today* show, Damon expressed contrition, saying. "I really wish I'd listened a lot more before I weighed in on this . . . I don't want to further anybody's pain with anything that I do or say . . . so for that I am really sorry . . . I should get in the back seat and close my mouth for a while" (229).

In making his original "spectrum of behavior" comments, Damon inadvertently ran headlong into the third belief—which places primacy on identity and identity-based claims of harm. When women who had suffered some of the harms that the #MeToo movement aims to address condemned Damon's comments, their identity was viewed on social media and then in the traditional media as conferring an absolute authority to decide what can be said about the movement, and who can say it. It no longer mattered that what Damon had said was factually incontestable: There *is* a difference between groping and rape; both of those behaviors *do* need to be confronted and eradicated, and they *shouldn't* be conflated.

In fact, if a female actor had made comments identical to Damon's, it is very unlikely that there would have been anything like the blowback that followed Damon's comments. But because Damon was male, and because he was told by a chorus of people on social media that he should, in essence, shut up, the conclusion—including by Damon himself—was that he needed to avoid discussing the topic. The title of a *Buzzfeed* article published after his *Today* show interview captures the climate well: "Matt Damon Says He Realizes He Needs to Shut Up for a While About Sexual Harassment" (230).

One could ask what the harm was in the criticisms directed at Damon. After all, the logic might go, as a wealthy and successful actor, he should know better than most that potential criticism comes with the territory if he's going to put himself in the public eye in relation to a matter of intense public interest. And, in the long run, Damon's career and public image are doing just fine. Less than a year later, in September 2018, Damon appeared on a *Saturday Night Live* episode parodying Brett Kavanaugh. So, what could be the cause for concern?

The answer is that the Damon episode illustrates a phenomenon that extends well beyond Damon. One consequence of the third belief (the primacy of identity and identity-based claims of harm) is an overly reductionist, binary view of the world: People are either viewed as having the proper identity to comment on an issue with moral authority, or they are viewed as lacking that identity and, as a result, lacking the right to say anything at all. This is a dramatic oversimplification that impoverishes dialog. The fact that identity matters should not mean that it is the *only* thing that matters.

There are many issues on which a person's identity confers a greater moral authority to speak on a particular issue. People who have been targets of sexual harassment or worse have a greater moral authority to speak on those issues than those who haven't. Women are disproportionately targeted by sexual harassment, and therefore generally have greater moral authority to speak on it than men. But higher moral authority to speak on a topic shouldn't mean an *absolute* authority to censor and otherwise control dialog. It is one thing to give—as we should—heightened deference and respect to those who speak from personal experience. It is quite another to use social media attacks as a mechanism to purge from the public discourse everyone who has failed to pass the identity filter applicable to a particular issue.

12.2.3 The Rao Nomination

On campus, people deemed to have transgressed by saying something counter to one of the core beliefs can come under pressure to issue what amount to rit-ualized apologies. The same dynamic occurs off campus as well. As discussed earlier, one example of this is the set of apologies offered by Facebook's Joel Kaplan and Andrew Bosworth after Kaplan was photographed attending the September 2018 Senate Judiciary Committee hearing on Kavanaugh's con-firmation. In that case, apologies were offered in relation to a recent action. Another important and interesting class of apologies relates to present-day atonement for opinions or actions taken in the past.

People who rise to positions of prominence have always had their past writings scrutinized. When properly contextualized, this scrutiny is an im-portant part of the vetting process. To take one example, it is eminently reasonable—in fact, necessary—to examine the previous judicial opinions of a judge who is being considered for a seat on a higher court. But given the ease with which digital searches can now be performed, it is reasonable to ask what weight should be given to things written decades ago and in a completely different professional context. Should the author be granted some latitude due to these differences in context and to the intervening passage of multiple decades? Or should the author be required to answer for long-ago controversial statements as if those statements had been published yes-terday? In the current climate, the latter approach has become the default.

Consider the February 2019 confirmation hearings for Neomi Rao, who was nominated to the D.C. Circuit Court of Appeals seat that had been re-cently vacated by Brett Kavanaugh. As has become standard practice, opponents of the nomination searched her past publication record for poten-tially problematic statements. In this case, the searchers found paydirt—not in any judicial opinions (Rao had not previously been a judge)—but rather in columns she had written decades earlier when she was an undergraduate at Yale University in the mid-1990s.

Most of the press and criticism focused on her assertion, published in an October 1994 column in the *Yale Daily Herald*, that if a woman "drinks to the point where she can no longer choose, well, getting to that point was part of her choice" (231). This assertion took central stage in her February 5 confir-mation hearing. Senator Joni Ernst (R-IA) said to Rao, "I've had a chance to review a number of your writings while you were in college and they do give me pause. And not just from my own personal experiences but regarding a

oh my god.

message that we are sending young women everywhere." After the hearing, Senator Kamala Harris (D-CA), who had also cited Rao's college writings during the hearing, tweeted, "Neomi Rao's prior writings about sexual assault are completely unacceptable and her responses to my questions today were deeply troubling" (232). About a week later, Rao penned an apology in the form of a letter sent to the Senate Judiciary Committee. In it, she stated that:

> they weren't just insensitive though.

> I particularly regret the insensitivity demonstrated in my remarks on rape and sexual assault. While responding to events and debates on campus, I failed to recognize the hurt that my words could cause a survivor of such crimes. I recognize now the arguments I made might discourage a victim from coming forward or from seeking help. With little knowledge or experience, I lacked perspective of how this might be perceived by others, particularly victims of sexual assault. (233)

Rao's apology sounds heartfelt, and there's certainly a good chance that it is. But whether or not Rao actually believed she should have to apologize for the things she wrote in the 1990s, the apology was clearly constructed with the goal of *sounding* heartfelt. This was apology as ritual—a step that Rao and her advisors likely concluded had to be taken in order to maximize her chances of a successful confirmation process.

It is possible to find some of her 1990s opinions disturbing while also being disturbed by the ways they were used against her in a Senate Judiciary Committee hearing a quarter of a century later. Do we really want to create a culture in which people who aspire to positions of authority spend their entire lives being careful to limit their opinions to anodyne statements that they can be sure will still be viewed as anodyne decades into the future? And do we really want to limit all positions of authority in the future to people who have approached their public engagement in such a calculated manner? Or are we better off fostering a climate that encourages the expression of a wide range of opinions, even when some of those opinions might be viewed as problematic, either in the present or in future decades? Apologies such as that offered by Rao have consequences well beyond her confirmation process, because they create pressure on anyone who aspires to obtain a highly visible professional position to avoid creating a written record with extensive commentary on hot-button topics.

> yeah. i don't want to elect a rape apologist

13

Solutions

13.1 Cultivating Open Discourse

In light of a culture in American academia that is unwelcoming to debate and free inquiry on a growing number of topics, it's natural to ask whether there are frameworks from outside the academy that provide lessons that could be valuable in improving academic discourse. The answer is yes. Across time and place, innumerable groups have grappled with ways to disagree, to debate, to resolve disputes, and to attempt to build understanding and bridge differences.

While the emergent role of social media in the current environment makes it harder to find direct historical analogs, there is still much to be learned by examining discourse and dispute resolution in other cultural, religious, and historical contexts. Of course, no one culture, society, or other group singularly holds the answer to the challenge of how people should best engage with one another on complex and potentially divisive topics. However, we needn't put a model—or the culture with which it is associated—through a purity test in order to learn something valuable from it.

For instance, Ancient Greece, which is often referred to as the birthplace of democracy, provides a useful example of the importance of participation in public discourse, a core democratic principle that ties directly to a valuation of the debate over ideas. As Oxford political scientist Teresa Bejan described in a 2017 *Atlantic* article, the Greek terms *isegoria* and *parrhesia* relate to the theory of freedom to express ideas and speak one's mind. Although they are invoked together, they are distinct concepts: *isegoria* refers to the idea of the equality of citizens to take part in public speech and debate and *parrhesia* refers to the ability to say more or less whatever one wants to whomever one chooses. Bejan explains that the competing ideals we see playing out in the campus context echo millennia-old challenges:

> When student protesters claim that they are silencing certain voices—via no-platforming, social pressure, or outright censorship—in the name of

Unassailable Ideas. Ilana Redstone and John Villasenor, Oxford University Press (2020). © Oxford University Press.
DOI: 10.1093/oso/9780190078065.001.0001.

isegoria and parrhesia

free speech itself, it may be tempting to dismiss them as insincere, or at best confused . . . To a generation convinced that hateful speech is itself a form of violence or "silencing," pleading the First Amendment is to miss the point. Most of these students do not see themselves as standing against free speech at all. What they care about is the *equal right* to speech, and equal access to a public forum in which the historically marginalized and excluded can be heard and count equally with the privileged. This is a claim to *isegoria*, and once one recognizes it as such, much else becomes clear—including the contrasting appeal to *parrhesia* by their opponents, who sometimes seem determined to reduce "free speech" to a license to offend. (234, emphasis in original)

Bejan also observed in relation to the U.S. Constitution that:

> [T]he genius of the First Amendment lies in bringing *isegoria* and *parrhesia* together, by securing the equal right and liberty of citizens not simply to "exercise their reason" but to speak their minds. It does so because the alternative is to allow the powers-that-happen-to-be to grant that liberty as a *license* to some individuals while denying it to others. (234, emphasis in original)

None of this erases the irony that both the Ancient Greeks and the Framers of the Constitution had extraordinarily problematic and exclusionary definitions of who counted as a citizen—and therefore of who could benefit from these lofty principles. To echo a point we noted earlier (and that many others have made), these classical frameworks can teach us something despite the flaws in the cultures within which they arose, not because of those flaws.

One needn't look to Ancient Greece to see examples of the importance of debate. As Margaret Goldberg noted in a 1985 Ph.D. dissertation at the University of Illinois at Urbana-Champaign, debate plays a central role in Tibetan Buddhist monastic education, where the formalized practice is used "to help create an understanding of the accurate description of reality" (235, p. 39). The goal of the interaction is for "the questioner to elicit an incorrect commitment from the answerer and then force him to explicitly change that commitment" (235, p. iii). Goldberg explained that:

Each round of debate consists of topic search, topic selection, evidence search, presentation of proof, and reformulation of the topic. The evidence search forces the answerer to think through the details and implications of his initial formulation of the topic. Presentation of proof almost always consists of showing that in the process of the evidence search, the answerer has asserted a direct contradiction to his original formulation of the topic . . . The iterative nature of the debate process makes it highly probable that agreement upon the <u>formulation</u> at least approaches agreement as to belief. (235, p. 8, emphasis in original)

Formalized frameworks for debate are important both because they can make it easier to reach resolution on the issue under consideration and because the very existence of these frameworks elevates the role and utility of discourse. Discourse on contentious topics is also closely tied to dispute resolution, which is another area with models that are valuable and instructive to study.

An example from Native Hawaiian culture is illustrative. In *hoʻoponopono*, as Manu Meyer explained in a 1995 article, "the first step . . . is the choice of a *haku* (facilitator). In ancient Hawaii, the haku was usually a male member of the healing, professional class, known as the kahuna. Today, haku are most often respected elders—male or female—who are not involved" (236, p. 31, italics and parentheses in original) in the matter under discussion. As Meyer explains, participants agree in advance to a set of conditions including: "All words and deeds that are part of the hoʻoponopono will be shared in an atmosphere of *ʻoia iʻo* (the essence of truth)," "A spirit of aloha is shared by the participants, or they are committed to reinstating that spirit," and "The chosen haku is a fair and impartial channel through which the hoʻoponopono can be done" (236, p. 31, italics and parentheses in the original).

While *hoʻoponopono* was traditionally "practiced only between immediate family members" (236, p. 30). its teachings are valuable in a much broader context. *Hoʻoponopono* is a framework through which people who disagree can come to a resolution through a process that places priority on preservation of the relationship; it is, as Meyer described it, a "relationship-centered resolution process" (236, p. 31). Elevating awareness of the distinction between relationships on the one hand and issues of contention on the other hand can facilitate dialog that is less likely to stray into personal attacks. And, it can help create a climate in which disputes can be more effectively contextualized, and in which the parties remain cognizant not only of the issue in dispute but also of the benefit to resolving things in a way that will facilitate harmonious and productive future interactions.

Traditional African societies provide another valuable reference framework. In a 2017 paper, Kariuki Muigua writes that "traditional African communities had institutions and mechanisms which were effective in handling and managing conflicts among the people" (237, p. 2). He describes a set of conflict-resolution mechanisms including a kinship system with relations "geared towards preventing conflict" and that could "create or restore relationships that could have been damaged by conflict," as well as a consensus-based approach under which "resolutions were attained on the basis of consensus rather than on [a] winner-takes-all approach" (237, pp. 9–10). Relatedly, Dejo Olowom, dean of the law school at the American University of Nigeria, wrote in a 2018 paper that

> Broadly speaking . . . African indigenous conflict resolution systems characteristically focus on agreements through deliberations, negotiations and reflections to ascertain facts and clear up problems. . . . The outcome is, ideally, a sense of harmony, mutual participation and obligation as well as interchange among conflicting sides. (238, p. 12)

Olowom also explained that

> Mediation ranks as the most popular dispute-settling tool in traditional Africa . . . Mediation normally avoids [an] explicit parade of power, win-lose mindset, social blemishes, and acrimony that are normally associated with adjudication . . . As a conflict resolution method, mediation helps to achieve a settlement through negotiation, conciliation, persuasion, inducement, and compromise. (238, p. 12)

Of course, there is significant variation across different African societies. Thus, it is instructive to look at a specific example. The Raya in northern Ethiopia use a conflict-resolution framework called *Mezard*, which as Yonas Berhe described in a 2012 master's thesis at Mekelle University in Ethiopia, aims "to address the cause of conflict" and "to build solidarity and belongingness" both within the Raya community and with "their neighboring societies" (239, p. 5).

Berhe explained that a council of elders plays a central role in *Mezard*, with "elders chosen for membership of the council for their high moral standards in the community." Their age gives them "skill and wisdom in handling disputes and an ability to analyze and advise disputants," and they are viewed as "patient, impartial, [and] free from favoritism" (239, p. 40). According to an interview Berhe conducted with a prominent elder, they "carefully argue for certain issues and convince the conflicting parties to accept the proposed alternative of decision" (239, p. 39). By employing "persuasion rather than threat of force," elders seek a "win-win solution" with the goal of "repairing severed relations among the disputants based on truth, conviction or remorse, sanction, accountability for justice, and forgiveness" (239, p. 39). While noting that *Mezard* has some drawbacks, Berhe concluded that it is "most of the time a win-win approach" that aims to "sustain further peace" and that "ensures an ease of intermixing [of] the conflicting parties" in a region where "their mode of living is highly interdependent" (239, p. 58).

Native American dispute-resolution approaches provide another important set of perspectives. In a 1997 law review article, James Zion and Robert Yazzie, who were at the time of publication respectively Solicitor to the Courts of the Navajo Nation and Chief Justice of the Navajo Nation, addressed Native American dispute-resolution systems, explaining that "[t]here are hundreds—if not thousands—of Indian groups in the Americas. There are many different language families . . . Therefore, it is impossible to state general principles about Indian law with accuracy. There are some things, however, which are most likely universal or nearly so" (240, p. 73). Zion and Yazzie then provided a contrast with European law and Native American law, writing that:

> European law is essentially a "vertical" system which is built on hierarchies of power. . . . In contrast, Indian traditional legal systems are "horizontal" . . . Vertical systems use hierarchies of power and authority, backed by force and coercion, to operate their legal systems. Horizontal systems are essentially egalitarian and function using relationships. (240, p. 74)

They also noted that in Navajo culture, the parties in a dispute "develop a plan of action to end the dispute through consensus and agreement. That plan describes the duties of each participant to mend relationships" (240, p. 79) and that in "Navajo peacemaking, which does not utilize punishment, people are free to 'talk out' the problem fully and get at the psychological barriers which impede a practical solution" (240, p. 81).

We next consider Islamic frameworks. In a 2017 article in the *International Journal of Cross Cultural Management* on Islamic conflict-management principles, Akram Abdul Cader described *Tahkīm*:

> In this model, a third-party arbitrator is chosen to mitigate conflict between parties. Arbitration occurs after the conflict takes place, in many instances during escalation. The arbitrator must have attributes of justice, fairness, knowledge, and wisdom. (241, p. 351)

Cader also explained the SNT model, where the acronym comes from "*Shura* (council), *Nasīha* (advice), and *Ta'awun* (mutual cooperation)" (241, p. 352, emphasis in original):

> The nature of *Shura* is to consult with nonpartisan individuals alongside the stakeholders and parties involved in the conflict. [With] *Nasīhah* . . . [i]nvolved parties are given advice or feedback toward corrective action, thereby increasing the probability of a favorable outcome. Based on consultation and advice, concerned parties are encouraged to cooperate with other upon good (*Ta'awun*). The purpose of cooperation is to create a positive atmosphere and reduce possible tension resulting from conflict. (241, p. 352, emphasis in original, internal citations omitted)

In a 1999 paper titled "Islamic Mediation Techniques for Middle East Conflicts," George E. Irani discussed *sulh* (settlement) and *musalaha* (reconciliation), which he explained "are alternative and indigenous forms of conflict control and reduction. The sulh ritual, which is an institutionalized form of conflict management and control, has its origins in tribal and village contexts" (242, p. 11). He then quotes from a paper by Laurie E. King-Irani that explains that the "sulh ritual stresses the close link between the psychological and political dimensions of communal life through its recognition that injuries between individuals and groups will fester and expand if not acknowledged, repaired, forgiven and transcended" (242 [the original Irani paper], p. 11, quoting 243).

A final example looks to Judaism. Consider the example of disagreements between the Houses of Hillel and Shamai. The names come from two of the early leading thinkers on Jewish law. Shamai tended to be stricter and Hillel more liberal in their interpretations. The two houses were opposed on many issues, including divorce and the value of white lies (244), and engaged in difficult conversations about topics on which they had very different viewpoints. Debates and disagreements between the two houses played an important role in shaping interpretations of Jewish law, so much so that the Talmud, a collection of rabbinical commentaries, recorded over 300 different disagreements between them.

The existence of a core text built upon debate and disagreement has shaped Jewish approaches to dispute resolution. In the book *Fundamentals of Jewish Conflict Resolution*, Rabbi Howard Kaminsky wrote that there are:

> six fundamental commandments that play a pivotal role in the prevention of destructive conflict and serve major functions throughout the entire process of interpersonal conflict resolution. The six commandments . . . encompass some of the most basic interpersonal obligations and prohibitions of Judaism—to love one's neighbor, the prohibition against hatred, the prohibition against physical violence, and the commandments that pertain to verbal abuse, which enjoin an individual from cursing, embarrassing, or saying hurtful things to another person. (245, p. 110)

Collectively, frameworks such as those we have just described have much to teach us. They remind us that many different cultures and religions have developed approaches to address disagreement, to facilitate debate, and to attempt to resolve conflicts peacefully through discussion. This observation is both obvious and at the same time useful, as it helps provide a broader contextual lens through which we can examine the challenges to discourse on American campuses. The fact that history is replete with examples of disputes that did *not* experience a peaceful, amicable resolution strengthens, rather than undermines, the importance of learning and practicing civil discourse.

When looking at how different groups have addressed discourse and dispute resolution, a commonly occurring theme is an emphasis on the preservation of relationships. This is tied to the recognition that the relationship between the parties can often far outlast the particular issue of contention, and that the parties therefore have a shared incentive not only to resolve that particular issue, but to do so in a way that will not poison opportunities for future engagement and collaboration. These incentives operate particularly powerfully in contexts involving disputes between people who are members of very small groups, which can be as small as members of an immediate family. But the value in preserving relationships has resonance in larger groups as well—including campuses,

preserve relationships

which, after all, are also communities in which people have years-long or even decades-long associations. And, these associations are often characterized by a need for repeated interactions, including some in which people who were on opposite sides of one issue in the past may find themselves aligned on the same side of a different issue in the future.

The frameworks we have just discussed underscore not only that disagreement is a normal feature of human interactions, but that the *ability* to disagree is crucial. Engaging constructively with the concept of disagreement and with those with whom we disagree is a skill that many cultures have sought to cultivate, and that campus communities should cultivate as well.

Against this backdrop, it is also important to note that the current environment has the very important complicating factor of social media, which can act in ways that undermine or sidestep the community-based incentives that provide such an important foundation in traditional frameworks for debate and dispute resolution. Of course, there are communities on social media as well, many of which provide an invaluable complement to and in some cases replacement for offline communities.

But, particularly in relation to call-out culture, social media communities can also be fleeting, forming and dissolving over weeks or days and digitally convening, ever so briefly, people who may never again interact with one another. With social media, people can and commonly do launch verbal fusillades against targets they have never met in the past and will never meet in the future. Attackers on social media may perceive little downside to these attacks. There is no previous relationship to preserve and no future relationship to cultivate. There is little or no pressure to engage civilly. In some cases, there may be incentives to engage uncivilly, given that more extreme positions tend to attract more attention. Another factor is that there is no investment needed to launch a social media attack; there is no need to travel anywhere or to invest significant time or energy. Physical distance is irrelevant with social media, as the target of ire can just as easily be on the other side of the world as down the street. And the gratification, coming in the form of endorsements such as likes or retweets, can come quickly, often within hours.

The removal of community-based incentives for civil discourse is one of the most challenging consequences of social media, and one with impacts not only on academia but also on the whole of society. But there are good reasons why academia should be an environment in which solutions can be developed and implemented. Academia is, after all, a place where rational discourse on all manner of topics should be routine. With that in mind, and recognizing that these are challenges to which there is no ideal solution, we offer a set of recommendations that we believe could help create a more tolerant and open campus climate.

13.2 Recommendations

In this section we present a series of recommendations that could collectively serve as a framework for faculty, staff, and students to construct more tolerant and open campus environments. We also recognize that many other groups are working to foster dialog both on and off campus, including on-campus student groups such as BridgeUSA, as well as larger-scale efforts through organizations such as Sustained Dialog, Heterodox Academy, and the Foundation for Individual Rights in Education. Our hope is that the recommendations we present in this section will complement the work of those groups, and more broadly, that they will be valuable to anyone interested in building campus environments with greater dialog, increased intellectual diversity, reduced political polarization, and increased civility.

Recommendation 1: Faculty should provide their students with the opportunity to engage with a diverse range of perspectives. Putting this recommendation into practice involves multiple challenges. The first is generic in relation to the culture regarding teaching, the second relates to the relative political homogeneity among administrators, and the third arises from the political costs that often accompany calls for increased "viewpoint diversity."

First, questions of how—and to what extent—universities should provide input into faculty teaching are complex in ways that go far beyond the issues explored in this book. Some mechanisms for providing feedback are widely accepted, such as teaching evaluations filled out by students at the end of a course and feedback from peer faculty members who attend a sample lecture being given by their colleagues.

Both of these approaches are retrospective, in that they involve considering teaching that has already occurred and generating after-the-fact feedback that can be used for improving future teaching. And, both approaches have their pros and cons. For example, student evaluations have the advantage of being able to bring information to light that might be otherwise unavailable to a university (e.g., that a professor is particularly responsive to, or particularly unresponsive to, after-class requests from students to clarify a topic addressed in class).

Peer teaching evaluations, which involve a faculty member sitting in on the lecture of a colleague, have the advantage of producing feedback by someone who has far more personal teaching experience than most students. But peer evaluations suffer from a sampling problem—they are typically based on attendance at a single session (or, if more than one, a very small number of class sessions). In addition, they can be problematic when there is a mismatch between the teaching style preferred by the evaluator and the style employed by the faculty member under evaluation. That said, the general consensus in higher education is that student and peer teaching evaluations, despite their drawbacks, are a valuable way both to gauge teaching effectiveness and to provide feedback aimed at improving future teaching.

Prospective input on teaching can be more controversial, particularly if it risks being viewed as impeding a faculty member's right to design and conduct classes without interference from administrators. Professors readily accept that the high-level *content* of a course, at least for some courses, can be dictated by the university. For example, an introductory biology class typically has a specific set of topics that anyone teaching that class must cover, as failure to do so would negatively impact students taking follow-on classes. However, faculty tend to bristle when they are told *how* to teach particular topics. As a result, administrative mandates regarding the specifics of how to teach are viewed with skepticism, and an instruction from deans or other campus administrators to bring more viewpoint diversity into college teaching would not be welcomed by many faculty members.

A second challenge is that, potential faculty objections to being told how to teach aside, it is not at all clear that administrators would be motivated to push for a more diverse range of perspectives in the classroom. In the October 2018 op-ed in the *New York Times* (105) discussed previously in the chapter on tenure, Sarah Lawrence College politics professor Samuel J. Abrams described surveying "a nationally representative sample of roughly 900 'student-facing' administrators." Abrams found that "the 12-to-one ratio of liberal to conservative college administrators makes them the most left-leaning group on campus," and concluded that "a *fairly* liberal student body is being taught by a *very* liberal professoriate—and socialized by an *incredibly* liberal group of administrators" (105).

To be clear, the relative lack of diversity among the political views of administrators doesn't lead inescapably to the conclusion that they don't see value in political diversity in the classroom. But it certainly suggests that there are few institutional pressures to counter a political monoculture, particularly when that monoculture is strongly present among the very administrators whose support would be essential to an effort to bring more viewpoint diversity into classrooms.

The third challenge to implementing this recommendation is that for many people in the academic ecosystem, there is no political gain associated with arguing for more viewpoint diversity in the classroom. In fact, there is more likely a political cost. An administrator who argues for the inclusion in classes of perspectives that his or her peers disagree with will not be optimizing future career advancement opportunities. In addition, the dialog on viewpoint diversity is often completely lacking in nuance, making it hard to have a rational conversation about bringing more of it into classes. A faculty member who proposes increased viewpoint diversity in courses might be accused of wanting to bring "hate speech" into the classroom.

In any reasonably objective sense, that would be a false accusation. But given the current climate on campus in which there is a tendency to assert that almost any disagreeable opinion violates one or more campus policies, the objection would undoubtedly arise. Consider a faculty member who believes, for example, that to present arguments against the recently enacted California law placing quotas on the minimum number of female board members for publicly held, California-based companies is tantamount to an endorsement of sexism. Such a person might see no problem at all with concluding that a classroom discussion should only consider one side of the issue—that is, a position that the California law is necessary and good, and that no reasonable person could argue otherwise.

Thus, this recommendation raises the question of where the impetus to broaden teaching will come from. There may be some campuses where the president or other top administrators take the initiative to build a campus culture that seeks to engage with diverse views. On campuses where the high-level administrators are indifferent to or hostile to viewpoint diversity, impetus can come from lower in the management hierarchy. Department heads who value diverse perspectives can encourage the faculty in the units they oversee to keep that in mind in their teaching. In addition, individual faculty are well positioned to engage on this issue on their own, as they are the ones in direct contact with students in their classes. Professors who want to bring a more diverse set of perspectives into their classes don't have to ask anyone; they can just take the initiative to do it directly through their own teaching.

Finally, students also have a role to play. Through teaching evaluations, students can and should provide positive feedback to instructors who work to bring viewpoint diversity to their classes, and they should also note when classes are taught in a way that only promotes the instructor's personal views.

It is also important to recognize that while no subject is completely free from sociopolitical questions, some (e.g., history or English literature) are far more intertwined with such questions than others (e.g., math or physics). This is not to say that these questions never arise in math or physics, but that they arise less frequently, and are less central to the decision regarding what material to cover and how to cover it. A calculus instructor teaches subject matter that is far less laden with sociopolitical overtones than a literature instructor.

Instructors of courses in which teaching inevitably involves sociopolitical choices—for example, of which readings to assign in a literature class, or of how to present a lecture on complex sociopolitical issues such as immigration, affirmative action, or education policy—should make explicit efforts to include a diverse range of viewpoints. Thus, under this model, an economics instructor who believes that capitalism has failed and that socialism should replace it would nonetheless include in his or her course some readings by authors extolling the benefits of capitalism and would discuss them in a way that isn't dismissive. This can be particularly challenging because it asks the instructor to present materials arguing positions he or she might not agree with. But that is far preferable to denying students the opportunity to engage with a broad range of perspectives.

We also note that there is an irony in even needing to call for increased viewpoint diversity in college teaching. Colleges are supposed to be places of ideas and free inquiry, where students are given the tools to engage with multiple perspectives and to form their own opinions based on a complex set of sometimes competing arguments.

We can offer some additional perspectives on teaching viewpoint diversity based on the experience of one of us (Redstone) creating and teaching two unique courses at the University of Illinois. One, titled *Bigots and Snowflakes: Living in a World Where Everyone Else Is Wrong* (and discussed earlier in this book), was devoted to the topic of viewpoint diversity on campus. The other was a more conventional *Social Problems* course— part of the sociology curriculum at many universities—but, in contrast to presenting the material from a largely singular viewpoint, it was taught from a wide range of political perspectives. Between the two courses, there were opportunities to have a series of open discussions about the nature of some of the challenges facing academia and society more broadly, as well as their causes and possible solutions.

Topics covered over the course of the semester included conceptions of masculinity, social media in news dissemination, white privilege, assimilation, immigration, definitions of racism, dead-naming, the relationship between the relationship between sex assigned at birth and gender identity, marijuana legalization, the opioid epidemic, politics in the classroom, definitions of anti-Semitism, policing and minority communities, sexual harassment, policies on the use of race in school admissions, and the persistence of segregation in K-12 schools. All of these topics were taught in a highly interactive manner, and in an environment that encouraged the respectful voicing of a diverse range of social and political perspectives. The resulting classroom discussions provided a far greater range of views on these topics than is encountered in many college courses.

The *Bigots and Snowflakes* course presented valuable lessons on teaching diverse perspectives, though it is in a sense anomalous because it is a course designed from the ground up specifically with that goal in mind. On the one hand, the course was successful in that students learned to engage with a broad range of perspectives. However, the fact that the course was needed in the first place reflects a broader failure of campus culture more generally—by no means unique to the University of Illinois—to sufficiently address viewpoint diversity in instruction. More fundamentally, we certainly would not define success through the introduction of courses designed to teach viewpoint diversity. Success will occur when college instructors consider it part of their jobs to teach multiple perspectives, including ones that don't necessarily align with their own. This is by far the best way to put students in a strong position to engage with the most complex and pressing sociopolitical issues confronting society.

Recommendation 2: People with positions of authority in universities— a group that includes faculty, department chairs, deans, university executives, and student-facing administrators—should give greater thought to how their own communications might inadvertently narrow the range of dialog deemed permissible. As in any other large organization, people in universities often issue official communications to people who are below them in the hierarchy. Professors send e-mails to the students in their classes; department chairs and deans communicate with the faculty members in their respective departments and schools; and university presidents and provosts send communications to the entire campus community. Perhaps more than is often realized, these communications contain explicit and implicit messaging that shapes campus expectations about the scope of permissible discourse. When a campus authority figure weighs in on one side of a contentious current social or political issue, this inevitably alters the dialog by attaching a negative valence to the unsupported opinion. People who agree with the authority figure will be emboldened to speak out, while those who disagree perceive a social penalty for doing so and will be incentivized to stay quiet.

Two solutions can mitigate this. First, in some cases it may be advisable for the authority figure to adopt a more neutral tone—explaining, for example, that the issue at hand is contentious, and urging respectful debate. If the authority figure believes it is best to offer a personal opinion in support of one side of the issue, he or she should also include a statement recognizing that reasonable people can disagree, and that such disagreement is exactly what is to be expected in a vibrant intellectual community.

In making this recommendation, we emphasize that it applies to situations in which there is a reasonable debate to be had. Not all situations fall in that category. If there has been an incident of racist graffiti at a university, the university president can and should issue a statement of condemnation, full stop. There is no legitimate debate on whether such graffiti is acceptable. But many of the contentious issues that lead to communications from campus authority figures do not fall into this category; rather, they pertain to issues on which reasonable people can hold divergent views.

Just as importantly, campus leaders can actively impede viewpoint diversity by what they chose *not* to say. When campus leaders fail to quickly and unequivocally come to the defense of professors who are targeted by calls for dismissal based on something they have written or said that should clearly fall within the protections of academic freedom, the resulting chilling effect narrows tolerance for viewpoint diversity, both on-campus and—if the incident has garnered broader visibility—beyond. This chills dialog, making it less likely that people with views deemed outside the academic mainstream will express them.

Recommendation 3: Avoid mandating viewpoint diversity. One of our concerns with the current campus environment is the extent to which the laudable goal of improving diversity in regards to areas such as race and gender is being achieved through a lengthening list of mandatory activities that theoretically will further that goal, but may not do so in practice. One example of this is the mandatory written diversity statements we discussed earlier that some colleges are now requiring from people who are applying to faculty positions and/or already-hired faculty who are going through the internal promotion process.

We are not convinced that faculty who are compelled to write accounts describing their contributions to diversity will, as a consequence, believe more strongly in it or take more actions to foster it. Thus, for analogous reasons, we recommend avoiding any sort of compulsory actions in relation to improving viewpoint diversity. We would oppose requiring faculty to prove that they have introduced more viewpoint diversity into their courses, and we would oppose any sort of hiring quota that would mandate that a department have on their faculty at least a certain number of people who hold views that are sociopolitically distinct from those that are dominant in their department or on their campus.

In addition, attempting to mandate viewpoint diversity treats the symptom and not the problem. The problem is a narrowing of discourse stemming from the three beliefs we have discussed in this book. Administrative mandates in relation to viewpoint diversity would likely have the unintended consequence of increasing faculty skepticism on this issue, and would therefore be counterproductive. *humility*

Recommendation 4: Faculty and other members of campus communities should recognize the role of humility in promoting productive discourse and a diverse range of perspectives. Most tenured faculty members have earned the highest possible graduate degrees in their fields of study. They have been hired into their positions from among an extraordinarily large and qualified pool of applicants. In their research, they are often recognized nationally and internationally for advancing the state of knowledge itself. Many of them have spent their entire lives being told that they are highly intelligent. In their teaching, they are accustomed to spending untold hours as authority figures, standing in front of classrooms full of people who pay high tuition bills in order to learn from them.

These factors do not engender humility. While there are exceptions, the same can be said for administrators, many of whom are faculty members who as they rose up through the ranks obtained positions of increasing managerial authority.

Unsurprisingly, assistant professors and adjunct instructors—likely due in part to their more tenuous job security—often have more humility than tenured faculty members. And, all else being equal, that humility helps make them better teachers. This is yet another reason why the low compensation rates paid to adjunct faculty are shameful.

In short, while there are plenty of exceptions, there is a lot of arrogance on university faculties. Some of the consequences are relatively harmless. For example, intra-campus squabbles over resources such as space can become pretty contentious due to the egos involved. But the lack of humility among faculty has another more problematic consequence: a greater tendency to dismiss opposing points of view, accompanied by a lower willingness to entertain the prospect that their own views may be wrong.

We are not suggesting that all faculty members (or administrators) fit this mold. There are professors who are humble, and who gladly entertain multiple points of view (and who almost never squabble in faculty meetings!). But, as a group, faculty members tend to have less humility than people in the general population.

While faculty represent only a small part of a university community's population in percentage terms, their influence far outweighs their numbers. Faculty exert control over hiring of new tenure-track faculty and of adjunct instructors, faculty directly or indirectly help determine a college's admissions policies, and they play a key role in programmatic decisions. Decisions to create a new department, major, or interdisciplinary program do not generally happen without the blessing of the faculty. Faculty are certainly not the only constituency that influences the culture of a college—after all, in some respects students are far more influential, as they should be given that they are the primary reason that a college exists—but they exert an extremely strong influence in the classroom in terms of what, by whom, and how material is taught. The advice that it is good to remember that none of us has a monopoly on truth is valuable for everyone, and particularly so for college faculty.

What does this mean in practice? For starters, department chairs, deans, and others who help set the culture for their faculty can emphasize the value of acknowledging that there are multiple views that one might reasonably hold on complex issues. Part of that process also likely entails a greater recognition among faculty that some strongly held opinions are based on a set of assumptions and beliefs that not everyone shares. It would not be an overstatement to say that intellectual humility is what makes real dialog and real learning possible, and thus that humility is one of the most important ingredients of a thriving academic culture.

While our call for greater humility is particularly relevant to faculty given the key role they play in setting the tone for discourse in the classroom, and by extension on campus more broadly, it is also relevant to everyone in the campus community. Humility doesn't necessarily mean a lack of conviction, or an inability to make and stand by arguments, or a need to downplay expertise acquired over years of experience. But it does require a certain openness of thought and a recognition of the limits of one's own knowledge. The value of humility in all manner of contexts is illustrated by considering it has arrogance as an antonym—a trait that few people would call admirable, and one that certainly isn't conducive to either learning or to productive discourse.

Campuses are supposed to be places of intellectual growth. And they are places where *everyone* learns—not only students, but also faculty, administrators, and staff members, all of whom share the privilege of spending time in a place dedicated to the advancement of knowledge and to the skills facilitating that advancement. People learn best when they are aware that there are things that they do not know, or could know better, and that there is value in hearing and giving thoughtful consideration to perspectives other than their own.

Recommendation 5: Administrators and those in positions of authority should avoid allowing online mobs to shape decisions. A university culture that gives administrators more confidence to resist social media–driven calls for censorship will be one that is more open, expansive, and conducive to free inquiry. For college administrators, standing up to a social media mob demanding punishment of a faculty member who has published research or engaged in expression deemed transgressive is challenging. This is particularly the case for administrators who have personal views that align with those expressed by the people who are protesting via social media. An additional complication is that social media mobs often make what amount to demands of administrators (e.g., to censure, or fire, or not rehire a particular instructor), and administrators then face the choice of either acceding to the demands and placating the mob, or refusing to do so and becoming the target of its ire. In such circumstances, the path of least resistance for administrators is to do what the social media mob demands.

But if colleges are going to take back the seat at the table that Twitter and other social media have claimed in policing campus discourse, more fortitude by administrators in relation to resisting social media–driven censorship pressures is imperative. The best way to promote this fortitude is from the top.

Consider the April 2019 example of University of the Arts president David Yager's response to protestors demanding the firing of Camille Paglia. Paglia, a tenured professor of humanities and media studies, was viewed by some as transgressive because of her comments on the #MeToo movement and transgender issues. But one doesn't need to agree with Paglia's comments to support her right to make them. In a response to the campus community that is a good example of how high-level administrators can support academic freedom, Yager wrote the following:

> Unfortunately, as a society we are living in a time of sharp divisions—of opinions, perspectives and beliefs—and that has led to decreased civility, increased anger and a "new normal" of offense given and taken. Across our nation it is all too common that opinions expressed that differ from another's—especially those that are controversial—can spark passion and even outrage, often resulting in calls to suppress that speech.
>
> That simply cannot be allowed to happen. I firmly believe that limiting the range of voices in society erodes our democracy. Universities, moreover, are at the heart of the revolutionary notion of free expression: promoting the free exchange of ideas is part of the core reason for their existence. That open interchange of opinions and beliefs includes all members of the UArts community: faculty, students and staff, in and out of the classroom. We are dedicated to fostering a climate conducive to respectful intellectual debate that empowers and equips our students to meet the challenges they will face in their futures. (246)

In colleges where the top leaders are staunch defenders of academic freedom, even if doing so makes them unpopular in certain corners of the campus or the social media world, academic deans and department chairs will be more likely to adopt a similar culture of promoting and defending academic freedom. And, conversely, when the top leaders of a college fail to defend academic freedom, that culture will propagate throughout the college as well.

Although David Yager is a university president, one does not need to have such a high position to take a stand against online mobs. This is a stand that could and should be taken by administrators at all levels in the university.

Recommendation 6: People on campuses should personalize connections with people with whom they disagree. Hostility thrives when we dehumanize one another. It's much more difficult to feel animosity or hostility to those who think differently when they are seen as people facing their own challenges and having their own vulnerabilities. Earlier, we discussed the role that social media can play in impeding exactly such an environment. Another way to contextualize this is by considering the contact hypothesis proposed in the mid- 20th century by Harvard psychologist Gordon Allport.

Allport's original hypothesis was that contact between two groups can promote tolerance and acceptance, but only when the groups have equal status and shared goals (247). However, while these conditions were once considered necessary for the positive effects of intergroup contact, more recent research has shown beneficial effects of contact in a broader set of circumstances. In their 2006 meta-analysis using "713 independent samples from 515 studies," UC Santa Cruz psychology professor Thomas Pettigrew and Boston College psychology professor Linda Tropp wrote:

> Allport's conditions are not essential for intergroup contact to achieve positive outcomes. In particular, we found that samples with no claim to these key conditions still show significant relationships between contact and prejudice. Thus, Allport's conditions should not be regarded as necessary for producing positive contact outcomes, as researchers have often assumed in the past. Rather, they act as facilitating conditions that enhance the tendency for positive contact outcomes to emerge. (248, p. 766)

As Pettigrew and Tropp have shown, more recent research building on Allport's work suggests that contact on its own, even in the absence of the other stipulations, can be sufficient to promote tolerance and acceptance, although the effect may be more positive if the other criteria are met (248, 249). Collectively, it appears that contact with a range of viewpoints that differ from one's own can have beneficial effects in a wide range of circumstances.

Applying this to the campus setting, more opportunities should be created for all community members to engage with people who think differently from them. On most campuses, one can find students, faculty, staff, and administrators who do not necessarily hold views aligning in every way with the dominant on-campus worldview. Yet, many of them choose to remain silent out of fear of the criticism that they would receive if they were to speak out. In creating an environment in which they too are comfortable sharing their perspectives and their views, the humanization process to which Allport refers can begin to flourish.

Recommendation 7: People in academia should be more willing to tolerate uncomfortable opinions. Sometimes one has to be willing to hear opinions that might be difficult or to have a contentious conversation. And there's simply no way that's going to happen when the *de facto* rules for discourse are centered around the requirement to avoid saying anything that anyone might deem uncomfortable or offensive.

Scholarly evidence points to the importance of discomfort in dialog as well. In his 1984 article "Dynamic Disequilibrium: The Intelligence of Growth," University of Oregon education professor Bruce Joyce wrote:

> If the environment is too comfortable or "reliable" the learners may be satisfied at the stage of concrete thinking where the ability to integrate new information and form new conceptual systems is limited indeed. To impel learners to diverge from the familiar sets of concepts that enable them to view the world in "blacks and whites," the environment must be dissatisfying in some ways. (250, p. 27)

Going to even earlier work, in his 1960 book "Education and the Human Quest" (251), University of Chicago education professor Herbert Thelen discussed the importance of conflict in life generally and in education specifically:

> It is unfortunate that the word *conflict* has become a dirty word, for our emotional reactions to the term blind us to the fact that without conflict neither growth nor education would be possible. In our Organization-Man society we tend to assume that conflict is all bad and destructive, not realizing that it is ridiculous to think of a universal fact as anything but a universal fact. It is true that we may deal with conflict in ways that are stultifying and destructive; but we may also deal with conflict in ways that lead to individual enlightenment and social cohesion. Man has both capabilities, and the task of education is to enable man to develop the constructive capability to the full. (251, as reproduced in part in 252, p. 145, emphasis in original)

According to Thelen, one of the ways of dealing with is through "inquiry." He wrote:

> [Inquiry] is the way of insight, of learning, of consciousness of methods, of diagnosis, speculation, hypothesis-testing. This capability probably began with the use of tools, which required the ability to distinguish between self

and object, organism and environment, cause and effect. Such distinctions require consciousness, language, and the ability to learn from one's own and others' experiences. This way tries to deal with stress through reflection on the situation, which includes oneself as actor. It involves discipline and the ability to curb tendencies to act out, the ability to live with tension and challenge long enough to formulate a plan. (252, p. 146)

The last part of Thelen's sentence, "live with tension and challenge long enough to formulate a plan," is particularly worthy of emphasis. Learning to live with discomfort long enough to come up with a plan or a solution is a skill that can be learned and exercised just like any other.

With these teachings in mind, we emphasize the value of creating a classroom and broader campus environment that asks students to think outside of their comfort zones. The goal, of course, is not provocation for its own sake. Rather, the goal is to build an on-campus culture that recognizes that when discourse is circumscribed by prohibitions on the expression of any ideas that any party to the exchange finds uncomfortable, the ability to engage in inquiry suffers. We also emphasize that an increased willingness to engage with uncomfortable perspectives in no way implies any sort of commitment to agree with or endorse them. Rather, the commitment is merely to listen, to give thought to a view of the world as seen from a very different perspective, and to reflect upon one's own opinions accordingly.

Recommendation 8: Expand formal institutional definitions of "diversity" to include viewpoint diversity. Given the enormous financial, programmatic, bureaucratic, employment, and other investments that universities are making to address diversity and inclusion, it is ironic that diversity definitions are not particularly inclusive. The University of California's formal diversity definition (253), which applies across all of the UC campuses, provides an illustrative example. According to a formal policy adopted by the governing body of UC, diversity is:

the variety of personal experiences, values, and worldviews that arise from differences of culture and circumstance. Such differences include race, ethnicity, gender, age, religion, language, abilities/disabilities, sexual orientation, gender identity, socioeconomic status, and geographic region, and more. (253)

With respect to viewpoint diversity, this definition is notably deficient. It cites "worldviews that arise from differences of culture and circumstance," suggesting a characterization that omits viewpoint differences arising among people who hail from *similar* cultures and circumstances. Yet differences of worldviews *within* cultures and circumstances are abundant, as anyone who has tried to talk politics at Thanksgiving dinner can confirm. Moreover, in enumerating the usual list of attributes associated with diversity (race, ethnicity, gender, etc.), the UC definition promotes the idea that those attributes alone are the primary drivers of "personal experiences, values, and worldviews."

Of course, some people do indeed identify most strongly with affinity groups that fall into one of these enumerated categories. For instance, it is perfectly reasonable for someone to consider their race (or gender, or one of the other categories listed in the UC definition) as the central attribute shaping their worldview. But it is also perfectly reasonable to have a world-view that is *not* primarily shaped by one of the UC-approved categories.

There are many people for whom different types of affinity groups, or none at all, might form the most strongly felt underpinnings of their identity and be the strongest drivers of their worldviews. The list of categories that can serve as foundations of identity is essentially endless: immigrants, math prodigies, cancer survivors, introverts, lovers of literature, veterans, and so on. The point is not to suggest that these are mutually exclusive. A Latino immigrant who is also a math prodigy can claim affinity to all three of those groups—that is, to being Latino, an immigrant, and a math prodigy.

And that is precisely one of the key problems with the UC diversity definition, as well as with the many other similarly worded diversity definitions that enumerate similar identity group categories: These definitions pay insufficient heed to the fact that every one of us embodies a complex mix of simultaneous identities. That extraordinary multidimensionality—with the enormous number of combinations and permutations of multilayered identities that result—is the foundation of true diversity. The UC definition risks flattening this multidimensional space, stripping it of texture and pushing us to see the world through the lens of the particular subset of enumerated categories.

And what of the counterargument that, given both history and the current societal context, there is an imperative to elevate awareness of attributes like race, religion, gender, sexual orientation, etc., in diversity definitions? After all, it is certainly the case that unimaginable harms have occurred because of oppression based on these very categories. Many of the ills in contemporary American society can be directly or indirectly tied to prejudices related to the categories listed in the UC definition.

That counterargument has a lot of merit. The best way to respect that counterargument is to retain the list of currently enumerated categories while also amending the text elsewhere to convey that it is not limiting. Thus, a more encompassing UC definition of diversity would be (with new text shown in italics):

> the variety of personal experiences, values, and *social and political* worldviews, *including but not limited to those* that arise from differences of culture and circumstance. Such differences include race, ethnicity, gender, age, religion, language, abilities/disabilities, sexual orientation, gender identity, socioeconomic status, and geographic region, and more.

The modifications introduced above accomplish several goals. First, inserting "social and political" before "worldviews" provides explicit acknowledgement of the differences in perspectives that can exist along those two different axes. In addition, this change indicates institutional recognition that a campus community benefits when there is variety in these dimensions. Notably, this provides a counterweight to the on-campus pressures to form a political and social monoculture. Second, adding "including but not limited to" makes clear that variations in worldviews can be, but are not necessarily, tied to differences of culture and circumstance. While the list of categories remains unchanged, the use of "not limited to," even though it is in the sentence preceding the enumerated list, helps make the overall definition more expansive.

While the changes discussed above are customized to the specific language used by UC, the diversity definitions used by other universities can be improved using analogous approaches. For example, consider the University of Illinois' Diversity Values Statement, which refers to the:

> diversity of worldviews, histories, and cultural knowledge across a range of social groups including race, ethnicity, gender identity, sexual orientation, abilities, economic class, religion, and their intersections. (254)

As did the UC definition, the Illinois definition calls out specific "social groups" and implies a tie between those groups and "worldviews." In this respect, it is open to critiques similar to those we raised in relation to the UC definition. An improved definition would be (with new text in italics):

> diversity of *social and political* worldviews, histories, and cultural knowledge across a range of social groups *including but not limited to* race, ethnicity, gender identity, sexual orientation, abilities, economic class, religion, and their intersections.

Why does any of this matter? First, contributions to diversity have become a formal consideration in hiring and promotion through incentives to (and sometimes requirements placed on) faculty members to submit documentation identifying their contributions to diversity. A more inclusive and expansive definition of diversity will provide a greater range of opportunities to contribute to its improvement. Second, broader definitions of (and understandings of) diversity can help disrupt the feedback loop that has contributed to creating an on-campus environment in which identity politics sometimes swamps all else. Unsurprisingly, diversity definitions crafted in such an environment tend to give primacy to the same set of identity categories that dominate on-campus discourse. By contrast, the definitional changes suggested here, if adopted, would help to indicate that these categories are contributors to, but not necessarily determinants of, worldviews.

A third reason why diversity definitions matter is that diversity is often addressed hand in hand with inclusion. This illustrates yet another irony of the current on-campus environment: Despite the proliferation of university websites, programs, and faculty-authored documents that make liberal use of words like "inclusion" and "inclusive," campuses are not particularly inclusive for those who hold views that are out of step with the on-campus mainstream. Campuses at which the climate supports a broader view of diversity will be truly more inclusive environments.

14

Conclusion

We've made the case that the academic enterprise is limited by a set of three beliefs. The first is that anything that aims to undermine traditional power structures or frameworks is automatically deemed good and therefore not subject to truly objective evaluation; the second is that discrimination is the sole cause of all unequal group outcomes; and third is that everything must be viewed through the lens of identity. These beliefs are held in place in part through a social media culture that operates directly through call-out campaigns, outrage, and public shaming in response to perceived transgressions. Social media operate indirectly as well, by creating incentives not to risk taking any position, publishing any research, or making any statement that runs counter to any of these beliefs. We've described how these factors combine to limit the research that gets done, the courses that are taught, and how academic institutions are run.

Why is this so important? One answer lies in the unique position that higher education holds in society. As the authors of a 2008 paper in the *Annual Review of Sociology* wrote, "as the organizational instantiation of intellectual progress, the university is the secular temple of modern societies" (208, p. 134). In addition to serving as centers for knowledge production, universities shoulder the responsibility of educating leaders, innovators, and much of the professional workforce of the future. What occurs on campus reaches far beyond its borders, and often garners the attention of a much broader audience.

As such, a spotlight is placed upon academia's successes, its failures, its controversies, and the environment in which they all unfold. Moreover, due to communications technology advances in recent decades, the spread of information and the reach of social media mean that people outside of the academic community are able to view, evaluate, and weigh in on what happens inside academia in a way that would previously have been impractical. In many respects, these changes are beneficial. For example, to the extent that the modern communications environment has lowered the barriers to information flow to and from academia, the work in academia becomes that much

Unassailable Ideas. Ilana Redstone and John Villasenor, Oxford University Press (2020). © Oxford University Press.
DOI: 10.1093/oso/9780190078065.001.0001.

more accessible to broader society. But not all of the change is positive. As we have discussed, when academic researchers, teachers, and administrators come under pressure to comply with the most censorious and judgmental voices in the social media ecosystem—or when those researchers, teachers, and administrators themselves amplify the same restrictive views—free inquiry and discourse suffer.

As we've also pointed out in this book, much of what is of concern in the current academic climate could be ameliorated with a broader recognition of the value of debate, dissent, and consideration of divergent viewpoints. The ability to have engaged, thoughtful conversations on issues where divergence—and sometimes strident divergence—exists is critical for a functional society. Of necessity, this will sometimes mean exposure to views that we find lacking, shortsighted, misinformed, and at times offensive. As uncomfortable as that might sometimes make us, the alternative—to censor all views, all research, and all approaches to classroom teaching that risk creating discomfort—is much worse.

If America's colleges cease to be places of free inquiry, American society will become less open and less innovative and will provide fewer opportunities. We write this with full knowledge that historically, and to a significant extent today, American opportunities have not been open to all. We do not believe that the important continued work of creating a more open and equitable society needs to come at the cost of restricting free inquiry at colleges. In fact, it's more likely that the opposite is true: that progress toward greater equity in American society will be enhanced if American higher education promotes a culture that elevates inquiry and discourse.

One thing that history very clearly teaches us is that in no era has American society had all the right answers. With that lesson in mind, it would be myopic to assume that anyone today—including anyone on college campuses—has all the right answers to today's many complex sociopolitical questions. If we are going to move toward those answers, colleges need to be places where people are free to think outside the box, question assumptions, and propose new ways of seeing, analyzing, and engaging with some of the most pressing challenges facing society. Inevitably, that process will be imperfect and messy. And, inevitably, it will sometimes lead to collisions with the dominant orthodoxy of the moment. Those collisions may at times be uncomfortable, but an academy and a society structured to permit them to occur will in the long run be freer, more prosperous, and more open.

References

1. University of Illinois. *Campus Commitment Statements*. Last updated August 31, 2018. Available at *http://inclusiveillinois.illinois.edu/commitment.html*. Accessed February 8, 2020.
2. Villasenor J, Akresh IR. *3 Ways That Colleges Suppress a Diversity of Viewpoints*. 2018. Chronicle of Higher Education. Last updated September 28, 2018. Available at *https://www.chronicle.com/article/3-Ways-That-Colleges-Suppress/244673*. Accessed February 8, 2020.
3. National Center for Education Statistics. *Number of degree-granting postsecondary institutions and enrollment in these institutions, by enrollment size, control, and classification of institution*. Fall 2017. National Center for Education Statistics. Available at *https://nces.ed.gov/programs/digest/d18/tables/dt18_317.40.asp*. Accessed February 8, 2020.
4. American Association for University Professors. The Annual Report on the Economic Status of the Profession, 2017–2018. *Academe*. March–April 2018.
5. National Center for Science and Engineering Statistics. *Federal Science and Engineering Obligations to Academic Institutions Increase 2%; Support to HBCUs Declines 17%*. NCSES; 2019.
6. Lukianoff G, Haidt J. *The Coddling of the American Mind*. Penguin Press; 2018.
7. Furedi F. *What's Happened to the University?* Routledge; 2017.
8. Ben-Porath SR. *Free Speech on Campus*. University of Pennsylvania Press; 2017.
9. Wittington KE. *Speak Freely: Why Universities Must Defend Free Speech*. Princeton University Press; 2018.
10. Zimmerman J. *Campus Politics: What Everyone Needs to Know*. Oxford University Press; 2016.
11. Bloom A. *The Closing of the American Mind*. Simon & Schuster; 1987.
12. MacDonald H. *The Diversity Delusion: How Race and Gender Pandering Corrupt the University and Undermine Our Culture*. St. Martin's Press; 2018.
13. Kimball R. *Tenured Radicals: How Politics Has Corrupted Our Higher Education*. Harper & Rowe; 1990.
14. Campbell B, Manning J. *The Rise of Victimhood Culture: Microaggressions, Safe Spaces, and the New Culture Wars*. Palgrave Macmillan; 2018.
15. Friedersdorf C. *The Most Common Error in Media Coverage of the Google Memo*. 2017. The Atlantic. Last updated August 8, 2017. Available at *https://www.theatlantic.com/politics/archive/2017/08/the-most-common-error-in-coverage-of-the-google-memo/536181/*. Accessed February 8, 2020.
16. Obama B. *Barack Obama's Keynote Address at the 2004 Democratic National Convention*. 2004. PBS News Hour. Last updated July 27, 2004. Available at *https://www.pbs.org/newshour/show/barack-obamas-keynote-address-at-the-2004-democratic-national-convention*. Accessed February 8, 2020.
17. Fukuyama F. *Against Identity Politics*. 2018. Foreign Affairs. Last updated September/October 2018. Available at *https://www.foreignaffairs.com/articles/americas/2018-08-14/against-identity-politics-tribalism-francis-fukuyama*. Accessed February 8, 2020.

18. Sowell T. *A Conflict of Visions*. William Morrow and Company; 1987.

19. McArdle M. *Why the New Yorker's concerns about normalizing Steve Bannon miss the point*. 2018. The Washington Post. Last updated September 4, 2018. Available at *https://www.washingtonpost.com/opinions/why-the-new-yorkers-concerns-about-normalizing-steve-bannon-miss-the-point/2018/09/04/d7149932-b085-11e8-9a6a-565d92a3585d_story.html*. Accessed February 8, 2020.

20. Deb S, Peters JW. *New Yorker Festival Pulls Steve Bannon as Headliner Following High-Profile Dropouts*. 2018. New York Times. Last updated September 3, 2018. Available at *https://www.nytimes.com/2018/09/03/arts/bannon-new-yorker-festival-remnick.html*. Accessed February 8, 2020.

21. Kay G. *University sued over constitutionality of Bias Response Team*. 2018. Michigan Daily. Last updated May 8, 2018. Available at *https://www.michigandaily.com/section/news-briefs/university-sued-over-constitutionality-bias-response-team*. Accessed February 8, 2020.

22. University of Chicago. *https://college.uchicago.edu/student-life/aims-education*. Accessed February 8, 2020.

23. Shweder R. Fundamentalism for Highbrows: The Aims of Education Address at the University of Chicago. *Academe*. 1994;80(6):13–21.

24. *The Berkeley Riots*. 1964. Harvard Crimson. Last updated December 9, 1964. Available at *https://www.thecrimson.com/article/1964/12/9/the-berkeley-riots-preports-in-the/*. Accessed February 8, 2020.

25. Dean A. *"Lived Experience Matters"—But Not More Than Everything Else*. 2016. Prospect. Last updated August 17, 2016. Available at *https://www.prospectmagazine.co.uk/politics/lived-experience-matters-but-not-more-than-everything-else*. Accessed February 8, 2020.

26. Merriam-Webster. *Definition of microaggression*. Available at *https://www.merriam-webster.com/dictionary/microaggression*. Accessed February 8, 2020.

27. Merriam-Webster. *Definition of trigger warning*. Available at *https://www.merriam-webster.com/dictionary/trigger%20warning*. Accessed February 8, 2020.

28. Singal J. *Colleges Are Defining 'Microaggressions' Really Broadly*. 2016. New York Magazine. Last updated September 8, 2016. Available at *http://nymag.com/intelligencer/2016/09/colleges-are-defining-microaggressions-really-broadly.html*. Accessed February 8, 2020.

29. Seltzer S. *Teaching Trigger Warnings: What Pundits Don't Understand About the Year's Most Controversial Higher-Ed Debate*. 2015. Flavorwire. Last updated May 27, 2015. Available at *http://flavorwire.com/520346/teaching-trigger-warnings-what-pundits-dont-understand-about-the-years-most-controversial-higher-ed-debate*. Accessed February 8, 2020.

30. Filipovic J. *We've Gone Too Far with 'Trigger Warnings'*. 2014. The Guardian. Last updated March 5, 2014. Available at *https://www.theguardian.com/commentisfree/2014/mar/05/trigger-warnings-can-be-counterproductive*. Accessed February 8, 2020.

31. University of California Office of the President. *Tool: Recognizing Microaggressions and the Messages They Send*. 2014. Available at *https://web.archive.org/web/20150615153008/https://www.ucop.edu/academic-personnel-programs/_files/seminars/Tool_Recognizing_Microaggressions.pdf*. Accessed February 8, 2020.

32. Experian Marketing Services' Simmons Connect. *Average Number of Texts Sent and Received per Month, by Age*. 2013. Marketing charts last updated March 20, 2013. Available at *https://www.marketingcharts.com/industries/telecom-industries-27993/*

attachment/experian-text-message-activity-by-age-mar2013.   Accessed   February 8, 2020.

33. Burke K. *How Many Texts Do People Send Every Day?* 2016. Text Request. Last updated May 18, 2016: Available at *https://www.textrequest.com/blog/how-many-texts-people-send-per-day/* Accessed February 8, 2020.

34. @TwitterIR. *Q4 and Fiscal Year 2018 Letter to Shareholders.* 2019. Twitter. Last updated February 7, 2019: Available at *https://s22.q4cdn.com/826641620/files/doc_financials/2018/q4/Q4-2018-Shareholder-Letter.pdf.* Accessed February 8, 2020.

35. Research ZE. *Snap (SNAP) Q1 Earnings and Revenues Surpass Estimates.* 2019. Yahoo! Finance. Last updated April 24, 2019. Available at *https://finance.yahoo.com/news/snap-snap-q1-earnings-revenues-160304797.html.* Accessed February 8, 2020.

36. Hootsuite. *The Global State of Digital in 2019 Report.* 2019. Available at *https://hootsuite.com/pages/digital-in-2019#accordion-115547.* Accessed February 8, 2020.

37. Hootsuite. *Digital 2019: The United States of America.* 2019. Available at *https://hootsuite.com/pages/digital-in-2019#accordion-115547.* Accessed February 8, 2020.

38. Mehrabian A. *Silent Messages: Implicit Communication of Emotions and Attitudes.* Wadsworth Publishing Company; 1972.

39. Mehrabian A, Ferris SR. Inference of Attitudes from Nonverbal Communication in Two Channels. *Journal of Consulting Psychology.* 1967;31(3):248–252.

40. Mehrabian A, Wiener M. Decoding of Inconsistent Communications. *Journal of Personality and Social Psychology.* 1967;6(2):109–114.

41. Lapakko D. Communication is 93% Nonverbal: An Urban Legend Proliferates. *Communication and Theater Association of Minnesota Journal.* 2007;34:7–12. Note: citing Lapakko D. Three Cheers for Language: A Closer Examination of a Widely Cited Study of Nonverbal Communication. *Communication Education.* 1997;46(1):63–67 at p. 65.

42. Forbes RJ, Jackson PR. Non-Verbal Behaviour and the Outcome of Selection Interviews. *Occupational and Organizational Psychology.* 1980;53(1):65–72.

43. Zeki CP. The Importance of Non-Verbal Communication in Classroom Management. *Procedia—Social and Behavioral Sciences.* 2009;1(1):1443–1449.

44. Turkle S. *Reclaiming Conversation: The Power of Talk in a Digital Age.* Penguin Books; 2015.

45. Boatwright RG, Shaffer TJ, Sobieraj S, Young DG, eds. *A Crisis of Civility? Political Discourse and Its Discontents.* Routledge; 2019.

46. Carr N. *The Shallows: What the Internet Is Doing to Our Brains.* W.W. Norton and Company; 2011.

47. Turkle S. *Alone Together: Why We Expect More from Technology and Less from Each Other.* Basic Books; 2011.

48. Haynes T. *Dopamine, Smartphones & You: A Battle for Your Time.* 2018. Harvard University: Science in the News. Last updated May 1, 2018. Available at *http://sitn.hms.harvard.edu/flash/2018/dopamine-smartphones-battle-time/.* Accessed February 8, 2020.

49. Burrow AL, Rainone N. How Many Likes Did I Get?: Purpose Moderates Links between Positive Social Media Feedback and Self-Esteem. *Journal of Experimental Social Psychology.* 2017;69:232–236.

50. Hong S. Who Benefits from Twitter? Social Media and Political Competition in the U.S. House of Representatives. *Government Information Quarterly.* 2013;30(4):464–472.

51. Suler J. The Online Disinhibition Effect. *CyberPsychology & Behavior.* 2004;7(3):321–326.

52. Brooks D. *How We Destroy Lives Today.* 2019. New York Times. Available at *https:// www.nytimes.com/2019/01/21/opinion/covington-march-for-life.html.* Accessed February 8, 2020.

53. More in Common. *Hidden Tribes.* 2018. Last updated 2018. Available at *https:// hiddentribes.us/about.* Accessed February 8, 2020.

54. Cohn N, Quealy K. *The Democratic Electorate on Twitter Is Not the Actual Electorate.* 2019. New York Times. Last updated April 9, 2019. Available at *https://www.nytimes. com/interactive/2019/04/08/upshot/democratic-electorate-twitter-real-life.html.* Accessed February 8, 2020.

55. Elon University. *The Future of Free Speech, Trolls, Anonymity and Fake News Online.* 2017. Last updated March 28, 2017. Available at *http://www.elon.edu/e-net/Article/ 145850.* Accessed February 8, 2020.

56. Beam A, Melley B. *Students in 'MAGA' Hats Mock Native American after Rally.* 2019. AP News. Last updated January 19, 2019. Available at *https://www.apnews.com/58d9e 567819346d185893e200ef440ea.* Accessed February 8, 2020.

57. Beam A, Melley B. *Students in 'MAGA' Hats Mock Native American after Rally.* 2019. ABC News. Last updated January 19, 2019. Available at *https://abcnews.go.com/US/ wireStory/diocese-investigates-students-mock-native-american-60492670.* Accessed February 8, 2020.

58. Mervosh S. *Viral Video Shows Boys in 'Make America Great Again' Hats Surrounding Native Elder.* 2019. New York Times. Last updated January 19, 2019. Available at *https://www.nytimes.com/2019/01/19/us/covington-catholic-high-school-nathan-phillips.html.* Accessed February 8, 2020.

59. Guardian Staff and Agencies. *Outcry after Kentucky Students in Maga Hats Mock Native American Veteran.* 2019. The Guardian. Last updated January 19, 2019. Available at *https://www.theguardian.com/us-news/2019/jan/20/outcry-after-kentucky-students-in-maga-hats-mock-native-american-veteran.* Accessed February 8, 2020.

60. Beam A, Melley B. *Catholic High School Students in 'MAGA' Hats Mock Native American after D.C. Rally, Could Face Expulsion.* 2019. Chicago Tribune. Last updated January 19, 2019. Available at *https://www.chicagotribune.com/news/nationworld/ ct-kentucky-students-in-maga-hats-mock-native-american-20190119-story.html.* Accessed February 8, 2020.

61. WCPO staff. *Diocese report finds Covington Catholic students did nothing wrong in viral Washington incident.* 2019. WCPO Cincinnati. Last updated February 13, 2019. Available at *https://www.wcpo.com/news/local-news/kenton-county/diocese-of-covington-releases-report-on-covcath-viral-video-incident.* Accessed February 8, 2020.

62. Associated Press. *Diocese finds Kentucky students didn't start confrontation.* 2019. ABC News. Last updated February 13, 2019. Available at *https://abcnews.go.com/ US/wireStory/kentucky-bishop-covington-students-instigators-61052603.* Accessed February 8, 2020.

63. Friedersdorf C. *Chelsea Clinton in the Hall of Mirrors.* 2019. The Atlantic. Last updated March 21, 2019. Available at *https://www.theatlantic.com/ideas/archive/2019/03/ chelsea-clinton-gets-caught-call-out-culture/585397/.* Accessed February 8, 2020.

64. Ronson J. *How One Stupid Tweet Blew Up Justine Sacco's Life.* 2015. New York Times. Last updated February 12, 2015. Available at *https://www.nytimes.com/2015/02/15/*

magazine/how-one-stupid-tweet-ruined-justine-saccos-life.html. Accessed February 8, 2020.

65. Vingiano A. *This is How a Woman's Offensive Tweet Became the World's Top Story*. 2013. Buzz Feed News. Last updated December 21, 2013. Available at *https://www.buzzfeednews.com/article/alisonvingiano/this-is-how-a-womans-offensive-tweet-became-the-worlds-top-s*. Accessed February 8, 2020.

66. Spangler T. *IAC Fires PR Chief Justine Sacco After Firestorm over AIDS Tweet*. 2013. Variety. Last updated December 21, 2013. Available at *https://variety.com/2013/biz/exec-shuffle-people-news/iac-fires-pr-chief-justine-sacco-after-firestorm-over-aids-tweet-1200984675/*. Accessed February 8, 2020.

67. Williamson KD. *When the Twitter Mob Came for Me*. 2018. Wall Street Journal. Last updated April 20, 2018. Available at *https://www.wsj.com/articles/when-the-twitter-mob-came-for-me-1524234850*. Accessed February 8, 2020.

68. Grynbaum MM. *The Atlantic Cuts Ties with Conservative Writer Kevin Williamson*. 2018. New York Times. Last updated April 5, 2018. Available at *https://www.nytimes.com/2018/04/05/business/media/kevin-williamson-atlantic.html*. Accessed February 8, 2020.

69. Wolfson S. *New York Times racism row: how Twitter comes back to haunt you*. 2018. The Guardian. Last updated August 3, 2018. Available at *https://www.theguardian.com/technology/2018/aug/03/sarah-jeong-new-york-times-twitter-posts-racism*. Accessed February 8, 2020.

70. Concha J. *Sarah Jeong out at New York Times editorial board*. 2019. The Hill. Last updated September 28, 2019. Available at *https://thehill.com/homenews/media/463503-sarah-jeong-out-at-new-york-times-editorial-board*. Accessed February 8, 2020.

71. Peiser J. *Times Stands by Editorial Board Member after Outcry Over Old Tweets*. 2018. New York Times. Last updated August 2, 2018. Available at *https://www.nytimes.com/2018/08/02/business/media/sarah-jeong-new-york-times.html*. Accessed February 8, 2020.

72. Flier J. *As a Former Dean Harvard Medical School, I Question Brown's Failure to Defend Lisa Littman*. 2018. Quillette. Last updated August 31, 2018. Available at *https://quillette.com/2018/08/31/as-a-former-dean-of-harvard-medical-school-i-question-browns-failure-to-defend-lisa-littman/*. Accessed February 8, 2020.

73. Frank A, Gleiser M. *A Crisis at the Edge of Physics*. 2015. New York Times. Last updated June 5, 2015. Available at *https://www.nytimes.com/2015/06/07/opinion/a-crisis-at-the-edge-of-physics.html*. Accessed February 8, 2020.

74. Kay J. *Jonathan Kay on the Tyranny of Twitter: How Mob Censure Is Changing the Intellectual Landscape*. 2017. National Post. Last updated August 11, 2017. Available at *https://nationalpost.com/news/world/jonathan-kay-on-the-tyranny-of-twitter-how-mob-censure-is-changing-the-intellectual-landscape*. Accessed February 8, 2020.

75. Vance T. *Chancellor Vitter responds to Ole Miss faculty member's social media post*. 2018. The Daily Mississippian. Last updated October 14, 2018. Available at *https://thedmonline.com/breaking-chancellor-vitter-responds-to-ole-miss-faculty-members-social-media-post/*. Accessed February 8, 2020.

76. Flaherty C. *Last-Minute Tenure Threat*. 2019. Inside Higher Education. Last updated May 17, 2019. Available at *https://www.insidehighered.com/news/2019/05/17/governing-board-university-mississippi-debates-professors-tweets*. Accessed February 8, 2020.

77. Mississippi Public Universities. *Statement from the Board of Trustees of State Institutions of Higher Learning.* 2019. Mississippi Public Relations. Last updated May 16, 2019. Available at *http://www.mississippi.edu/pr/newsstory.asp?ID=1524#.XN3FpZPd4bY.twitter.* Accessed February 8, 2020.

78. American Association of University Professors. *1940 Statement of Principles on Academic Freedom and Tenure.* 1940. Last updated 1970. Available at *https://www.aaup.org/file/1940%20Statement.pdf.* Accessed February 8, 2020.

79. Duke University Faculty Handbook. *Appendix C. Academic Freedom and Academic Tenure.* 2017. Available at *https://provost.duke.edu/sites/default/files/FHB_App_C.pdf.* Accessed February 8, 2020.

80. Tufts University Office of the Provost and Senior Vice President. *Academic Freedom, Tenure & Retirement.* Available at *https://provost.tufts.edu/policies/academic-freedom-tenure-retirement/.* Accessed February 8, 2020.

81. University of Illinois Board of Trustees. *Statutes.* 2013. Last updated January 24, 2013. Available at *https://www.bot.uillinois.edu/governance/statutes.* Accessed February 8, 2020.

82. Marquette University. *Handbook for Full-Time Faculty.* 2013. Available at *http://www.marquette.edu/provost/documents/faculty-handbook.pdf.* Accessed February 8, 2020.

83. University of California Office of the President. *Academic Freedom.* 2003. Available at *https://www.ucop.edu/academic-personnel-programs/_files/apm/apm-010.pdf.* Accessed February 8, 2020.

84. *Brandenburg v. Ohio,* 395 U.S. 444 (1969).

85. *Watts v. United States,* 394 U.S. 705 (1969).

86. *Matal v. Tam,* 137 S. Ct. 1744 (2017).

87. Gersen JS. *Laura Kipnis' Endless Trial by Title IX.* 2017. The New Yorker. Last updated September 20, 2017. Available at *https://www.newyorker.com/news/news-desk/laura-kipniss-endless-trial-by-title-ix.* Accessed February 8, 2020.

88. Kipnis L. *Sexual Paranoia Strikes Academe.* 2015. Chronicle of Higher Education. Last updated February 27, 2015. Available at *http://laurakipnis.com/wp-content/uploads/2010/08/Sexual-Paranoia-Strikes-Academe.pdf.* Accessed February 8, 2020.

89. Kipnis L. *My Title IX Inquisition.* 2015. Chronicle of Higher Education. Last updated May 29, 2015. Available at *http://5d5.3dd.myftpupload.com/wp-content/uploads/2010/08/My-Title-IX-Inquisition-The-Chronicle-Review-.pdf.* Accessed February 8, 2020.

90. Kalven Committee. *Report on the University's Role in Political and Social Action.* 1967. University of Chicago. Available at *http://www-news.uchicago.edu/releases/07/pdf/kalverpt.pdf.* Accessed February 8, 2020.

91. Shweder R. *In Defense of the No Action Option: Institutional Neutrality, Speaking for Oneself, and the Hazards of Corporate Political Opinions.* 2015. Available at *https://humdev.uchicago.edu/sites/humdev.uchicago.edu/files/uploads/Shweder/AAAtalk2015Kalvenfin.pdf.* Accessed February 8, 2020.

92. Shweder R. *Targeting the Israeli Academy: Will Anthropologists Have the Courage to Just Say 'No'?* 2017. Huffington Post. Last updated March 25, 2017. Available at *https://www.huffingtonpost.com/richard-a-shweder/targeting-the-israeli-aca_b_9540974.html.* Accessed February 8, 2020.

93. American Association for University Professors. *Tenure.* Available at *https://www.aaup.org/issues/tenure.* Accessed February 8, 2020.

94. Friedersdorf C. *Stripping a Professor of Tenure Over a Blog Post*. 2015. The Atlantic. Last updated February 10, 2015. Available at *https://www.theatlantic.com/education/archive/2015/02/stripping-a-professor-of-tenure-over-a-blog-post/385280/*. Accessed February 8, 2020.

95. *Marquette Philosophy Instructor: "Gay Rights" Can't Be Discussed in Class Since Any Disagreement Would Offend Gay Students*. 2014. Marquette Warrior. Last updated November 9, 2014. Available at *http://mu-warrior.blogspot.com/2014/11/marquette-philosophy-instructor-gay.html*. Accessed February 8, 2020.

96. *A Letter to the Marquette Community:*. 2014. Marquette Wire. Last updated November 25, 2014. Available at *https://marquettewire.org/3902776/tribune/viewpoints/reader-submission-mcadamss-treatment-of-instructor-is-deplorable/*. Accessed February 8, 2020.

97. Holz R. *Letter to John McAdams*. 2015. Last updated January 30, 2015. Available at *https://docs.google.com/file/d/0B4jS38HQ3f8dSDhNX1FQRnlpcTQ/edit*. Accessed February 8, 2020.

98. *McAdams v. Marquette Univ.*, 914 N.W.2d 708, 714 (Wis. 2018).

99. *McAdams v. Marquette Univ.*, 914 N.W.2d 708, 715 (Wis. 2018).

100. *McAdams v. Marquette Univ.*, 914 N.W.2d 708, 715 (Wis. 2018).

101. *McAdams v. Marquette Univ.*, 914 N.W.2d 708, 716 (Wis. 2018).

102. *McAdams v. Marquette Univ.*, 914 N.W.2d 708, 712 (Wis. 2018).

103. *McAdams v. Marquette Univ.*, 914 N.W.2d 708, 732 (Wis. 2018).

104. Supreme Court of Wisconsin. *John McAdams, Plaintiff-Appellat, v. Marquette University, Defendant-Respondent*. 2018. Available at *https://www.wicourts.gov/sc/opinion/DisplayDocument.pdf?content=pdf&seqNo=215236*. Accessed February 8, 2020.

105. Abrams SJ. *Think Professors are Liberal? Try School Administrators*. 2018. New York Times. Last updated October 16, 2018. Available at *https://www.nytimes.com/2018/10/16/opinion/liberal-college-administrators.html*. Accessed February 8, 2020.

106. Soave R. *Sarah Lawrence Professor's Office Door Vandalized After He Criticized Leftist's Bias*. 2018. Reason.com. Last updated November 2, 2018. Available at *https://reason.com/blog/2018/11/02/sarah-lawrence-professor-samuel-abrams*. Accessed February 8, 2020.

107. Office of the President Sarah Lawrence College. *Letter to Students, Staff, and Faculty*. 2018. Last updated November 6, 2018. Available at *https://www.sarahlawrence.edu/about/leadership/president/ccj_slc_110618.pdf*. Accessed February 8, 2020.

108. Diaspora Coalition. *DEMANDS: Westlands Sit-In 50 Years of Shame*. 2019. The Phoenix. Last updated March 11, 2019. Available at *http://www.sarahlawrencephoenix.com/campus/2019/3/11/demands-westlands-sit-in-50-years-of-shame*. Accessed February 8, 2020.

109. Flaherty C. *When Students Want to Review a Tenured Professor*. 2019. Inside Higher Education. Last updated March 13, 2019. Available at *https://www.insidehighered.com/news/2019/03/13/students-sarah-lawrence-want-review-tenure-conservative-professor-who-criticized*. Accessed February 8, 2020.

110. Judd CC. *A Message from President Judd*. 2019. Sarah Lawrence College. Last updated March 12, 2019. Available at *https://www.sarahlawrence.edu/news-events/news/2019-03-12-a-message-from-president-judd-nb.html*. Accessed February 8, 2020.

111. UCLA Office of Equity, Diversity and Inclusion. *Equity, Diversity, and Inclusion (EDI) Statement FAQs*. 2018. Last updated June 25, 2018. Available at *https://ucla. app.box.com/v/edi-statement-faqs*. Accessed February 8, 2020.

112. UC San Diego Center for Faculty Diversity and Inclusion. *Contributions to Diversity Statements*. 2018. Available at *https://facultydiversity.ucsd.edu/recruitment/ contributions-to-diversity.html*. Accessed February 8, 2020.

113. Berkeley Office for Faculty Equity & Welfare. *Guidelines for Applicants Writing Statements*. 2018. Available at *https://ofew.berkeley.edu/guidelines-applicants-writing-statements*. Accessed February 8, 2020.

114. Oregon State University. *Promotion and Tenure Guidelines*. 2018. Available at *https:// facultyaffairs.oregonstate.edu/faculty-handbook/promotion-and-tenure-guidelines*. Accessed February 8, 2020.

115. Pomona College. *How to Prepare a Diversity Statement*. 2018. Available at *https:// www.pomona.edu/administration/academic-dean/faculty-jobs/how-prepare-diversity-statement*. Accessed February 8, 2020.

116. UCLA Equity, Diversity, and Inclusion. *Sample Guidance for Candidates*. Available at *https://equity.ucla.edu/programs-resources/faculty-search-process/faculty-search-committee-resources/sample-guidance/*. Accessed February 8, 2020.

117. Flier J. *Against Diversity Statements*. 2019. Chronicle of Higher Education. Last updated January 3, 2019. Available at *https://www.chronicle.com/article/Against-Diversity-Statements/245400*. Accessed February 8, 2020.

118. Zucker KJ, Lawrence AA, Kreukels BPC. Gender Dysphoria in Adults. *Annual Review of Clinical Psychology*. 2016;12:217–247.

119. Littman L. *Rapid-Onset Gender Dysphoria in Adolescents and Young Adults: A Study of Parental Reports*. 2018. PLOS ONE. Last updated August 16, 2018. Available at *https://journals.plos.org/plosone/article?id=10.1371/journal.pone.0214157#sec011*. Accessed February 8, 2020.

120. *Brown Research First to Describe Rapid-Onset Gender Dysphoria*. 2018. Last updated August 22, 2018. Available at *http://archive.is/M8a3Z#selection-1029.0-1033.246*. Accessed February 8, 2020.

121. Serano J. *Everything You Need to Know About Rapid Onset Gender Dysphoria*. 2018. Medium. Last updated August 22, 2018. Available at *https://medium.com/@ juliaserano/everything-you-need-to-know-about-rapid-onset-gender-dysphoria-1940b8afdeba*. Accessed February 8, 2020.

122. Serano J. *Rapid Onset Gender Dysphoria, scientific debate, and suppressing speech*. 2018. Medium. Last updated August 28, 2018. Available at *https://medium.com/@ juliaserano/rapid-onset-gender-dysphoria-scientific-debate-and-suppressing-speech-fd88a83bcd60*. Accessed February 8, 2020.

123. *Statement by PLOS ONE staff*. 2018. PLOS ONE. Last updated August 27, 2018. Available at *https://journals.plos.org/plosone/article/comment?id=10.1371/annota-tion/2a4269d4-90ab-4f26-bf00-1348cc787ca8*. Accessed February 8, 2020.

124. Brown University. *Updated: Brown Statements on Gender Dysphoria Study*. 2019. Last updated March 19, 2019. Available at *https://www.brown.edu/news/2019-03-19/gender*. Accessed February 8, 2020.

125. *Brown University and PLoS ONE: Defend Academic Freedom and Scientific Inquiry*. 2018. ipetitions. Available at *https://www.ipetitions.com/petition/brown-university-and-plos-one-defend-academic*. Accessed February 8, 2020.

126. Littman L. Correction: Parent Reports of Adolescents and Young Adults Perceived to Show Signs of a Rapid Onset of Gender Dysphoria. *PLOS ONE.* 2019;14(3):e0214157.

127. Brandelli Costa A. Formal Comment on: Parent Reports of Adolescents and Young Adults Perceived to Show Signs of a Rapid Onset of Gender Dysphoria. *PLOS ONE.* 2019;14(3):e0212578.

128. Kay J. *An Interview With Lisa Littman, Who Coined the Term 'Rapid Onset Gender Dysphoria.'* 2019. Quillette. Last updated March 19, 2019. Available at *https:// quillette.com/2019/03/19/an-interview-with-lisa-littman-who-coined-the-term-rapid-onset-gender-dysphoria/.* Accessed February 8, 2020.

129. *Brown University Bulletin.* 2018–2019. Available at *https://bulletin.brown.edu/foreword/.* Accessed February 8, 2020.

130. Tuvel R. In Defense of Transracialism. *Hypatia.* 2017;32(2):263–278.

131. Jaschik S. *Journal Apologizes for Article on 'Transracialism.'* 2017. Inside Higher Education. Last updated May 2, 2017. Available at *https://www.insidehighered.com/ quicktakes/2017/05/02/journal-apologizes-article-transracialism.* Accessed February 8, 2020.

132. *Open Letter to Hypatia.* Available at *https://docs.google.com/forms/d/1efp9C0MHch_ 6Kfgtlm0PZ76nirWtcEsqWHcvgidl2mU/viewform?ts=59066d20&edit_ requested=true.* Accessed March 28, 2019.

133. Board of Hypatia. *Hypatia News.* 2017. Available at *https://archive.is/kVrLb.* Accessed February 8, 2020.

134. Weinberg J. *Hypatia's Associate Editors Resign.* 2017. DailyNous. Last updated July 24, 2017. Available at *http://dailynous.com/2017/07/24/hypatias-associate-editors-resign/.* Accessed February 8, 2020.

135. Bermúdez JL. *Defining 'Harm' on the Tuvel Affair.* 2017. Inside Higher Education. Last updated May 5, 2017. Available at *https://www.insidehighered.com/views/2017/ 05/05/real-damage-done-flare-over-philosophers-journal-article-essay.* Accessed February 8, 2020.

136. Gilley B. The Case for Colonialism. 2017. Note: Original paper published at *https:// www.tandfonline.com/doi/abs/10.1080/01436597.2017.1369037.* Paper also available at *http://www.web.pdx.edu/~gilleyb/2_The%20case%20for%20colonialism_ at2Oct2017.pdf.*

137. Prashad V. *Tweet.* 2017. Twitter. Last updated September 11, 2017. Available at *https://web.archive.org/web/20170918032706/https:/twitter.com/vijayprashad/ status/907409225558740993.* Accessed February 8, 2020.

138. Flaherty C. *Is Retraction the New Rebuttal?* 2017. Inside Higher Education. Last updated September 19, 2017. Available at *https://www.insidehighered.com/news/ 2017/09/19/controversy-over-paper-favor-colonialism-sparks-calls-retraction.* Accessed February 8, 2020.

139. Prashad V. *Letter of Resignation from Members of the Editorial Board of Third World Quarterly.* 2017. Twitter. Last updated September 11, 2017. Available at *https://www. facebook.com/photo.php?fbid=10214329786508248&set=a.1048612385268&type=3 &theater.* Accessed February 8, 2020.

140. Brought to Life: Exploring the History of Medicine. *Miasma Theory.* UK Science Museum. Available at *http://broughttolife.sciencemuseum.org.uk/broughttolife/ techniques/miasmatheory.* Accessed February 8, 2020.

141. Alfred R. *Dec. 30, 1924: Hubble Reveals We Are Not Alone.* 2009. Last updated December 30, 2009. Available at *https://www.wired.com/2009/12/1230hubble-first-galaxy-outside-milky-way/*. Accessed February 8, 2020.

142. Hubble E. A Relation between Distance and Radial Velocity among Extra-Galactic Nebulae. *Proceedings of the National Academy of Sciences of the United States of America.* 1929;15(3):168–173.

143. Drescher J. Out of DSM: Depathologizing Homosexuality. *Behavioral Science.* 2015;5(4):565–575.

144. Beard A. *Women Respond Better than Men to Competitive Pressure.* 2017. Harvard Business Review. Last updated November–December 2017. Available at *https://hbr.org/2017/11/women-respond-better-than-men-to-competitive-pressure.* Accessed February 8, 2020.

145. Low E. *Are Women Better Investors than Men? Here's What the Studies Say.* 2018. Investor's Business Daily. Last updated July 16, 2018. Available at *https://www.investors.com/news/women-investing-stocks-outperform-men-studies/.* Accessed February 8, 2020.

146. Goodman L, Zhu J, Bai B. *Women Are Better than Men at Paying Their Mortgages.* Urban Institute; 2016.

147. Frymorgen T. *Women Really Are Stronger Than Men, According to Study.* 2018. BBC. Last updated Janaury 10, 2018. Available at *https://www.bbc.co.uk/bbcthree/article/7b6484fb-3b00-46d6-a557-ac2a0b6f8591.* Accessed February 8, 2020.

148. Carson E. *Women Are Better in Tech Than Men, Says a Report.* 2017. CNET. Last updated November 17, 2017. Available at *https://www.cnet.com/news/women-are-better-in-tech-than-men/.* Accessed February 8, 2020.

149. Martin C. *Arthur Sakamoto on Paradigms in Sociology: Half Hour of Heterodoxy #14.* 2017. Heterodox Academy. Last updated October 10, 2017. Available at *https://heterodoxacademy.org/arthur-sakamoto-on-paradigms-in-sociology-half-hour-of-heterodoxy-14/.* Accessed February 8, 2020.

150. Lilienfeld SO. Microaggressions: Strong Claims, Inadequate Evidence. *Perspectives on Psychological Science.* 2017;12(1):138–169.

151. *Perspectives on Psychological Science.* 2017. Sage Journals. Last updated January 2017. Available at *http://journals.sagepub.com/toc/PPS/12/1* Accessed February 8, 2020.

152. Garfield E. *The History and Meaning of the Journal Impact Factor.* 2006. JAMA. Last updated January 4, 2006. Available at *http://garfield.library.upenn.edu/papers/jamajif2006.pdf.* Accessed February 8, 2020.

153. Sharma M, Sarin A, Gupta P, Sachdeva S, Desai AV. Journal Impact Factor: Its Use, Significance and Limitations. *World Journal of Nuclear Medicine.* 2014;13(2):146.

154. Sokal AD. Transgressing the Boundaries: Towards a Transformative Hermeneutics of Quantum Gravity. *Social Text.* 1996;46(47):217–252.

155. Lindsay JA, Boghossian P, Pluckrose H. *Academic Grievance Studies and the Corruption of Scholarship.* 2018. Areo Magazine. Last updated October 2, 2018. Available at *https://areomagazine.com/2018/10/02/academic-grievance-studies-and-the-corruption-of-scholarship/.* Accessed February 8, 2020.

156. Kuntz M. The Postmodern Assault on Science. *EMBO Reports.* 2012;13(10):885–889.

157. Scherr RE, Robertson AD. Unveiling Privilege to Broaden Participation. *The Physics Teacher.* 2017;55:394–397.

158. Kaufman R. *Aztec, Maya Were Rubber-Making Masters.* 2010. National Geographic. Last updated June 30, 2010. Available at *https://news.nationalgeographic.com/news/2010/06/100628-science-ancient-maya-aztec-rubber-balls-beheaded/.* Accessed February 8, 2020.

159. Maugh TH, II. *Mayas mastered rubber long before Goodyear.* 2010. Los Angeles Times. Last updated May 31, 2010. Available at *http://articles.latimes.com/2010/may/31/science/la-sci-rubber-20100531.* Accessed February 8, 2020.

160. Schmidt P. *Ancestors of Science: Complex Iron Smelting and Prehistoric Culture in Tanzania.* 2005. Science. Last updated May 27, 2005. Available at *http://www.sciencemag.org/careers/2005/05/ancestors-science-complex-iron-smelting-and-prehistoric-culture-tanzania.* Accessed February 8, 2020.

161. *Boomerang.* National Museum of Australia. Available at *http://www.nma.gov.au/exhibitions/symbols_of_australia/boomerang.* Accessed May 26, 2019.

162. Burko L. Unveiling Nonsense to Save Physics. *The Physics Teacher.* 2017;56(4).

163. Gutiérrez R. Why (Urban) Mathematics Teachers Need Political Knowledge. *Journal of Urban Mathematics Education.* 2013;6(2):7–19.

164. Gutiérrez R. Political Conocimiento for Teaching Mathematics: Why Teachers Need It and How to Develop It. In: Kastberg SE, Tyminksi AM, Lischka AE, Sanchez WB, eds. *Building Support for Scholarly Practices in Mathematics Methods.* Information Age Publishing; 2017:11–38.

165. College Pulse. *Free Expression on College Campuses.* 2019. College Pulse. Last updated May 2019. Available at *https://kf-site-production.s3.amazonaws.com/media_elements/files/000/000/351/original/Knight-CP-Report-FINAL.pdf.* Accessed February 8, 2020.

166. Crawford JT, Jussim L, eds. *Politics of Social Psychology.* Routledge; 2018.

167. Smith C. *The Sacred Project of American Sociology.* Oxford University Press; 2014.

168. Gross N. *Professors Are Overwhelmingly Liberal. Do Universities Need to Change Hiring Practices?* 2016. Los Angeles Times. Last updated May 20, 2016. Available at *http://www.latimes.com/opinion/op-ed/la-oe-gross-academia-conservatives-hiring-20160520-snap-story.html.* Accessed February 8, 2020.

169. Simon RM. The Conflict Paradigm in Sociology and the Study of Social Inequality: Paradox and Possibility. *Theory in Action.* 2013;9(1):1–31.

170. Haskell DM. *Suppressing TVO Video, Stifling Free Speech, Is Making Wilfrid Laurier Unsafe.* 2017. The Star. Last updated November 15, 2017. Available at *https://www.thestar.com/opinion/contributors/2017/11/15/suppressing-tvo-video-stifling-free-speech-is-making-wilfrid-laurier-unsafe.html.* Accessed February 8, 2020.

171. Lam P. *Why Wilfrid Laurier University's President Apologized to Lindsay Shepherd.* 2017. CBC. Last updated November 24, 2017. Available at *https://www.cbc.ca/news/canada/kitchener-waterloo/wilfrid-laurier-university-president-explains-apology-to-lindsay-shepherd-1.4417809.* Accessed February 8, 2020.

172. *Apology from Laurier President and Vice-Chancellor Deborah MacLatchy.* 2017. Wilfred Laurier. Last updated November 21, 2017. Available at *https://wlu.ca/news/spotlights/2017/nov/apology-from-laurier-president-and-vice-chancellor.html.* Accessed February 8, 2020.

173. Naughton KAN, Eastman N, Perrino N. *Speaking Freely: What Students Think About Expression at American Colleges.* Foundation for Individual Rights in Education; October 2017.

174. Stevens S. *The Campus Expression Survey: Summary of New Data.* Heterodox Academy; 2017.

175. Gillette. *We Believe: The Best Men Can Be.* 2019. Last updated January 13, 2019. Available at *https://www.youtube.com/watch?v=koPmuEyP3a0.* Accessed February 8, 2020.

176. Villanova University (2019). "Diversity and inclusion" question used in teaching evaluations.

177. Sheehan CA, Wilson JM. *A Mole Hunt for Diversity 'Bias' at Villanova.* 2019. Wall Street Journal. Last updated March 29, 2019. Available at *https://www.wsj.com/articles/a-mole-hunt-for-diversity-bias-at-villanova-11553898400.* Accessed February 8, 2020.

178. Donohue RPM. (2019). Email to Villanova Community.

179. Community College Research Center. *Community College FAQs.* 2018. Teachers College, Columbia University. Available at *https://ccrc.tc.columbia.edu/Community-College-FAQs.html.* Accessed February 8, 2020.

180. National Center for Education Statistics. *Table 303.30: Total fall enrollment in degree-granting postsecondary institutions, by level and control of institution, attendance status, and sex of student: Selected years, 1970 through 2027.* Available at *https://nces.ed.gov/programs/digest/d17/tables/dt17_303.30.asp.* Accessed February 8, 2020.

181. Ma J, Baum S. *Trends in Community Colleges: Enrollment, Prices, Student Debt, and Completion.* 2019. College Board. Last updated April 2016. Available at *https://trends.collegeboard.org/sites/default/files/trends-in-community-colleges-research-brief.pdf.* Accessed February 8, 2020.

182. Jaschik S. *Professors and Politics: What the Research Says.* 2017. Inside Higher Education. Last updated February 27, 2017. Available at *https://www.insidehighered.com/news/2017/02/27/research-confirms-professors-lean-left-questions-assumptions-about-what-means.* Accessed February 8, 2020.

183. Urista M, Wei S. 2018. Campus Expression Survey—Linn-Benton Community College, personal communication (2018).

184. Wenatchee Valley Community College. *Diversity Requirement for Graduation.* Available at *https://www.wvc.edu/students/support/diversity/graduation-diversity-requirement.html.* Accessed February 8, 2020.

185. Everett Community College. *Diversity Course Requirement for Associate Degrees.* Available at *https://www.everettcc.edu/programs/diversity-requirement.* Accessed February 8, 2020.

186. Anne Arundel Community College. *About the Diversity Requirement.* Available at *https://catalog.aacc.edu/content.php?catoid=23&navoid=7220.* Accessed February 8, 2020.

187. Community College of Philadelphia. *Degree Requirements.* Available at *https://www.ccp.edu/college-catalog/degree-requirements.* Accessed February 8, 2020.

188. Kissel A. *FIRE in 'Chronicle of Higher Education': Adjuncts Need Academic Freedom, Too, and Outside Organizations Do What Faculty Colleagues Often Won't.* 2008. Last updated September 30, 2008. Available at *https://www.thefire.org/fire-in-chronicle-of-higher-education-adjuncts-need-academic-freedom-too-and-outside-organizations-do-what-faculty-colleagues-often-wont/.* Accessed February 8, 2020.

189. Evans CG. *Working Off-Track: Adjunct Labor in Higher Education.* Publicly Accessible Penn Dissertations, University of Pennsylvania; 2018. Note: For the 22%

figure from the 1960s, citing Schuster JH, Finkelstein MJ. *The American Faculty: The Restructuring of Academic Work and Careers.* 2006. Johns Hopkins University Press.

190. American Association for University Professors. *The Inclusion in Governance of Faculty Members Holding Contingent Appointments.* 2014. Available at *https://www.aaup.org/report/inclusion-governance-faculty-members-holding-contingent-appointments.* Accessed February 8, 2020.

191. Schneider A. *To Many Adjunct Professors, Academic Freedom is a Myth.* 1999. Chronicle of Higher Education. Last updated December 10, 1999. Available at *https://www.chronicle.com/article/To-Many-Adjunct-Professors/24384.* Accessed February 8, 2020.

192. Byrne JP. Academic Freedom of Part-Time Faculty. *Journal of College and University Law.* 2001;27(3):583–593.

193. Stern CS, Choper JH, Gray MW, Wolfson RJ. The Status of Part-Time Faculty. *Academe.* 1981;67(1):29–39.

194. Clausen J, Swidler E-M. Academic Freedom from Below: Toward an Adjunct-Centered Struggle. *AAUP Journal of Academic Freedom.* 2013;4:1–26.

195. Steinbaugh A. *University of Northern Colorado Defends, Modifies 'Bias Response Team' as Criticism Mounts and Recording Emerges.* 2016. Foundation for Individual Rights in Education. Last updated July 7, 2016. Available at *https://www.thefire.org/university-of-northern-colorado-bias-response-team-recording-emerges/.* Accessed February 8, 2020.

196. *University of Northern Colorado Bias Response Incident 2015009902.* 2015. Available at *https://www.documentcloud.org/documents/2902168-University-of-Northern-Colorado-Bias-Response.html.* Accessed February 8, 2020.

197. Silvy T. *Professor Breaks Silence in University of Northern Colorado academic freedom case.* The Tribune. Last updated July 8, 2016. Available at *https://www.greeleytribune.com/news/local/professor-breaks-silence-in-university-of-northern-colorado-academic-freedom-case/.* Accessed February 8, 2020.

198. Silvy T. *Rise of Bias Response Teams at University of Northern Colorado, across country signals shift in how universities deal with inclusion.* 2016. The Tribune. Last updated April 26, 2016. Available at *https://www.greeleytribune.com/news/local/rise-of-bias-response-teams-at-university-of-northern-colorado-across-country-signals-shift-in-how-universities-deal-with-inclusion/.* Accessed February 8, 2020.

199. Silvy T. *University of Northern Colorado's handling of speech deemed offensive raises questions, concerns.* 2016. The Tribune. Last updated June 28, 2016. Available at *https://www.greeleytribune.com/news/local/university-of-northern-colorados-handling-of-speech-deemed-offensive-raises-questions-concerns/.* Accessed February 8, 2020.

200. Silvy T. *University of Northern Colorado retreats from embattled Bias Response Team.* 2016. The Tribune. Last updated September 7, 2016. Available at *https://www.greeleytribune.com/news/local/university-of-northern-colorado-retreats-from-embattled-bias-response-team/.* Accessed February 8, 2020.

201. Melchior JK. *The Bias Response Team is Watching.* 2018. Wall Street Journal. Last updated May 8, 2018. Available at *https://www.wsj.com/articles/the-bias-response-team-is-watching-1525806702.* Accessed February 8, 2020.

202. *Appointment and Promotion.* 2019. University of California Office of the President. Last updated October 1, 2018. Available at *https://ucop.edu/academic-personnel-programs/_files/apm/apm-285.pdf.* Accessed February 8, 2020.

203. Beauchamp Z. *Data Shows a Surprising Campus Free Speech Problem: Left-Wingers Being Fired for Their Opinions*. 2018. Vox. Last updated August 3, 2018. Available at *https://www.vox.com/policy-and-politics/2018/8/3/17644180/political-correctness-free-speech-liberal-data-georgetown*. Accessed February 8, 2020.

204. Hanlon A. *Are Liberal College Students Creating a Free Speech Crisis? Not According to Data*. 2018. NBC News. Available at *https://www.nbcnews.com/think/opinion/are-liberal-college-students-creating-free-speech-crisis-not-according-ncna858906*. Accessed February 8, 2020.

205. FIRE. *Disinvitation Report 2014: A Disturbing 15-Year Trend*. 2014. Last updated May 28, 2014. Available at *https://www.thefire.org/disinvitation-season-report-2014/*. Accessed February 8, 2020.

206. Beauchamp Z. *The Myth of a Campus Free Speech Crisis*. 2018. Vox. Last updated August 31, 2018. Available at *https://www.vox.com/policy-and-politics/2018/8/31/17718296/campus-free-speech-political-correctness-musa-al-gharbi*. Accessed February 8, 2020.

207. Levin S. *Arizona Republicans Move to Ban Social Justice Courses and Events at Schools*. 2017. The Guardian. Last updated January 13, 2017. Available at *https://www.theguardian.com/us-news/2017/jan/13/arizona-schools-social-justice-courses-ban-bill*. Accessed February 8, 2020.

208. Stevens ML, Armstrong EA, Arum R. Sieve, Incubator, Temple, Hub: Empirical and Theoretical Advances in the Sociology of Higher Education. *Annual Review of Sociology*. 2008;34:127–151.

209. Damore J. *Google's Ideological Echo Chamber*. 2017. Last updated July 2017. Available at *https://assets.documentcloud.org/documents/3914586/Googles-Ideological-Echo-Chamber.pdf*. Accessed February 8, 2020.

210. Pichai S. *Note to Employees from Sundar Pichai*. 2017. Google. Last updated August 8, 2017. Available at *https://www.blog.google/outreach-initiatives/diversity/note-employees-ceo-sundar-pichai/*. Accessed February 8, 2020.

211. Penny L. *James Damore is wrong. It's fine to discriminate against bigots and bullies*. 2018. The Guardian. Available at *https://www.theguardian.com/commentisfree/2018/jan/11/discriminate-conservatives-james-damore-suing-google-intolerance*. Accessed February 8, 2020.

212. Isaac M. *Rifts Break Open at Facebook Over Kavanaugh Hearing*. 2018. New York Times. Last updated October 4, 2018. Available at *https://www.nytimes.com/2018/10/04/technology/facebook-kavanaugh-nomination-kaplan.html*. Accessed February 8, 2020.

213. Seetharaman D. *Zuckerberg Faces Anger Over Facebook Executive's Kavanaugh Support*. 2018. Wall Street Journal. Last updated October 4, 2018. Available at *https://www.wsj.com/articles/zuckerberg-seeks-to-quell-employee-anger-over-facebook-executives-appearance-at-kavanaugh-hearing-1538687361*. Accessed February 8, 2020.

214. Seetharaman D. *Facebook's Zuckerberg Tells Employees to Respect Diverse Views of Colleagues*. 2018. Wall Street Journal. Last updated October 5, 2018. Available at *https://www.wsj.com/articles/facebooks-zuckerberg-tells-employees-to-respect-diverse-views-of-colleagues-1538767936*. Accessed February 8, 2020.

215. Chmielewski D. *Facebook Has Been Actively Courting Conservatives, But That Won't Stop It from Getting Spanked*. 2016. Recode. Last updated May 11, 2016. Available

at *https://www.recode.net/2016/5/11/11657580/facebook-conservative-bias-news-curation-gop*. Accessed February 8, 2020.

216. Kovach S. *Female Employee on the Google Memo: 'I Don't Know How We Could Feel Anything but Attacked by That.'* 2017. Business Insider. Last updated August 13, 2017. Available at *https://www.businessinsider.com/female-google-employee-responds-to-james-damore-memo-2017-8*. Accessed February 8, 2020.

217. Jackson K. *Tweet.* 2019. Twitter. Last updated February 19, 2019. Available at *https://web.archive.org/web/20190309123402/https:/twitter.com/KosokoJackson/status/1097910899371855874*. Accessed February 8, 2020.

218. Cook T. *Tamera Cook's Reviews—>A Place for Wolves.* 2019. Good Reads. Last updated February 22, 2019. Available at *https://www.goodreads.com/review/show/2725140484*. Accessed February 8, 2020.

219. Graham R. *Wolves: A YA Sensitivity Reader Watched His Own Community Kill His Debut Novel before It Was Ever Released.* 2019. Vox.com. Last updated March 4, 2019. Available at *https://slate.com/culture/2019/03/ya-book-scandal-kosoko-jackson-a-place-for-wolves-explained.html*. Accessed February 8, 2020.

220. Kantor E. *Sourcebooks Cancels Kosoko Jackson's YA Debut.* 2019. Publishers' Weekly. Last updated February 28, 2019. Available at *https://www.publishersweekly.com/pw/by-topic/childrens/childrens-book-news/article/79392-sourcebooks-cancels-kosoko-jackson-s-ya-debut.html*. Accessed February 8, 2020.

221. Jackson K. *Tweet.* 2018. Twitter. Last updated May 8, 2018. Available at *https://web.archive.org/web/20190502025255/https://twitter.com/KosokoJackson/status/993994643145674754*. Accessed February 8, 2020.

222. Alter A. *Y.A. Author Pulls Her Debut After Pre-Publication Accusations of Racism.* 2019. New York Times. Last updated January 31, 2019. Available at *https://www.nytimes.com/2019/01/31/books/amelie-wen-zhao-blood-heir-ya-author-pulls-debut-accusations-racism.html*. Accessed February 8, 2020.

223. Wen Zhao A. *To The Book Community: An Apology.* 2019. Twitter. Last updated January 30, 2019. Available at *https://web.archive.org/web/20190502025230/https://twitter.com/ameliewenzhao/status/1090706315440242688*. Accessed February 8, 2020.

224. Alter A. *She Pulled Her Debut Book When Critics Found It Racist. Now She Plans to Publish.* 2019. New York Times. Last updated April 29, 2019. Available at *https://www.nytimes.com/2019/04/29/books/amelie-wen-zhao-blood-heir.html*. Accessed February 8, 2020.

225. ABC News. *Matt Damon on Harvey Weinstein, Sexual Harassment and Confidentiality Agreements.* 2017. Available at *https://abcnews.go.com/Entertainment/video/matt-damon-harvey-weinstein-sexual-harassment-confidentiality-agreements-51796050*. Accessed February 8, 2020.

226. Eppolito S. *Here's What Matt Damon Said About #MeToo, and the Backlash That Followed.* 2017. Boston Globe. Available at *https://www.bostonglobe.com/arts/2017/12/19/here-what-matt-damon-said-about-metoo-and-backlash-that-followed/PNOjcVddMV9rQ13eqsDm4I/story.html*. Accessed February 8, 2020.

227. Fisher L. *Matt Damon Draws Backlash for Comments on Sexual Harassment and Assault.* 2017. ABC News. Available at *https://abcnews.go.com/Entertainment/matt-damon-draws-backlash-comments-sexual-harassment-assault/story?id=51860137*. Accessed February 8, 2020.

228. Caron C. *Matt Damon Draws Rebukes for Comments on the #MeToo Movement.* 2017. New York Times. Last updated December 17, 2017. Available at *https:// www.nytimes.com/2017/12/17/arts/matt-damon-metoo-movement.html.* Accessed February 8, 2020.

229. TODAYwithHoda&Jenna.*Tweet.*2018.Twitter.LastupdatedJanuary16,2018.Available at *https://web.archive.org/web/20190829161146/https://twitter.com/HodaAndJenna/ status/953291514125406211.* Accessed February 8, 2020.

230. Blackmon M. *Matt Damon Says He Realizes He Needs To Shut Up For A While About Sexual Harassment.* 2018. BuzzFeed News. Last updated January 16, 2018. Available at *https://www.buzzfeednews.com/article/michaelblackmon/matt-damon-apologizes.* Accessed February 8, 2020.

231. Rao N. *Shades of Gray.* 1994. The Yale Herald. Last updated October 14, 1994. Available at *https://assets.documentcloud.org/documents/5684266/01-Shades-of- Gray-Neomi-Rao.pdf.* Accessed February 8, 2020.

232. Harris K. *Tweet.* 2019. Twitter. Last updated February 5, 2019. Available at *https:// web.archive.org/web/20191203231044/https:/twitter.com/SenKamalaHarris/status/ 1092867347965186049.* Accessed February 8, 2020.

233. Rao N. *Letter.* 2019. Last updated February 11, 2019. Available at *https://www.ju- diciary.senate.gov/imo/media/doc/Letter%20from%20N.%20Rao%20to%20SJC.pdf.* Accessed February 8, 2020.

234. Bejan TM. *The Two Clashing Meanings of 'Free Speech.'* 2017. The Atlantic. Last updated December 2, 2017. Available at *https://www.theatlantic.com/politics/ar- chive/2017/12/two-concepts-of-freedom-of-speech/546791/.* Accessed February 8, 2020.

235. Goldberg ME. Argumentation and Understanding: A Study of Tibetan Religious Debate: A Dissertation. 1985. University of Illinois at Urbana-Champaign.

236. Meyer M. To Set Right—Ho'oponopono. *The Compleat Lawyer.* 1995, 30–35. https:// www.narf.org/nill/documents/peacemaking/1995-meyer-to-set-right.pdf

237. Muigua K. *Traditional Conflict Resolution Mechanisms and Institutions.* 2017. Available at *http://kmco.co.ke/wp-content/uploads/2018/08/Traditional-Conflict- Resolution-Mechanisms-and-Institutions-24th-October-2017.pdf.* Accessed February 8, 2020.

238. Olowu D. Indigenous Approaches to Conflict Resolution in Africa: A Study of the Barolong People of the North-West Province, South Africa. *Journal of Law and Judicial System.* 2018;1(1):10–16.

239. Berhe Y. *An Assessment of Indigenous Conflict Resolution Mechanism of Mezard in Rural Alamata Woreda, Tigray National Regional State, Ethiopia.* Mekelle University; 2013.

240. Zion JW, Yazzie R. Indigenous Law in North America in the Wake of Conquest. *Boston College International and Competitive Law Review.* 1997;20(1):55–84.

241. Cader AA. Islamic Principles of Conflict Management: A Model for Human Resource Management. *International Journal of Cross Cultural Management.* 2017;17(3):345–363.

242. Irani GE. Islamic Mediation Techniques for Middle East Conflicts. *Middle East Review of International Affairs.* 1999;3(2):1–17.

243. King-Irani LE. Rituals of Reconciliation and Processes of Empowerment in Post- War Lebanon. In: Zartman IW, ed. *Traditional Cures for Modern Conflicts: African Conflict Medicine.* Lynne Rienner; 1999.

244. Wikipedia. *Hillel and Shammai*. Wikipedia. Available at *https://en.wikipedia.org/wiki/Hillel_and_Shammai*. Accessed February 8, 2020.

245. Kaminsky H. *Fundamentals of Jewish Conflict Resolution: Traditional Jewish Perspectives on Resolving Interpersonal Conflicts*. Academic Studies Press; 2017.

246. Yager D. *Message from the President on Freedom of Expression*. 2019. University of the Arts. Last updated April 10, 2019. Available at *https://www.uarts.edu/node/43674*. Accessed February 8, 2020.

247. Allport G. *The Nature of Prejudice*. Addison-Wesley; 1954.

248. Pettigrew TF, Tropp LR. A Meta-Analytic Test of Intergroup Contact Theory. *Journal of Personality and Social Psychology*. 2006;90(5):751–783.

249. Pettigrew TF, Tropp LR. Does Intergroup Contact Reduce Prejudice: Recent Meta-Analytic Findings. In: Oskamp S, ed. *The Claremont Symposium on Applied Social Psychology: Reducing Prejudice and Discrimination*. Lawrence Erlbaum Associates Publishers; 2000:93–114.

250. Joyce BR. Dynamic Disequilibrium: The Intelligence of Growth. *Theory into Practice*. 1984;23(1):26–34.

251. Thelen HA. *Education and the Human Quest: Four Designs for Education*. Harper & Brothers; 1976.

252. Thelen HA. Education and the Human Quest: What's to Become of Johnny? *The School Review*. 1960;68(2):136–151.

253. Board of Regents. *Regents Policy 4400: Policy on University of California Diversity Statement*. 2010. University of California. Last updated September 16, 2010. Available at *https://regents.universityofcalifornia.edu/governance/policies/4400.html*. Accessed February 8, 2020.

254. *University of Illinois Diversity Values Statement*. Available at *https://www.inclusiveillinois.illinois.edu/mission.html*. Accessed February 8, 2020.

Index

For the benefit of digital users, indexed terms that span two pages (e.g., 52–53) may, on occasion, appear on only one of those pages.

AA. example
new/contradicting stuff has higher
                          burden of proof